1974

PERSONALITY

PERSONALITY
BIOSOCIAL BASES

DAVID R. HEISE
University of North Carolina / *Chapel Hill*

Rand McNally & Company • *Chicago* • *New York* • *San Francisco* • *London*

To Edgar F. Borgatta

Contents

Preface

Personality is biologically anchored; to ignore this fact in favor of interpretations exclusively in terms of learning, influence, and socio-cultural dynamics can detour us from understanding much human action. One of the intents of this book of essays and reprinted articles is to emphasize the point that the development of many behavioral regularities depends on biological givens operating in conjunction with environmental and social forces.

In addition, the book is meant to contribute constructively to the volatile debates about the relations of personality with heredity, sex, race, and age. As the debates continue in the 1970s, there is a need for more facts, more open-mindedness, and more appreciation of the complexity and intricacy of these issues.

The book is too brief to provide exhaustive coverage of all that is known about biosocial variables and personality. In the essays and in the selection of readings I have tried to serve two more limited goals. First, I have tried to accentuate the most reliable facts and, at the same time, to reexamine some ideas that are widely believed although they seem of doubtful validity. Second, I have emphasized fairly recent discoveries and somewhat novel theorizing in order to bring the issues into a fresh, up-to-date perspective.

Most of the reprinted articles were abridged for the sake of readability and to allow more materials to be included; scholars should consult the original sources when making citations.

DAVID R. HEISE

Acknowledgements

Colleagues and students in the Department of Sociology at Chapel Hill have my appreciation for keeping my thoughts honed and for reinforcing my interests in biosocial psychology. In particular, I want to thank Dick Cramer and John Reed for making special efforts to amplify my perspectives on race. Secretary Gert Rippy has my thanks for patiently typing draft after draft of the original essays in this volume.

Introduction

Distinctions of sex, age, and race are *biosocial,* meaning that in each case a biological difference is used to classify people into types that are assigned different statuses and roles in society. Sex and age distinctions serve as the foundation stones for social structure in all societies (Linton, 1945), and racial differences reinforce social structure in many societies, including our own.

It is widely believed that males and females, persons of different ages, and persons of different races show contrasts in psychological development and functioning. This book assembles some evidence about what kinds of differences really exist and why such differences might occur.

Few scientific topics are so difficult to study with detachment. Because biosocial distinctions gird the existing social structure, beliefs about personality differences among biosocial groups may serve to rationalize the system as it is, and so ideas in this area tend to be emotionally and morally loaded. Before turning to the more technical topics, it is desirable to consider briefly some of the ideological aspects of biosocial psychology.

Biosocial Elitism

Some people believe that biosocial distinctions naturally serve as building blocks of social structure because these distinctions provide an efficient means for assigning personalities to roles. For example, it may be argued that men, presumably more independent and competitive, should operate in the occupational world while women, supposedly more nurturant, should tend to families. The "emotionally stable" elders of society should have greater freedom and power whereas youths, who are "erratic and impulsive," need to be directed and disciplined. "Brighter" racial-ethnic groups should carry out the executive duties in society while "duller, but physically heartier," groups serve as workers. Such positions are called "elitist" because in effect they always support the privileges of some group or groups above those of others.

Elitist thinking about the social positioning of biosocial types involves two key assumptions. First, it is assumed that psychological differences between biosocial types are biologically inevitable and, second, that differences in capacities between biosocial categories are so pronounced that they can be used to allocate roles. However, both of these assumptions have only a limited foundation in reality.

The development of every general personality trait is environmentally determined to some degree (see Chapter 1) and so, theoretically, it would be possible to equalize the sexes, or races, or even age groups to some extent through environmental enrichment and compensatory socialization. A society willing to spend the resources could eliminate significant psychological differences between most biosocial types and, therefore, could eliminate the rationalization for using biosocial variables as a basis of discrimination; a society's decision not to do this is as much a reflection of its value system as it is a matter of "natural order." Sometimes this judgment is evaded by supposing that strong heritability of a trait implies that it can be modified only genetically. For example, it has been said that "the techniques for raising intelligence . . . probably lie more in the province of the biological sciences than in psychology and education" (Jensen, 1969: 108). But this conclusion is by no means necessarily or even probably true. Even though intelligence and a few other psychological traits develop predominately as a function of genes, there still is a substantial amount of environmental determination. As long as an environmental component exists, it theoretically is possible to effect major changes through environmental manipulations alone.

Oddly, an elitist argument has most validity, or at least most expediency, with respect to characteristics that are molded almost entirely by society rather than by genes. Through socialization, societies may manipulate some characteristics to the point where biosocial types have relatively little overlap. In fact, this does *not* appear to be the case for most abilities and personality traits, but it may be relatively true of self-identifications. For example, most males do identify with their masculinity and most females with their femininity, and in the process they subject themselves to the culturally defined self-attitudes and behavioral codes that correspond to these identities. The resulting constraints on character and behavior indeed may make males and females suitable for different positions. The male, culturally molded as an initiating, dominance-seeking creature, may be more comfortable in occupational roles where he can act decisively; the female, culturally pressured to adopt an accommodating, ingenuous style, may prefer the security of home and family life.

The fact that males and females generally are happiest in their culturally assigned roles does not prove that a division of labor based on sex is biologically justified, however; it may mean nothing more than that society at present successfully socializes males and females to identify with the roles assigned to them. Essentially the same perspective can be employed with other biosocial variations. The fact that youths seem to prefer adventure while elders lean toward respectability does not necessarily prove anything about the basic nature of youth versus older age; it may simply signify a society's success in defining different age identities and in getting people to identify with them. A society that has a caste system based on racial distinctions may be stable because persons in the lower castes identify with their status, believe they are inferior, and would feel uncomfortable in higher positions. But this does not prove that the lower caste groups really are inferior and therefore properly placed; it may mean only that society has been successful in teaching them "their place."

The second elitist assumption is that abilities and competencies are so contrasting across biosocial categories that they justify a discriminatory system simply as a matter of efficiency in assigning roles. In fact, this argument is largely irrelevant for the kinds of general personality traits that typically are mentioned—intelligence, independence, emotionality, etc. The average differences between biosocial types on these variables are so small relative to the amount of variation within groups that the information provided by knowing a person's biosocial type is of little value in assigning duties (Gottesman, 1968). For example, suppose two groups, A and B, show a fairly large average difference on a trait x, with B being higher than A. In normal populations this would imply that a person extremely high on trait x is much more likely to be from group B than from group A, and this seems to support the elitist position. But social discrimination works in the other direction, from knowledge of group to knowledge of trait. And knowing a person is in group A rather than B provides little information about his value on x since the variation among A's is so great and the distribution of A's mostly overlaps the distribution of B's. Trait x could be intelligence, independence, reaction speed, or emotional stability, and groups A and B could stand for females and males, blacks and whites, elderly and middle-aged, or youths and adults. In all such cases the allocation of status and duties on the basis of biosocial type is inefficient—and inequitable—because of the large variations within types.

Biosocial elitism can be viewed as undemocratic and restrictive of individual liberty, as discriminatory and unjust, and as judging people simplistically in terms of their anatomical features. Each individual must personally weigh elitism in terms of its competition with the other values implied by this statement. However, there should be no confusion about the logical status of elitist ideas. Elitist principles have provided, and still provide, a basis for allocating power, privileges, and duties in society. But that basis is not the only viable one, nor is it the most efficient one.

References

Gottesman, I. I.
    1968   "Biogenetics of race and class." Chapter 1 in Martin Deutsch, Irving Katz, and A. R. Jensen (eds.), Social Class, Race and Psychological Development. New York: Holt, Rinehart and Winston.

Jensen, A. R.
    1969   "How much can we boost IQ and scholastic achievement?" Harvard Educational Review 39 (Winter): 1-123. (Also pp. 1-123 in Environment, Heredity, and Intelligence. Cambridge, Massachusetts: Harvard Educational Review, Reprint Series, No. 2, 1969.)

Linton, Ralph.
    1945   The Cultural Background of Personality. New York: Appleton-Century-Crofts.

PERSONALITY

Part I
Genetics and Socialization

Genetic processes are involved in human development whenever an observable characteristic, or phenotype, is affected by a biochemical blueprint carried by an individual from the time of conception—the genotype. Genetic mechanisms account for the basic uniformity of the species and, paradoxically, for much of the diversity within the species.

Uniformity develops because all humans share fundamentally similar genotypes. This genotypic similarity makes all humans comparable in anatomy and biological functioning, it maintains characteristic features of the species such as upright posture and sapience, and it sets ultimate limits on the possibilities of human individuation. On the other hand, some of the diversity within the species develops out of the fact that all genotypes are not quite the same. For example, genes determine the physiological differences that split the species into two distinct sexes, and genes maintain the varieties of human types that constitute races. Genetic variations also produce physical idiosyncracies and affect some aspects of physiological functioning like hormonal levels. Certain aspects of psychological individuality have a genetic basis, too.

Genetic effects in human development are too important to ignore, but there is widespread confusion over the ways that genetic processes are significant in psychological development. It is best to begin by discarding the major misconception.

Genes versus Socialization

No *general* personality characteristic is known that is entirely controlled by genetic mechanisms. Environmental factors, which include social experiences and socialization, always are at least partially involved in the development of a general psychological trait. From a theoretical standpoint, this means that a strictly genetic analysis of any aspect of personality development always is incomplete. With respect to social policy it means that eugenic or biogenetic programs for population improvement may be the hardest roads rather than the only ones.

For example, the development of intelligence is predominately determined by genes (Chapter 1). Yet there still is a very substantial amount of environmental determination, therefore it theoretically is possible to effect major changes in intelligence through environmental manipulations alone. Suppose that we accept one of the typical estimates of the degree of genetic determination, namely, a heritability of 80 percent (using a terminology that will be explained later). Now in this situation, if the quality of everyone's genotypes were uniformly improved so that 50 percent of the population had genotypes as favorable as those held by the top 16 percent of the present population, then the mean I.Q. of the population would increase by 13.4 points. On the other hand, if environments were improved uniformly so that 50 percent of the population enjoyed environments as good as those now enjoyed by just the top 16 percent of the population, this theoretically would raise the mean I.Q. 6.7 points. The latter gain is about half as great as that from genotypic manipulation, thus, in a sense, environmental manipulations are about half as powerful as genetic manipulations even though intelligence is perhaps the most genetically determined of all general personality variables.

Programs to improve environments, even though difficult and

expensive, no doubt are more feasible strategies for population improvement than are programs involving eugenics or genetic manipulations. Neither scientists nor politicians really seem ready to set up programs employing selective mating or biogenetic manipulations for the sake of population improvement. In any case, a eugenic program involving controlled reproduction, even if it could be implemented, would not show appreciable effects for several generations. Eugenic control is not an answer to any immediate problem, whereas environmental treatments can have relatively fast effects on the character of a population.

Genetic Structuring of Socialization

Yet it should not be supposed that the genetic aspects of psychological development are only of esoteric interest. Genetically determined differences in physical and psychological traits structure socialization processes in several ways.

The genetically induced physical differences involved in age, sex, and race almost universally are the basis for assigning different social identities and statuses to people. People with different identities and statuses receive different experiences and, as a consequence, they develop different psychological characteristics. Thus one way that genetic mechanisms enter into socialization is by producing physical subtypes that are the basis of differential socialization. This issue, and its complications, will be examined later when age, sex, and race are directly the matters of concern.

Genetically determined variations in personality also may influence socialization processes. The existence of genetically determined traits implies that humans at birth are not totally plastic entities; at least with respect to genetically determined traits, an infant can be thought of as an embryonic form of a fairly specific adult psyche. Thus there is a sense in which socialization operates on a population with "preexisting" character, and the process of socialization is likely to be conditioned as a consequence.

Two characteristic phenomena of genetically influenced personality traits are especially relevant in the structuring of

3

socialization. The first is genetic variance: even if all persons in a population were raised in identical environments, there would be variations on a genetically determined trait because persons are born with different genotypes. The second basic phenomenon is genetic stability: the differences among persons on a genetically determined trait tend to continue over time, at least as long as the particular genetic mechanism is operating.

The existence of genetic variance on a trait is likely to structure socialization processes when a society seeks either to homogenize or diversify its population with respect to that trait. For example, a goal of homogamy may arise because a society places a strong negative valuation on certain states like intellectual deficiency or mental illness, and efforts are made to bring everyone within the "normal" range. If a trait has essentially no genetic component, then a goal of homogamy implies uniform socialization for all: generally speaking, the same treatment yields the same outcome. But if the trait has a significant genetic component, this is no longer true. A socialization treatment applied equally to all would not influence the genetic variance on the trait, and the outcome would be diversity. The only way to achieve homogamy is to use environmental treatments to *counteract* genetic potentials. Those with potential for the undesired state have to receive one treatment, while those with potential for the desired state receive another treatment or no special treatment at all. So genetic variance on a trait implies either that everyone in a population will not be equal on that characteristic or, if equality is to be the case, that everyone cannot be socialized equally.

Because of the requirements of a division of labor, societies sometimes seek to maximize diversity in psychological characteristics, especially aptitudes and talents. Maximizing diversity requires utilizing a variety of socialization treatments whether or not the trait involved has a genetic component. The socialization process is more efficient in the case of genetically controlled traits, however, if it is coordinated with the genetic potentials so that those with high potential are given treatments that develop that potential.

The phenomenon of genetic stability implies that some of the physical and psychological differences that appear among children tend to remain in effect for long periods of time. Such stable differences are likely to be employed by adults as anchors in their differentiation of children and, accordingly, genetically induced variations may structure socialization by serving as an early basis for different treatments. It has been noted that different treatments based on early assessment of potentials can either counteract or enhance genetic diversity when the treatments are related to the trait that was used in defining the socialization track. In order to appreciate the full implications of genetic stability, however, it needs to be added that differential treatments also may have secondary effects on development by affecting traits other than the one that led to differential treatment. For example, Moss (Chapter 3) found that infants with high irritability received different levels of cuddling and intimacy from their mothers than did children with low irritability; present theory suggests that secondary differences in character development might result from such variations in maternal treatment.

Genetic stability can affect socialization processes in another way. Basic aspects of personality such as intelligence, introversion-extroversion, and emotionality condition the way people respond to the world so that people differing on these traits actually can have different experiences even when they receive identical treatments. For example, an interpersonal event that is benign for most children may traumatize an especially emotional or timid child; thus the same experience could be associated with adjustment in some cases but lead to neurosis in others. Traits with a measure of genetic stability are liable to be especially important conditioners of experience because the consequences of the idiosyncratic responses have a chance to cumulate for each individual.

In summary, the existence of a genetic component in personality does not imply that the environment is irrelevant in the development of any psychological attributes. It does mean, however, that even from an early age children have some degree of character that structures and conditions their socialization processes.

5

1

Is personality inherited or is it the cumulated residue of individual experiences? This chapter reviews research showing that both genetic and environmental forces are active in many kinds of personality development. The review further reveals that the balance of influence between nature and nurture varies from trait to trait. The last section of the chapter discusses some of the abundant complexities involved in estimating the heritability of characteristics from research on human populations.

The Heritability of Personality
David R. Heise

Genetic processes do not affect all aspects of personality equally. Some traits are subject to a large amount of genetic determination while others are predominately or wholly a product of environmental conditions and learning experiences. This chapter reviews research findings about the heritability of some major personality variables. It should be noted that while there are enough studies to yield some interesting conclusions, nevertheless the entire area of personality-genetics is in an early stage of development. Findings concerning some of the variables listed below are meager and tentative, and other variables (notably those concerned with talents and aptitudes) are not discussed at all because of an apparent paucity of research.

At a number of points below, the research findings are summarized in terms of a heritability index or, equivalently, by a number indicating the "percent of variance explained by genotypes." This index varies from zero to 100. A value of zero indicates that a characteristic is completely determined by environmental and experiential factors; a value of 100 indicates complete genotypic determination; values in between indicate the relative balance of nurture and nature influences in development. Heritability indices are discussed in more detail in the final section of this chapter.

Intelligence
A rich body of empirical evidence on the heritability of intelligence

This paper was prepared especially for this volume.

shows that two-thirds or more of the total variance in intelligence is genetically determined (Spuhler & Lindzey, 1967:405). Recent results based on large samples of people, reliable measurements of intelligence, and sophisticated mathematical procedures indicate that a heritability of 80 percent is typical for a variety of populations and that the value possibly is higher—around 87 percent—for some urban populations in industrialized countries.

Erlenmeyer-Kimling and Jarvik (1963) collated a large number of studies reporting intelligence correlations among persons related by different degrees of kinship. Jensen (1969) used the figures, along with data from Burt's (1966) study of London children, to estimate the heritability of intelligence. He notes:

The Erlenmeyer-Kimling and Jarvik (1963) review was based on 52 independent studies of the correlations of relatives for tested intellectual abilities, involving over 30,000 correlational pairings from 8 countries in 4 continents, obtained over a period of more than two generations. The correlations were based on a wide variety of mental tests, administered under a variety of conditions by numerous investigators with contrasting views regarding the importance of heredity. . . . I applied [a] heritability formula to all the correlations for monozygotic and dizygotic (half their genes in common) twins reported in the literature and found an average heritability of .80 for intelligence test scores. (The correlations from which this heritability estimate was derived were corrected for unreliability.) Environmental differences *between* families account for .12 of the total variance, and differences *within* families account for .08. It is possible to derive an overall heritability coefficient from all the kinship correlations. . . . This composite value of H is .77, which becomes .81 after correction for unreliability (assuming .an average test reliability of .95). This represents probably the best single overall estimate of the heritability of measured intelligence that we can make. But, as pointed out previously, this is an average value of H about which there is some dispersion of values, depending on such variables as the particular tests used, the population sampled, and sampling error.

Identical Twins Reared Apart. The conceptually simplest estimate of heritability is, of course, the correlation between identical twins reared apart, since, if their environments are uncorrelated, all they have in common are their genes. The correlation (corrected for unreliability) in this case is the same as the heritability. . . . There have been only three major studies of MZ [monozygotic] twins separated early in life and reared apart. All three used individually administered intelligence tests. The correlation between Stanford-Binet I.Q.'s of 19 pairs of MZ twins reared apart in a study by Newman, Freeman, and Holzinger (1937) was .77 (.81 corrected for unreliability). The correlation between 44 pairs of MZ twins reared apart on a composite score based on a vocabulary test and Raven's Progressive Matrices was .77 (.81 corrected) in a study by Shields (1962). The correlation between 53 pairs on the Stanford-Binet was .86 (.91 corrected) in a study by Burt (1966). Twin correlations in the same group for height and for weight were .94 and .88, respectively.

The Burt study is perhaps the most interesting, for four reasons: (*a*) it is based on the largest sample; (*b*) the I.Q. distribution of the sample had a mean of 97.8 and a standard deviation of 15.3—values very close to those of the general population; (*c*) all the twin pairs were separated at birth or within their first six months of life; and (*d*) most important, the separated twins were spread over the entire range of socioeconomic levels (based on classification in terms of the six socioeconomic categories of the English census), and there was a slight, though nonsignificant, negative correlation between the environmental ratings of the separated twin pairs. When the twin pairs were rated for differences in the cultural conditions of their rearing, these differences correlated .26 with the differences in their I.Q.'s. Differences between the material conditions of their homes correlated .16 with I.Q. differences. (The corresponding correlations for a measure of scholastic attainments were .74 and .37, respectively. The correlation between the twins in scholastic attainments was only .62, indicating a much lower heritability than for I.Q.) (Jensen, 1969:48, 51–52).

Jinks and Fulker (1970) also analyzed the Burt (1966) data, using their complex and sophisticated formulas for estimating heritability. They arrived at a heritability of 87, and estimated more specifically that the overall variance in intelligence could be partitioned as follows: 38 percent due to *genetic* variations *within* families; 49 percent due to *genetic* variations *between* families; 8 percent due to *environmental* differences among the individuals *within* families; and 5 percent due to *environmental* variations *between* families.

The above studies leave very little room for doubting that performances on present-day intelligence tests are genetically determined to a large degree. Heritabilities of about 80 appear to be quite typical when calculations are based on samples of persons drawn from a single national population. However, this figure should not be presumed to apply to the human population as a whole (see last section of this chapter).

We would go far astray if we were to consider all the controversies that have arisen concerning the heritability of intelligence (e.g., see Harvard College, 1969). Yet one controversy is of special interest because the same basic issue arises repeatedly in discussing the heritability of other traits. The question is: Should heritability studies be focused on just the variable of "general intelligence" or on more specific aspects of intellectual ability?

An I.Q. score really is a composite score based on a person's performance with respect to several different intellectual abilities. These different forms of intelligence—such as the ability to apply abstract rules or to manipulate verbal, spatial, or numerical symbols—tend to correlate with one another, and this is what gives rise to the notion of general intelligence. But these abilities also are distinguishable theoretically (Guilford, 1972), they form distinct patterns in different racial and ethnic groups (Chapter 6), and they may be inherited to different degrees (Vandenberg, 1969). Thus it can be argued that scientific understanding of intellectual development would be advanced most by treating the measurements of the abilities separately rather than by summing measurements into a single score.

At a somewhat different level it can be argued that intellectual ability is not as important socially as is a person's achievement (Jensen, 1969:50), and achievements have a relatively low heritability, being a function of motivations, attitudes, and opportunities as well as intellectual ability (Jensen, 1969:58; Jinks & Fulker, 1970). Thus, perhaps less attention should be given to the development of intelligence and more attention should be given to those social conditions that enhance achievement orientations and that open up opportunities for achievement.

Both of these arguments have general currency in the study of the heritability of personality characteristics. Nearly every trait breaks down into components that could be studied separately. Moreover, the expression of any trait is always conditioned by its position within a personality configuration and by the situation under which expression can occur, so narrow concentration on the trait may lead to ignoring the behavior that is socially significant. In the near future, most studies no doubt will focus on relatively undifferentiated traits as a research economy. But ultimately the component traits will have to be studied to understand thoroughly the impact of genes on personality.

Introversion-Extroversion

Cattell, Blewett, and Beloff (1955) conducted a twin study measuring personality traits with a questionnaire form; from their heritability analysis, they concluded that the traits of aloofness versus sociability and adventuresome-boldness versus timidity are predominately inherited, and these are component traits of the more general dimension of introversion-extroversion. In a later study based on objective tests rather than questionnaires, variations in gregariousness were found to be mainly genetically determined (Cattell, Stice, & Kristy, 1957). Vandenberg (1967) reviewed a variety of studies on the heritability of personality, and it appeared that introversion-extroversion may be the most genetically controlled of all traits besides intelligence. Jinks and Fulker (1970), using sophisticated methods for calculating heritability, concluded that genes control about two-thirds of the variance in introversion-extroversion. On the basis of such reports the obvious conclusion is that variations in introversion-extroversion are more a function of genes than of environments.

A serendipitous finding arising out of the heritability studies of introversion-extroversion is that twins seem to polarize with respect to this characteristic, one becoming relatively introverted while the other becomes relatively extroverted (Jinks & Fulker, 1970). Thompson (1968), noting the phenomenon, suggested that it might occur because families encourage the development of differentiation in twins, but it is also plausible that twins develop these differences in interaction with one another and that a similar process occurs in siblings other than twins. One important aspect of this phenomenon is that it could account for a few discrepant estimates of heritability for the introversion-extroversion variable. Thompson (1968) reported some studies of twins that suggested low heritability of the trait, but the reported data are suitable only for comparing nature-nurture influences within families where this kind of arbitrary polarization occurs. Such studies do not account for the large genetic component existing between families.

Finally, it should be noted that the Cattell studies provide evidence suggesting that introversion-extroversion may break down into components differing in their heritability (Cattell, Blewett, & Beloff, 1955; Cattell, Stice, & Kristy, 1957).

Emotionality (Neuroticism)

Studies of the heritability of emotionality present a somewhat mixed picture. Eysenck and Prell (1951) estimated heritability at 80 percent for "general neuroticism," although heritability of component traits appeared to be much lower. Cattell found the trait to be mainly environmentally determined in his analyses based on questionnaire data (Cattell, Blewett, & Beloff, 1955) and also in analyses based on test data (Cattell, Stice, & Kristy, 1957). On the other hand, Jinks and Fulker (1970) estimated heritability of the trait at around 50 percent.

A more careful examination of the results from Cattell, Blewett, and Beloff (1955) and from Jinks and Fulker (1970) suggests an hypothesis concerning emotionality that may serve to resolve the discrepancies between reports. In both of these studies, it was found that emotionality is environmentally determined within families but not between families. Jinks and Fulker (1970:331) stated that "although environment is more important than genotype in producing differences between siblings, the differences in neuroticism observed between families are entirely genotypic in origin. Evidently cultural and class differences have no effect on this major personality dimension." If this finding replicates in other studies, then there is reason to believe that some of the discrepancies in heritability estimates between studies may be due simply to different emphases on between-family as opposed to within-family variation.

In any case, at present, the most plausible conclusion is that emotionality is determined by both heredity and environment. In addition, the finding that environmental effects are significant only within families suggests that nongenetic variations in emotionality may be a function mainly of internal family dynamics.

Dominance

Heritability studies of dominance are in agreement that environmental determination is important in the development of this trait. The analysis by Cattell, Blewett, and Beloff (1955) based on questionnaire measurements and the review by Thompson (1968) of other questionnaire data both indicate that environment and heredity are about equally involved in the development of dominance. (In addition, Cattell's analysis suggested that genetic differences are suppressed within families in favor of positional determination in terms of the family power structure.) However, later analyses by Cattell, Stice, and Kristy (1957) using objective test measurements indicated that variations in assertiveness and aggressiveness are almost entirely environmentally determined.

Too few studies are available to justify an estimate of heritability. However, it is fairly clear at this point that genetic determination is less involved in dominance than in the other personality characteristics discussed up to now.

Of some minor interest are a few selective breeding studies carried out on chickens (reviewed by DeFries, 1967). Some genetic control of dominance behavior and pecking order was found in these studies but most of the variance on the trait was environmentally determined.

Interests and Attitudes

Current theoretical perspectives provide little basis for supposing that specific interests and attitudes can be inherited. This is because interests and attitudes are conceived as affective responses to particular objects and categories, which in turn are conceived as being more or less arbitrarily defined at the cultural level. It is hard to imagine an interest in, say, stamp collecting being transmitted through genotypes when a person could not even know about stamps unless exposed to a culture where they exist. On the whole, heritability studies support this conceptualization. Most attitudes and interests do not appear to have any significant genetic component.

Nevertheless, some nonzero heritabilities of low value do arise for a few interests and attitudes. Vandenberg and Stafford (1967) found evidence for a genetic component in a third of the vocational preferences that they studied, and Thompson (1968) reports that significant heritabilities have been found for some religious attitudes. Given even a few instances of this kind, one must deal with the question of how heritability in interests and attitudes is to be interpreted.

First of all, it has to be understood that really no behavior is inherited. Genotypes are inherited, not phenotypes, and all behavioral and psychological variables are phenotypic, representing the complex products of genetic processes interacting with environments. Thus, heritability indices should be interpreted only as indicating how much people's genotypes determine their characteristics in the context of a given environment and not, as the term seems to imply, the extent to which parents' characteristics are passed on to children. With this viewpoint, there is no real anomaly involved in finding nonzero heritabilities for interests and attitudes. This simply means that some of the variation in interests and attitudes is associated with variation in genotypes. It does not mean that specific interests and attitudes are transmitted genetically from parents to child.

Even with the correct interpretation of heritabilities, a sense of discomfort is likely to remain in treating genetic determination of interests and attitudes as comparable to genetic control of, say, intelligence. Generally this problem is dealt with by proposing hierarchical causation: genes directly affect general personality dispositions like introversion-extroversion, and these in turn lead people to prefer certain activities and orientations in areas where their culture offers alternatives. Thus two levels of phenotypic development are proposed. The first level consists of basic characteristics that show comparable variations in all populations regardless of culture, although the style and content of expression might vary by culture. At the second level are characteristics so culture bound that they cannot sensibly be translated from one culture to another.

Finally, it should be noted that Jung (1956) did postulate direct genetic transmission of some specific attitudinal responses with his concept of archetypes. However, even this theory could not explain the heritabilities of vocational preferences as direct genetic transmission because the genetic imbedding of an archetype theoretically takes hundreds of generations.

Abnormal Behavior

Studies of the heritability of psychopathology and criminality are confronted with formidable problems. First, the variables themselves are only loosely defined and measurable so that assessment of the characteristics is usually on a rough clinical or legalistic basis. Second, adequate samples for the study of the phenomena are especially hard to acquire since almost by definition the abnormalities are present in only a small proportion of any general population. Rosenthal (1970) overcame these difficulties to some extent by reviewing a large number of studies appearing in both the American and European literature. Satisfactory quantitative estimates of heritability are yet to be obtained, but Rosenthal was able to reach a number of general conclusions.

"Genetic factors do contribute appreciably and beyond any reasonable doubt to the development of schizophrenic illness . . . . We know too . . . that nongenetic factors play an important role . . ." (Rosenthal, 1970: 132). Rosenthal's estimates of the heritability of schizophrenia calculated from data in nine different studies average out to around 50 percent, but this figure is highly tentative.

With respect to the manic-depressive syndrome, the data are considerably less adequate. Nevertheless, a variety of studies suggests that manic-depressive psychosis is subject to a very significant amount of genetic determination, and indeed this may be the dominant factor in its etiology.

Psychopathy is a psychiatric diagnostic category that has special social significance because of its rough identification with criminality or criminal potential. As Rosenthal notes, there is a long history of attributing criminality to genetic mechanisms. However, the evidence indicates quite the opposite: psychopathy is a characteristic that appears to be determined predominately by the environment, especially, it seems, by an oppressive and noxious early home life. Rosenthal concludes that genetic processes explain very little of the variations in criminal behavior and that certainly no single genotype is implicated.

Methods of Assessing Heritability

All of the studies cited above, dealing with the heritability of human personality traits, were nonexperimental in nature since experimentation using biochemical manipulations or selective breeding of humans simply is out of the question for ethical and practical reasons. So the first thing to understand about heritability studies of humans is that researchers do not manipulate genes and then observe whether traits change. Rather they find persons who naturally are similar or different in genotypic characteristics and then assess their psychological similarities.

Nonexperimental heritability studies are founded on the basic genetic principle that similarity in genotypes is a direct function of the degree of kinship between persons. Half of a child's genes are the same as those of either one of its parents, and on the average siblings also have half of their genes in common. In more distant relationships, genotypic similarity is less; e.g., a grandparent and grandchild or an uncle and nephew tend to have only a quarter of their genes in common. The closest relationship from a genetic standpoint occurs with identical, or monozygotic, twins: both develop from a single fertilized ovum and, consequently, have identical genotypes. These facts can be used to design a great variety of heritability studies ranging from the intergenerational analysis of a single family to a survey of a whole population at one point in time.

The most powerful designs make use of the genotypic identity between monozygotic twins, and twin studies of several types constitute the bulk of heritability research. Heritability studies involving identical twins are basically simple in their logic. Since twins from the same pair have the same genotype, one sees to what extent they also have similar phenotypes. If a trait is largely determined by genes, then identical twins should be more similar on the trait than persons with different genotypes. If a trait is not inherited, then there is no genetic constraint, and twins should be as dissimilar on the trait as unrelated persons.

The basic logic is simple, but a complication arises because identical twins are likely to experience very similar environments. Identical twins share the same prenatal environment, they are born at the same time and probably are assigned comparable status in the family, and for many years portions of their experience tend to be parallel. Hence it may not be entirely accurate to infer genetic determination of a trait just because identical twins are more similar on the trait than persons with different genotypes. This might be a consequence of their similar environments as well as, or instead of, their identical genes.

This problem typically is dealt with in one of two ways. First, an effort can be made to control the environmental factor by comparing identical twins with other pairs of persons who also have been raised in very similar environments but whose genotypes are not the same, namely, fraternal or dizygotic twins. Fraternal twins, like ordinary siblings, have only about half their genes in common. If monozygotic twins still are more similar than dizygotic pairs, it can be inferred that this similarity does not arise because of the experiences that they have in common. Thus one important type of twin study compares the degree of similarity among identical twins with the degree of similarity among fraternal twins.

Another approach is to make the environments of identical twins just as different as the environments of any two persons picked at random. Then when a pair of twins is compared with a pair of unrelated persons, the environmental factor is eliminated in the sense that it is equally present in both sets of differences, therefore similarity in environment cannot enter as a factor explaining any greater similarity between the twins. The environments of identical twins are "made" as different as the environments of people raised in different families by selecting only twins that have been reared apart from one another. It may come as a surprise that identical twins get separated and raised apart naturally, and frequently enough to be of use, but this does occur, and hundreds of such cases have been found and employed in research.

Of course, even these special research designs do not guarantee that the environmental factor is controlled. For example, because of their similar appearance, identical twins may receive more similar social treatments than fraternal twins. And twins, even when raised apart, do have some shared experiences during their nine-month prenatal period. Such problems mean that the results of a study employing a particular design almost always are subject to some ambiguities; confidence in whether a trait has a genetic component or not develops mainly as one sees the results of different kinds of studies converging.

Heritability Indices

Heritability studies rarely aim to determine whether a trait is a function of nature *or* nurture but rather to what extent each of these factors affects development, and quantification of information into an index requires the use of certain statistical procedures.

The basic quantifying concept used in heritability studies is the notion of variance. Variance is a mathematically defined quantity that measures the extent to which a set of humans (or any entities) differ on some measurable attribute. Variance can be interpreted as a kind of average of the differences between all pairs of individuals in the set, although in fact it is measured by averaging the squared difference between each individual and the group mean. What is interesting about variance is that it can be partitioned into parts associated with different comparisons, and the different components of variance can be used to calculate what proportion of the total variance on a trait is due to different effects. In heritability studies, variance is analyzed to see what proportion of the total variation on a trait is due to genetic effects and what proportion is due to environmental effects. The heritability index is defined as the percent of total variance that is due to genetic effects, i.e.,

$$\text{Heritability} = \frac{\text{genetic variance}}{\text{genetic variance} + \text{environmental variance}} \times 100.$$

To get a rough idea of how heritability indices actually are estimated, consider a simplified twin study. Suppose only identical twins reared apart are chosen for analysis. The total variance on a particular trait is a measure of the differences among all individuals in the sample, and this total variance can be partitioned into three components —the variance due to differences in genotypes between twins from different pairs, the variance due to variations in environment between twins in the same pair, and the variance due to variations in environment between twins in different pairs. In symbolic terms:

$$T = G + E_{\text{within}} + E_{\text{between}}$$

where T stands for the total variance, G stands for genetically determined variance resulting from differences in genotypes between pairs, E_{within} stands for variance arising from differences in environment experienced by twins in the same pairs, and E_{between} refers to environmental variations across pairs.

It is important to note that there is *not* a component due to genotypic differences within pairs since we are working only with monozygotic twins. Furthermore, it is to be noted that the environmental variations for twins in the same pair theoretically should be almost the same as those for twins in different pairs, since all subjects were reared in different homes. Assuming this is true, then the two environmental components of variance should be equal, i.e.:

$$E_{\text{within}} = E_{\text{between}} = E,$$

and
$$T = G + 2E.$$

A second measure of variance can be computed assessing only the differences between twins from the same pair. Since twins from the same pair have identical genotypes, these differences reflect only environmental effects, and this variance—call it W—is a direct measure of the environmental component: $W = E$. Now the two observed variances, T and W, can be used to solve for the two theoretical components of the total variance, E and G, i.e.

$$E = W, \qquad G = T - 2W.$$

The definition of a heritability index is the genetic variance divided by the total variance so we could write:

$$H = \frac{G}{G + 2E} \times 100 = \frac{T - 2W}{T} \times 100.$$

This would tend to underestimate the genetic component, however, because this particular sampling design artificially inflated the environmental variance by selecting only twins reared apart. A better index would show the genetic contribution in a hypothetical sample of unrelated persons reared in different families:

$$H = \frac{G}{G + E} \times 100 = \frac{T - 2W}{T - 2W + W} \times 100 = \frac{T - 2W}{T - W} \times 100.$$

Studies that employ monozygotic and dizygotic twins who have been reared together also can be used to estimate components of genetic and environmental variance, which in turn can be used to calculate a heritability index. One weakness of this design, however, is that estimates of heritability cannot be made using the total variance existing both between and within families. Rather, the heritability index is based only on the variance occurring within families.

Twin studies are difficult and expensive to conduct, and they are subject to their several weaknesses. Thus there have been efforts to develop still other designs for studying the inheritance of traits on the basis of observations on less restricted populations. The fundamental logic always is the same as above — persons are grouped according to the similarities in their genotypes and environments, then the phenotypic variance is partitioned according to these groupings to define components of variance associated with genetic determination and environmental determination. Once the different components of variance have been calculated, heritability can be estimated.

Variations in Heritability

Different studies rarely result in exactly the same estimates of heritability for a number of reasons:

1. *Sampling variations.* The average differences among persons in genotypes and in environmental backgrounds vary from study to study in part because the group of subjects in one study may be more similar in a particular way than those in another purely as a result of chance. Such chance variations in samples lead to variations in estimates of heritability, but statistical theory postulates that the different figures do tend to cluster around a true value for the population as a whole.

2. *Measurement reliability.* If errors are made in measuring a trait, then differences may seem to exist among persons who really are identical. Thus measurement errors generally increase the apparent differences or amount of variance in a group. In most study designs this extra error variance gets aggregated with environmental variance. So, generally, the overall effect of measurement imprecision is to inflate the proportion of variance attributed to environment; and studies that use less reliable measures tend to find greater amounts of environmental determination than do studies using more reliable measures.

3. *Variations in formulas.* Different estimates of heritability may occur because different formulas are used to calculate heritability. For example, it was noted above that studies of twins reared

together do not provide the same kind of information as do studies of monozygotic twins reared apart, and therefore the formula for estimating heritability necessarily is different in the two cases. For such reasons, two different studies might not agree concerning the heritability of a particular trait.
4. *Balance between genetic and environmental variance in the population.* Looking at the formula presented earlier, it is clear that a heritability index simply registers the balance of genotypic and environmental variance existing in the population being studied. However, this balance may vary from population to population. Some populations may have relatively more environmental variance than others, and some populations may have relatively more genetic variance than others. When such is the case, heritabilities will be found to vary across populations.

The first three sources of variability in heritability indices are methodological problems: they can be minimized by doing better research and adopting standard conventions. But the last kind of variability is not methodological — it is a problem arising from the nature of human populations and societies, and it is worth elaborating the point.

For convenience, suppose that the amount of genetic variance on a particular trait is constant for the species. Now suppose we look at a society where everyone experiences very nearly the same environment. In such a case, environmental variations on the trait are trivial, and almost all of the differences among people are a function of their differing genotypes. In such a society, heritability indices will indicate that the trait is genetically determined because most of the total variance on the trait has a genetic source. On the other hand, imagine a society in which there are immense differences in the environments and experiences of individuals. The genetic component for the trait remains the same, but now there also is likely to be a large environmental component, and heritability indices will indicate that the trait is only partially, perhaps even negligibly, determined by genetic factors.

So human characteristics more often will seem to be genetically controlled in simple societies and environmentally controlled in complex societies. Furthermore, the heritability of a trait may appear to change within a single society over time. If social change causes environments to become homogenized, heritabilities will increase; if environments become diversified, heritabilities will decline.

A heritability index is not a natural constant. It is only an indication of how genetic and environmental factors contribute to the development of a trait in a particular society at a particular time.

References

Burt, C. L.
  1966 "The genetic determination of differences in intelligence: a study of monozygotic twins reared together and apart." British Journal of Psychology 57: 137–153.

Cattell, Raymond B.; D. B. Blewett; and J. R. Beloff.
  1955 "The inheritance of personality: a multiple variance analysis determination of approximate nature-nurture ratios for primary personality factors in Q-data." American Journal of Human Genetics 7: 122–146.

Cattell, Raymond B.; G. F. Stice; and N. F. Kristy.
  1957 "A first approximation to nature-nurture ratios for eleven primary personality factors in objective tests." Journal of Abnormal and Social Psychology 54: 143–149.

DeFries, John C.
  1967 "Quantitative genetics and behavior: Overview and perspective." Pp. 322–339 in Jerry Hirsch (ed.), Behavior-Genetic Analysis. New York: McGraw-Hill.

Erlenmeyer-Kimling, L., and L. F. Jarvik.
  1963 "Genetics and intelligence: A review," Science 142: 1477–1479.

Eysenck, H. J., and D. B. Prell.
  1951 "The inheritance of neuroticism: An experimental study." Journal of Mental Science 97: 441–467.

Guilford, J. P.
  1972 "Thurstone's primary mental abilities and structure-of-intellect abilities." Psychological Bulletin 77: 129–143.

Harvard College.
  1969 Environment, Heredity, and Intelligence. Cambridge, Massachusetts: Harvard Educational Review Reprint Series, No. 2.

Jensen, A. R.
  1969 "How much can we boost IQ and scholastic achievement?" Harvard Educational Review 39 (Winter):1–123.

Jinks, J. L., and D. W. Fulker.
  1970 "Comparison of the biometrical genetical, MAVA, and classical approaches to the analysis of human behavior." Psychological Bulletin 73:311–349.

Jung, Carl G.
  1956 "On the psychology of the unconscious." Pp. 11–130 in Two Essays on Analytical Psychology. Translated by R. F. C. Hull. New York: Meredian Books.

Newman, H. H.; F. N. Freeman; and K. J. Holzinger.
  1937 Twins: A Study of Heredity and Environment. Chicago: University of Chicago Press.

Rosenthal, David.
  1970   Genetic Theory and Abnormal Behavior. New York: McGraw-Hill.

Shields, James.
  1962   Monozygotic Twins Brought Up Apart and Brought Up Together. London: Oxford University Press.

Spuhler. James N.. and Gardner Lindzey.
  1967   "Racial differences in behavior." Chapter 19 in Jerry Hirsch (ed.), Behavior-Genetic Analysis. New York: McGraw-Hill.

Thompson, W. R.
  1968   "Genetics and personality." Pp. 161-174 in Edward Norbeck, Douglas Price-Williams, and W. M. McCord (eds.), The Study of Personality: An Interdisciplinary Appraisal. New York: Holt, Rinehart, and Winston.

Vandenberg, Steven G.
  1967   "Hereditary factors in normal personality traits (as measured by inventories)." Recent Advances in Biological Psychiatry, 9:65-104.
  1969   "Human behavior genetics: present status and suggestions for future research." Merrill-Palmer Quarterly 15:121-154.

Vandenberg, Steven G., and Richard E. Stafford.
  1967   "Hereditary influences on vocational preferences as shown by scores of twins on the Minnesota vocational interest inventory." Journal of Applied Psychology 51:17-19.

2

While sex, race, and age are the most prominent biosocial variables, there are innumerable other biological distinctions that could be, and sometimes are, involved in social discrimination and the channeling of people into different socialization tracks. This chapter considers the social psychological significance of several such variations, for instance, somatotypes or body builds. An emphasis running throughout the chapter is that personality can be related to biological constitution through the medium of social interaction as well as through a direct genetic connection. In other words, constitutional differences may be related to personality development because people react in distinct ways to different constitutions and thereby nurture different personalities.

The Organism and Socialization

John A. Clausen

In the following pages, I wish to highlight some of the characteristics of the organism and its development that seem to me to merit sociological attention in research on socialization.

Socialization is an ongoing process with many phases, many changing tasks to be accomplished. Goals change, in accordance with age and social position. But insofar as we can speak of an ultimate goal, it is that the individual be prepared to deal with the requirements of full adult participation in his society. It is this goal that should be kept in mind as we consider some of the specific ways in which biological features may make a difference.

Biological Factors
in Behavioral Development

Donald Hebb (1958), who has contributed so much to the study of psychology as a biological discipline, notes six classes of factors influencing behavioral development: (1) genetic, that is, properties of

Revised version of a paper presented at the meetings of the American Sociological Association, Miami, Florida, August 30, 1966. The author is indebted to David C. Glass for helpful suggestions. The longitudinal research referred to in this paper is supported in part by a grant from the National Institute of Mental Health, MH–5300.

Abridged from the *Journal of Health and Social Behavior,* 8(1967):243–252, with permission of the American Sociological Association and the author.

the fertilized ovum; (2) prenatal chemical factors which exercise nutritive or toxic influence in the uterine environment; (3) postnatal chemical influences, which may be endogeneous to the organism, such as endocrine balance, or exogeneous, such as diet, drugs, etc.; (4) sensory experiences which are normally inevitable for all members of the species (for example, contact between mother and offspring in the case of all mammals); (5) sensory experiences that vary from one member of the species to another; and (6) traumatic events. A sociologist might well subdivide classes 4 and 5 to deal with experiences that are culturally prescribed for all persons of a given age and sex, those that are prescribed for certain categories of persons, those that are accepted alternatives and those that are culturally proscribed or devalued. Hebb's other classes could undoubtedly be subdivided and enlarged upon also. The list is a useful reminder of the variety (and potential interaction) of influences upon behavioral development. We may note that genetic, chemical and traumatic events may themselves be responsible for the individual's having experiences that vary from those of other members of the species. It is equally true that experiences in the socialization of the individual can influence not only such biologically relevant behaviors as dietary intake and intake of other chemicals, but also internal biochemical processes and the likelihood that the individual will be exposed to various types of trauma or injury.[1]

Genetic Factors

Theoretical statements of the interrelationships of heredity and environment in various circumstances (genetic pools and environments) have been available for several decades. Geneticists like Dobzhansky (1957; 1962) have given us formulations of the problem that show high sophistication in the treatment of social and cultural variables as well as in the realm of genetics. A whole field of behavioral genetics, relating primarily to infra-human species, has evolved and has produced impressive evidence on the nature of the interaction between heredity and environmental experience (see Fuller & Thompson, 1960). The existence of critical periods during which certain types of learning must occur if that learning is to be effective has been clearly documented for a number of species. For example, Harlow's research

1 For evidence on the relationship of maternal attitudes and child personality to children's accident experience, see Manheimer and Mellinger (1967).

on rhesus monkey infants, reared in isolation from age-mates, demonstrated conclusively that deprivation of early experience with peers irrevocably destroyed the heterosexual capabilities of these monkeys in adulthood (Harlow & Harlow, 1965).[2] Scott (1963:4) generalizes that "every highly social animal has a short period early in life in which the formation of primary social relationships takes place." The development of sensory modalities and of particular skills which entail learning to use the senses effectively is also closely scheduled for many species. Moreover, experimental studies have demonstrated that for a variety of species the effects of early experience are influenced by genotype or biological variation (Fuller & Thompson, 1960).

With humans, such experimental studies are not possible. We cannot manipulate genetic make-up, nor can we identify genotypes. Only in instances of genetically transmitted diseases or deformities are we able to put a genetically relevant label on an individual at birth. Some approach to valid labeling is essential if we are to study closely the interaction between genetic potentiality and socialization processes. Yet the tremendous number of gene combinations with which one deals in man may render infeasible any attempt to work with genotypes except as these are manifest in gross behavioral effects, at least until further advances are made in methodology. Our ability to go further in studying this particular aspect of the relationship between the organism and socialization may have to rest on crude approximations to labeling through (1) twin and family geneology studies or (2) our finding behavioral and temperamental tendencies or sensitivities that are manifest very early and that can serve as indicators of biological make-up.

Studies of monozygotic and dizygotic twins reveal a number of psychological characteristics whose variance is markedly greater for dizygotic twins (Vandenberg, 1967), but unfortunately we have almost no data on the ongoing socialization process in their families. Indeed, one of the major deficits in our knowledge derives from the fact that research has overwhelmingly dealt with outcome variables and not with how the outcomes came about. Sociologists have been prone to argue that identical twins are more likely to be reared alike than fraternal twins; some geneticists have denied this and others have attempted to estimate the effects of rearing by analyzing separately

2 It recently was discovered that the loss is not irrevocable (see Suomi & Harlow, 1972)—*Editor.*

their data on same-sex and opposite-sex fraternal twins. We badly need a sophisticated formulation and conceptualization of the kinds of socialization experiences that may make a difference and the application of such concepts in longitudinal studies of families with twins.

Systematic research on early differences in temperament and sensitivity is still in its infancy. There is evidence of a variety of differences between males and females in skin sensitivity and responsiveness in the neonatal period.[3] Individual differences within the sexes are greater than mean differences between the sexes in this respect, and it seems reasonable to predict that such variations influence caretaking practices and attitudes as well as the response of the infant to such practices. Girls appear to many parents to be much more pliant to the early demands put upon them by the imposition of training disciplines, though available research does not support the existence of clear differences in conformity at early ages.[4]

Another lead to the possibility of differences in responsiveness of the child comes from recent research on "cuddlers" and "noncuddlers"—children who like to be held and cuddled and those who respond by kicking and crying when they are held. It appears that such differences are in part related to the mother's enjoyment of sensual contact, but they are also significantly related to the sleeping patterns of the children ("cuddlers" sleep much longer), to the child's enjoyment of soft, cuddly toys and to reactions to any kind of physical restraint (Schaffer & Emerson, 1964).

Studies of infant conditioning (Papousek, 1967) and of autonomic responses (Bridger & Reiser, 1959) have also revealed individual differences which may have significance for socialization experience. A critical methodological problem is posed by the high lability of responses in the neonate (making reliable measurement of response tendencies extremely difficult) and the very rapid development of learned responses which depend on environmental and socialization influences.

Behavioral Correlates of Morphology

Another approach to the identification of constitutional attributes that may influence socialization and behavior is afforded by the study of

3 For a brief summary of relevant studies, see Hamburg and Lunde (1966:18).
4 For a summary of the literature on sex differences in conformity, see Maccoby (1966:329–330).

body build. Sheldon's classification of components or varieties of physique as endomorphic (soft, fat), mesomorphic (muscular, tough) and ectomorphic (thin, fragile) has been carefully developed and standardized (Sheldon, with Stevens & Tucker, 1940). His classification of personality components or varieties of temperament—viscerotonic, somatotonic and cerebrotonic—is less well accepted, and his attempts to demonstrate relationships between the two (Sheldon, with Stevens, 1942) have been rejected as methodologically indefensible by most psychologists and social scientists who have reviewed his work. Personality ratings are inevitably influenced by the rater's presuppositions as to what goes with what; Sheldon's ratings could hardly have failed to confirm his expectations. Yet there have been enough indications that somatotypes do have some relationship to behavior to merit further consideration. Gardner Lindzey (1967) notes five classes of mechanisms which might mediate relationships between morphology and behavior: (1) experiential events that influence both morphology and behavior or personality (as in the influence of certain types of maternal over-protectiveness on both overeating and timidity); (2) the facilitation of certain performances by physical characteristics such as height, strength and stride; (3) the recruitment or selection of individuals for social roles and activities on the basis of physical characteristics; (4) related to (2) and (3), the existence of cultural expectations as to the behavior or temperament of persons of given physique ("lean and hungry" types, "jolly fat people," etc.), regardless of the validity of the underlying rationale for the expectation; and (5) joint biological determinants of both behavior and physique, as brought about, for example, by genetic determinants or by endocrinological function. Sociologists have in general been willing to contemplate the first four of these mechanisms but have boggled at the fifth.

The data on relationships between physique and behavior available from independent assessments of the two realms do establish that there are significant correlations. If they are less high than the correlations reported by Sheldon, they are nevertheless not appreciably less than correlations between behavior and many variables of socialization experience presumed by social scientists to be important influences on adult personality. But the data thus far available do not permit us to establish what mechanisms account for the correlations between physique and behavior. Perhaps each accounts for some part of the relationship.

One's physique is certainly determined in large part by his heredity. It does not appear, however, that body type is inherited as a unit. For physique and temperament to be jointly determined by heredity would require that these complexes of traits be inherited as units through the operation of linked groups of genes. The one available study on the heritability of Sheldon's components, based on somatotyping of fraternal and identical twins by Osborne and DeGeorge (1959), found higher heritability coefficients for females than for males, but even for females the correlation was less than would be expected if somatotype were inherited as a unitary trait.

Nevertheless, it does appear that there are linkages between somatotype and other aspects of physical development. For example, body build is related to rate of maturing sexually, especially for girls, with mesomorphic girls maturing earlier and becoming more amply endowed while their ectomorphic peers are growing taller but less curvy (McNeill & Livson, 1963). Despite relationships between physique and the attainment of sexual maturity, we shall defer consideration of personality and behavioral differences associated with early or late maturing since the social significance of this event may entail different social implications than does body build.

How might somatotype modify socialization influences? Consider Sheldon's hypothesis that a *mesomorph* should tend toward *somatotonic* temperament, which he characterizes as high in aggressiveness, activity, need for power by dominance and low in sensitivity to others. As yet unpublished analyses of data from the Oakland Growth Study, by Glen Elder and the writer, give at least partial confirmation of Sheldon's hypotheses, especially among males. Somatotypes were ascertained by Sheldon from body photographs taken periodically through adolescence. Personality data were secured from self-report inventories, peer ratings and staff ratings (made before the publication of Sheldon's formulations) for this group of subjects who were intensively studied during their high school years in the 1930s. Boys high in mesomorphy were seen by their peers as getting into fights ($r = .63$), "active" ($r = .57$) and "daring" ($r = .58$), but these correlations vary somewhat by social class and by height above or below the median.

There seems but little doubt that in Western society physiques high on the mesomorphic component are regarded as most attractive, despite the recent trend to ectomorphic models in the world of fashion. Among the higher correlations found in our data between components of physique and social or psychological attributes of the individual are the .55 between mesomorphy and attractiveness (factor score derived from ratings in adolescence by adult observers). The differing correlations between somatotype and psychological characteristics among middle-class and working-class subjects suggest that the social meaning of the somatotype rather than genetic constitution accounts for a good deal of the variance. It remains to be seen whether further analysis, in longitudinal perspective, will reveal changing correlations by age groups as well.

Early vs. Late Maturing

Linked with morphology are such characteristics as stature and rate of maturing. The age at which the organism approaches full stature or reaches sexual maturity is somewhat influenced by diet and the conditions of life, but research on twins suggests that up to 90 percent of the variance in height is attributable to heredity and a large proportion of the variance in rate of maturing seems likewise to be genetically determined (see Bloom, 1964:34). In general, the child who is tall or short relative to his peers at the time of entrance into school will tend to maintain this position in adulthood; correlations between height at age eight and height at maturity average about .8 in various longitudinal studies, though the correlation drops a bit during puberty (Bloom, 1964:18-32). Early maturers achieve their maximum height at a younger age than do late maturers but they tend to be no taller at maturity than their late-maturing peers. Indeed, among females, late maturers tend to grow taller, and, as already noted, to be more ectomorphic.

Among males in the Oakland Growth Study at the Institute of Human Development, University of California, early maturers were most likely to make a favorable impression as to physique and to exhibit leadership and assurance in adolescence, according to analyses by Mary Jones (1965). Significant psychological differences betwen early and late maturers persist at least into the thirties. The early maturers, who appear to have acquired substantial social skills and assurance along with sexual maturity, scored higher at age 32 on C.P.I. [California Personality Inventory] scales of dominance, responsibility and desire to make a good impression, for example, while later maturers scored higher on flexibility, psychological mindedness and psychoneurotic tendencies. We cannot yet be certain whether these differences are largely the consequence of the adaptation of the early and late maturers to their social stimulus values in adolescence, or whether the organisms also differ in temperament (especially as a consequence of endocrinological differences) and other respects. The groups do *not* differ in tested intelligence.

Body build, height, weight and strength certainly affect the individual's choice of activities and his selection or recruitment for certain roles. This is equally true of attractiveness and of manifestly high intelligence, but sociologists have not attempted to examine the different developmental pathways of the homely and the beautiful, the very bright and the dull child, except as intelligence is related to school attainment.[5] The interactions of a biological attribute and a social behavior with important consequences for health are revealed in an examination of the relationships between cigarette smoking and various physical, psychological and social attributes of the subjects of the Oakland Growth Study. Early maturers were *less* likely to become smokers and late maturers *more* likely to become smokers than their peers, especially among males. The late maturers were more often smoking before they finished high school (in 1938–39), and more of them became heavy smokers subsequently (Clausen, 1967). One is tempted to interpret their smoking as evidence of a compensatory striving to appear mature, but the large number of other attitudinal and behavioral correlates suggests caution in offering interpretations.

Aberrant Development

Most of the research that has been directly concerned with investigating the effects of biological variation on socialization has dealt with instances of gross pathology, deficit, or consequences of illness or injury. For the study of influences on socialization, it is often irrelevant whether such deficit or disorder has come about through genetic mutation, prenatal influences, birth injury or subsequent illness. Among prenatal conditions that leave many infants impaired are the mother's contracting rubella in the first trimester of pregnancy, the effects of drugs like thalidomide or the use of hormone treatments during pregnancy. Premature birth and the process of birth itself account for a substantial amount of neurological damage. Early blindness, deafness or crippling as a consequence of various diseases of childhood account

---

5   An excellent review of research on intelligence and school attainment which explores a number of aspects of behavioral genetics is contained in Eckland (1967).

for additional instances of aberrant physical development. With notable exceptions, sociologists have been interested in the influences of such conditions primarily as they lead to stereotyping or, to use a term that has become increasingly fashionable, "stigmatization." The person whose morphology is grossly variant from population norms, the person with an obvious sensory defect, the brain-injured child with his emotional lability, short attention span and disordered behavior, are all subject to labels that stigmatize. In some instances, the attribute that leads to stereotypic responses from others will have trivial influence on ability to master the tasks of normal development; in others, those tasks will be made much more difficult and problematic of attainment. Stigmatization inevitably affects identity to some degree, but the nature of the social matrix surrounding the individual at crucial developmental phases may make an enormous difference on whether a physical deficit becomes the core of identity or merely one attribute among many.

The past decade has produced evidence of a much greater prevalence of neurological damage in surviving infants than had hitherto been suspected (Pasamanick & Knobloch, 1966). Such children show various limitations in adaptive capacity or learning ability, ranging from highly circumscribed deficits to generalized depression of intelligence. Quite clearly they need learning environments that can make maximal use of sensorimotor channels that are relatively unimpaired, while bypassing those in which the child is most deficient (Eisenberg, 1964).

We know from a number of studies that parental attitudes toward a child that is early perceived as vulnerable or defective will be different from parental attitudes toward normal offspring. As Eisenberg (1964:70) notes, "Parental behavior may be so skewed as to induce in the child the very patterns of behavior we would have recognized as psychogenic had the presence of brain damage not preempted our attention." He goes on to raise a number of highly pertinent questions for research. For example, what kind of parental socialization practices are most successful in dealing with the outbursts of seemingly uncontrollable behavior manifested by such children? Eisenberg (1964:70) suggests that: "Such children plead for external controls upon their behavior; permissive childrearing practices multiply the problem and increase the [child's] burden of guilt."

Whether or not they recognize the nature of the child's needs, parents of children who are congenitally impaired appear to respond more protectively and intrusively to these children than do parents of normal children. Many of the parental behaviors which appear to be implicated in the etiology of schizophrenia, duodenal ulcer, asthma and a number of other psychiatric and psychosomatic disorders are also found *in response to* deficits of clearly biological origin.[6] This is not to say that the theories of psychogenic origin are necessarily invalid, but rather that the interactions between parental socialization behavior and the nature of the particular organism being socialized must be studied with a recognition that causal influences work in both directions.

Parental overprotection may take place even when impairment is very minor. Stephen Richardson (1964) has noted how a single functional impairment may jeopardize the child's opportunity to gain experiences necessary for his socialization. He cites research indicating, for example, that a normally intelligent child with mild cerebral palsy (leading to motor impairment of the legs) is less likely than a child without such motor impairment to be given increasing responsibility with increasing age, to be liked by his peers, and to be permitted to explore his environment.

Sex Differences

Students of socialization research have been especially interested in the learning of sex identity and sex-appropriate behaviors. Maccoby's recent volume, *The Development of Sex Differences* (1966), summarizes theory and research on this topic from biological, psychological, social and cultural perspectives. In all societies, males and females differ not merely in primary sex characteristics but also in secondary sex attributes such as height, musculature and body hair. The degree of sexual dimorphism can be influenced by both genetic and cultural factors (see D'Andrade, 1966). In all human populations, men tend to be taller, heavier and stronger than women, but the relative differences between the sexes in height, weight and strength vary substantially from one population to another. Both sexual selection and social roles play a part in determining the size of such differences. Yet we have very little

---

6 Some of the relevant evidence is presented by Bell (1964). He also discusses a methodological strategy for attempting to resolve alternative interpretations of the observed correlations between family patterns and child disorders.

research that relates to the process of achieving sex identity or, for that matter, to socialization for sexual competence.

Studies of persons born with sexual anomalies that rendered original sex assignment ambiguous (most often females with congenital adrenal hyperplasia) suggest that the gender role assigned in the first three years is more important than chromosomal, gonadal or hormonal sex in determining the individual's sexual identification in later life (Hampson & Hampson, 1965). In other words, "labeling" of sex can to a large extent determine how the individual will be regarded, and will regard himself, even when such labeling is erroneous. That erroneous labeling is likely to lead to severe social disabilities and psychological problems for the individual is obvious.

The Labeling of Bodily Processes

Sociologists have, as noted above, been much concerned with the effects of stigmatizing labels. We have devoted less attention to the way in which the individual comes to label his own feelings and bodily states. Zborowski's (1952) insightful analysis of cultural components in responses to pain contained a number of hypotheses as to how socialization agents teach the child to label his feelings and actions when hurt or sick. One would like to have direct observational data bearing on such hypotheses. Does the child reared in a family of Christian Scientists come to label his discomforts differently than one who receives prompt medical attention when ill with diarrhea or bronchitis?

Recent research by Schacter (1964) has demonstrated the importance of the labeling of bodily states in determining response to injections of epinephrine. Even more impressive is his research on obesity. Starting with Hilde Bruch's (1961) hypothesis that obese persons have not been taught in childhood to discriminate between hunger feelings and such states as fear, anger and anxiety, Schacter (1967) has conducted experiments which document that the obese do not label as "hunger" the same set of bodily symptoms as do normals. Unlike normal subjects, the obese ate as much on a full stomach as on an empty stomach, and whereas normals ate appreciably less when in a fear-inducing situation, the obese ate somewhat more in this situation than in a less threatening one.

A Plea for Observational Study

Study of the interaction of biological make-up and socialization experience requires direct repeated observation of the socialization process as well as repeated assessment of the individuals undergoing socialization. The past two decades have witnessed a tremendous advance in knowledge of the nature of the infant's behavioral repertoire, largely because of the very great increase in systematic observation by physiologists, psychologists and pediatricians. Sociologists have seldom engaged in such observation. Sociological surveys reveal attitudes and reported socialization practices and experiences but they cannot answer such crucial questions as: (1) In what situations or circumstances do behaviors of children with particular biological attributes or deficits call forth different responses from the environment? and (2) Under what conditions do the same environmental influences produce quite different effects in the child? I am aware that "the same influences" are never *really* the same. Unique meanings are evolved, which is precisely the process that needs to be studied.

There are many basic questions begging for investigation. What are the consequences for parents with low energy level having a child with an inordinately high energy level? Or the reverse? Parents with unrealistically high or unrealistically specialized expectations for their children often apply pressures for performance that lead to rebellion or to frustration for both parent and child. But what happens when the child *is able to meet* those expectations? The life histories of a number of outstanding scholars and athletes suggest that sometimes unusual excellence results. Can we learn how to maximize the fit between what is biologically given and what is to be done in the course of socialization?

Conclusion

Recent developments relevant to the topic of this paper have been so varied as to make even a summary difficult. Studies of primate behavior in natural habitats and in experimental settings have added new dimensions to comparative research on learning.[7] Careful studies of species-specific behavior by ethologists with backgrounds in zoology, psychology and anthropology have given new and scientifically respectable meaning to the term *instinct*.[8] Neurophysiological and biochemical processes mediating behavior in stressful situations are under

7 See, for example, DeVore (1965) and Schrier, Harlow, and Stollnitz (1965).
8 Good examples are Schiller (1957), Rheingold (1963), and Marler and Hamilton (1966).

study (see, for example, Liederman & Shapiro, 1964; Glass & Pfaff-man, 1967). The emergence of medical sociology and the increasing participation of sociologists in research teams containing physicians and physiologists have created opportunities for sociologists to become more knowledgeable about the nature of man as an organism. Publications of the proceedings of the ongoing series of conferences on biological aspects of behavior sponsored by the Russell Sage Foundation and the Rockefeller University will help to make available to sociologists some of the crucially important recent developments in other fields.[9] There is an opportunity for major advances if we can incorporate some of this recently acquired knowledge in research on the development of the person in society.

References

Bell, Richard Q.
  1964 "The effect on the family of a limitation in coping ability in the child: A research approach and a finding." Merrill-Palmer Quarterly 10:129–142.

Bloom, Benjamin S.
  1964 Stability and Change in Human Characteristics. New York: Wiley.

Bridger, Wagner H., and Morton F. Reiser.
  1959 "Psychophysiologic studies of the neonate: An approach toward the methodological and theoretical problems involved." Psychosomatic Medicine 21:265–276.

Bruch, Hilde.
  1961 "Transformations of oral impulses in eating disorders: A conceptual approach." Psychiatric Quarterly 35:458–481.

Clausen, J. A.
  1967 "Adolescent antecedents of cigarette smoking: Data from the Oakland Growth Study." Social Science and Medicine 1(December):357–382.

D'Andrade, Roy.
  1966 "Sex differences and cultural institutions," in Eleanor E. Maccoby (ed.), The Development of Sex Differences. Stanford, California: Stanford University Press.

DeVore, Irven (ed.).
  1965 Primate Behavior: Field Studies of Monkeys and Apes. New York: Holt, Rinehart and Winston.

9 In addition to Glass and Pfaffman (1967), see Glass (1967).

Dobzhansky, Theodosius.
1957   "The biological concept of heredity as applied to man." Pp. 11-19 in The Nature and Transmission of the Genetic and Cultural Characteristics of Human Population. New York: Milbank Memorial Fund.
1962   Mankind Evolving. New Haven, Connecticut: Yale University Press.

Eckland, Bruce K.
1967   "A sociologist's perspective on behavior genetics." American Sociological Review 32(April):173-194.

Eisenberg, Leon.
1964   "Behavioral manifestations of cerebral damage." Pp. 61-73 in H. G. Birch (ed.), Brain Damage in Children: The Biological and Social Aspects. Baltimore: Williams and Wilkins.

Fuller, John L., and William R. Thompson.
1960   Behavior Genetics. New York: Wiley.

Glass, David C.
1967   "Genetics and social behavior." Items 21(March):1-5.

Glass, David C., and Carl Pfaffman (eds.)
1967   Biology and Behavior: Neurophysiology and Emotion. New York: Rockefeller University Press and Russell Sage Foundation.

Hamburg, David A., and Donald T. Lunde.
1966   "Sex hormones in the development of sex differences in human behavior," in Eleanor E. Maccoby (ed.), The Development of Sex Differences. Stanford, California: Stanford University Press.

Hampson, John, and Joan Hampson.
1965   "The development of gender role," in Frank Beach (ed.), Sex and Behavior. New York: Holt, Rinehart and Winston.

Harlow, Harry F., and Margaret K. Harlow.
1965   "The affectional systems." Pp. 287-334 in A. M. Schrier, H. F. Harlow, and F. Stollnitz (eds.), Behavior of Nonhuman Primates. Volume 2. New York: Academic Press.

Hebb, Donald O.
1958   A Textbook of Psychology. Philadelphia: W. B. Saunders.

Jones, Mary Cover.
1965   "Psychological correlates in somatic development." Child Development 36:899-911.

Leiderman, P. H., and David Shapiro (eds.)
1964   Psychobiological Approaches to Social Behavior. Stanford, California: Stanford University Press.

Lindzey, Gardner.
1967   "Morphology and behavior," in James H. Spuhler (ed.), Genetic Diversity and Human Behavior. Viking Fund Publications in Anthropology, No. 45. Chicago: Aldine.

Maccoby, Eleanor E. (ed.)
1966   The Development of Sex Differences. Stanford, California: Stanford University Press.

McNeill, David, and Norman Livson.
1963 "Maturation rate and body build in women." Child Development 34(March):25–32.

Manheimer, D. I., and G. D. Mellinger.
1967 "Personality characteristics of the child accident repeater." Child Development 38(June):497–513.

Marler, Peter, and W. J. Hamilton.
1966 Mechanisms of Animal Behavior. New York: Wiley.

Osborne, R. H., and F. V. DeGeorge.
1959 Genetic Basis of Morphological Variation. Cambridge, Massachusetts: Harvard University Press.

Papousek, Hanus.
1967 "Genetics and child development," in James H. Spuhler (ed.), Genetic Diversity and Human Behavior. Viking Fund Publications in Anthropology, No. 45. Chicago: Aldine.

Pasamanick, Benjamin, and Hilda Knobloch.
1966 "Retrospective studies on the epidemiology of reproductive casualty: Old and new." Merrill-Palmer Quarterly 12:7–26.

Rheingold, Harriet (ed.)
1963 Maternal Behavior in Mammals. New York: Wiley.

Richardson, Stephen A.
1964 "The social environment and individual functioning," in H. G. Birch (ed.), Brain Damage in Children: The Biological and Social Aspects. Baltimore: Williams and Wilkins.

Schacter, Stanley.
1964 "The interaction of cognitive and physiological determinants of emotional state," in P. H. Leiderman and David Shapiro (eds.), Psychobiological Approaches to Social Behavior. Stanford, California: Stanford University Press.
1967 "Cognitive effects on bodily functioning: Studies of obesity and overeating," in David C. Glass and Carl Pfaffman (eds.), Biology and Behavior: Neurophysiology and Emotion. New York: Rockefeller University Press and Russell Sage Foundation.

Schaffer, H. R., and P. E. Emerson.
1964 "Patterns of response to physical contact in early human development." Journal of Child Psychology and Psychiatry 5(June):1–13.

Schiller, Claire H. (ed.)
1957 Instinctive Behavior. New York: International Universities Press.

Schrier, A. M.; H. F. Harlow; and F. Stollnitz (eds.)
1965 Behavior of Nonhuman Primates. 2 volumes. New York: Academic Press.

Scott, J. P.
1963 "The process of primary socialization in canine and human infants." Monographs of the Society for Research in Child Development 28(No. 1).

Sheldon, William H. (with collaboration of S. S. Stevens).
1942 The Varieties of Temperament: A Psychology of Constitutional Differences. New York: Harper.

Sheldon, William H. (with collaboration of S. S. Stevens and W. B. Tucker).
  1940   The varieties of Human Physique: An Introduction to Constitutional Psychology. New York: Harper.

Suomi, S. J., and Harry F. Harlow.
  1972   "Social rehabilitation of isolate-reared monkeys." Developmental Psychology 6:487–496.

Vandenberg, Steven G.
  1967   "Hereditary factors in psychological variables in man, with a special emphasis on cognition," in James H. Spuhler (ed.), Genetic Diversity and Human Behavior. Viking Fund Publications in Anthropology, No. 45. Chicago: Aldine.

Zborowski, Mark.
  1952   "Cultural components in responses to pain." Journal of Social Issues 8:16–30.

3

This chapter reports a study of mother-child interaction in early infancy. Three of the findings are especially provocative: (1) on the average, boys and girls display differences in irritability and activity almost from the time of birth; (2) during the first few weeks, many aspects of the mothers' differential treatment of the sexes are a direct response to this constitutional difference between the sexes; yet (3) other sex-linked variations in maternal behavior seem to occur simply from the mothers' identifications of infant gender. Thus the study demonstrates three key mechanisms that can give rise to personality variations — genetically linked constitutional differences, social reactions to constitutional states, and socialization routines generated by social stereotyping alone.

Sex, Age, and State as Determinants of Mother-Infant Interaction

Howard A. Moss

Observational studies of the infant are necessary in order to test existing theoretical propositions and to generate new propositions based on empirical evidence. In addition, the infant is an ideally suitable subject for investigating many aspects of behavior because of the relatively simple and inchoate status of the human organism at this early stage in life. Such phenomena as temperament, reactions to stimulation, efficacy of different learning contigencies, perceptual functioning, and social attachment can be investigated while they are still in rudimentary form and not yet entwined in the immensely complex behavioral configurations that progressively emerge.

The research to be reported in this paper involves descriptive-normative data of maternal and infant behaviors in the naturalistic setting of the home. These data are viewed in terms of how the infant's experience structures potential learning patterns. Although the learning process itself is of primary eventual importance, it is necessary initially to

Presented at The Merrill-Palmer Institute Conference on Research and Teaching of Infant Development, February 10–12, 1966, directed by Irving E. Sigel, chairman of research. The conference was financially supported in part by the National Institute of Child Health and Human Development. The author wishes to express his appreciation to Mrs. Helen McVey and Miss Betty Reinecke for their assistance in preparing and analyzing the data presented in this paper.

Abridged from the *Merrill-Palmer Quarterly,* 13(1967):19–36, with permission of the *Quarterly* and the author.

identify the organizational factors, in situ, that structure learning opportunities and shape response systems.

A sample of 30 first-born children and their mothers were studied by means of direct observations over the first 3 months of life. Two periods were studied during this 3-month interval. Period one included a cluster of three observations made at weekly intervals during the first month of life in order to evaluate the initial adaptation of mother and infant to one another. Period two consisted of another cluster of three observations, made around 3 months of age when relatively stable patterns of behavior were likely to have been established. Each cluster included two 3-hour observations and one 8-hour observation. The 3-hour observations were made with the use of a keyboard that operates in conjunction with a 20-channel Esterline-Angus Event Recorder. Each of 30 keys represents a maternal or infant behavior, and when a key is depressed it activates one or a combination of pens on the recorder, leaving a trace that shows the total duration of the observed behavior. This technique allows for a continuous record showing the total time and the sequence of behavior. For the 8-hour observation the same behaviors were studied but with the use of a modified time-sampling technique. The time-sampled units were one minute in length and the observer, using a stenciled form, placed a number opposite the appropriate behaviors to indicate their respective order of occurrence. Since each variable can be coded only once for each observational unit, a score of 480 is the maximum that can be received. The data to be presented in this paper are limited to the two 8-hour observations. The data obtained with the use of the keyboard will be dealt with elsewhere in terms of the sequencing of events.

The mothers who participated in these observations were told that this was a normative study of infant functioning under natural living conditions. It was stressed that they proceed with their normal routines and care of the infant as they would if the observer were not present. This structure was presented to the mothers during a brief introductory visit prior to the first observation. In addition, in order to reduce the mother's self-consciousness and facilitate her behaving in relatively typical fashion, the observer emphasized that it was the infant who was being studied and that her actions would be noted only in relation to what was happening to the infant. This approach seemed to be effective, since a number of mothers commented after the observations were completed that they were relieved that they were not the ones being studied. The extensiveness of the observations and the frequent use of informal conversation between the observer and mother seemed to contribute further to the naturalness of her behavior.

The observational variables, mean scores and sample sizes are presented in Table 1. These data are presented separately for the 3-week and the 3-month observations. The inter-rater reliabilities for these variables range from .74 to 1.00 with a median reliability of .97. Much of the data in this paper are presented for males and females separately, since by describing and comparing these two groups we are able to work from an established context that helps to clarify the theoretical meaning of the results. Also, the importance of sex differences is heavily emphasized in contemporary developmental theory and it is felt that infant data concerning these differences would provide a worthwhile addition to the literature that already exists on this matter for older subjects.

The variables selected for study are those which would seem to influence or reflect aspects of maternal contact. An additional, but related consideration in the selection of variables was that they have an apparent bearing on the organization of the infant's experience. Peter Wolff (1959), Janet Brown (1964), and Sibylle Escalona (1962) have described qualitative variations in infant state or activity level and others have shown that the response patterns of the infant are highly influenced by the state he is in (Bridger, 1965). Moreover, Levy (1958) has demonstrated that maternal behavior varies as a function of the state or activity level of the infant. Consequently, we have given particular attention to the variables concerning state (cry, fuss, awake active, awake passive, and sleep) because of the extent to which these behaviors seem to shape the infant's experience. Most of the variables listed in Table 1 are quite descriptive of what was observed. Those which might not be as clear are as follows: *attends infant* — denotes standing close or leaning over infant, usually while in the process of caretaking activities; *stimulates feeding* — stroking the infant's cheek and manipulating the nipple so as to induce sucking responses; *affectionate contact* — kissing and caressing infant; *stresses musculature* — holding the infant in either a sitting or standing position so that he is required to support his own weight; *stimulates/arouses infant* — mother provides tactile and visual stimulation for the infant or attempts to arouse him to a higher activity level; and *imitates infant*

Table 1. Mean Frequency of Maternal and Infant Behavior at 3 Weeks and 3 Months

Behavior	3-Week Observation		3-Month Observation[a]	
	Males[b] ($N = 14$)	Females ($N = 15$)	Males[b] ($N = 13$)	Females ($N = 12$)
Maternal variables				
Holds infant close	121.4	99.2	77.4	58.6
Holds infant distant	32.2	18.3	26.7	27.2
Total holds	131.3	105.5	86.9	73.4
Attends infant	61.7	44.2	93.0	81.8
Maternal contact				
(holds and attends)	171.1	134.5	158.5	133.8
Feeds infant	60.8	60.7	46.6	41.4
Stimulates feeding	10.1	14.0	1.6	3.6
Burps infant	39.0	25.9	20.9	15.3
Affectionate contact	19.9	15.9	32.8	22.7
Rocks infant	35.1	20.7	20.0	23.9
Stresses musculature	11.7	3.3	25.8	16.6
Stimulates/arouses infant	23.1	10.6	38.9	26.1
Imitates infant	1.9	2.9	5.3	7.6
Looks at infant	182.8	148.1	179.5	161.9
Talks to infant	104.1	82.2	117.5	116.1
Smiles at infant	23.2	18.6	45.9	46.4
Infant variables				
Cry	43.6	30.2	28.5	16.9
Fuss	65.7	44.0	59.0	36.0
Irritable (cry and fuss)	78.7	56.8	67.3	42.9
Awake active	79.6	55.1	115.8	85.6
Awake passive	190.0	138.6	257.8	241.1
Drowsy	74.3	74.7	27.8	11.1
Sleep	261.7	322.1	194.3	235.6
Supine	133.7	59.3	152.7	134.8
Eyes on mother	72.3	49.0	91.0	90.6
Vocalizes	152.3	179.3	207.2	207.4
Infant smiles	11.1	11.7	32.1	35.3
Mouths	36.8	30.6	61.2	116.2

[a] Four of the subjects were unable to participate in the 3-month observation. Two moved out of the area, one mother became seriously ill, and another mother chose not to participate in all the observations.

[b] One subject who had had an extremely difficult delivery was omitted from the descriptive data but is included in the findings concerning mother-infant interaction.

— mother repeats a behavior, usually a vocalization, immediately after it is observed in the infant.

The sex differences and shifts in behavior from 3 weeks to 3 months are in many instances pronounced. For example, at 3 weeks of age mothers held male infants about 27 minutes more per 8 hours than they held females, and at 3 months males were held 14 minutes longer. By the time they were 3 months of age there was a decrease of over 30 percent for both sexes in the total time they were held by their mothers. Sleep time also showed marked sex differences and changes over time. For the earlier observations females slept about an hour longer than males, and this difference tended to be maintained by 3 months with the female infants sleeping about 41 minutes longer. Again, there was a substantial reduction with age in this behavior for both sexes; a decrease of 67 and 86 minutes in sleep time for males and females, respectively. What is particularly striking is the variability for these infant and maternal variables. The range for sleep time is 137-391 minutes at 3 weeks and 120-344 minutes at 3 months, and the range for mother holding is 38-218 minutes at 3 weeks and 26-168 minutes for the 3-month observation. The extent of the individual differences reflected by these ranges seem to have important implications. For instance, if an infant spends more time at a higher level of consciousness this should increase his experience and contact with the mother, and through greater learning opportunities, facilitate the perceptual discriminations he makes, and affect the quality of his cognitive organization. The finding that some of the infants in our sample slept a little over 2 hours, or about 25 percent of the observation time and others around 6 hours or 75 percent of the time, is a fact that has implications for important developmental processes. The sum crying and fussing, what we term irritability level of the infant, is another potentially important variable. The range of scores for this behavior was from 5-136 minutes at 3 weeks and 7-98 at 3 months. The fact that infants are capable through their behavior of shaping maternal treatment is a point that has gained increasing recognition. The cry is a signal for the mother to respond and variation among infants in this behavior could lead to differential experiences with the mother.

Table 2 presents t-values showing changes in the maternal and infant behaviors from the 3-week to the 3-month observation. In this case, the data for the males and females are combined since the trends, in most instances, are the same for both sexes. It is not surprising that there

Table 2. Changes in Behavior between 3 Weeks and 3 Months ($N = 26$)

Maternal Variables	t-values	Infant Variables	t-values
Higher at 3 weeks:		*Higher at 3 weeks:*	
Holds infant close	4.43****	Cry	2.84***
Holds infant distant	.56	Fuss	1.33
Total holds	4.00****	Irritable (cry and fuss)	1.73*
Maternal contact		Drowsy	9.02****
(holds and attends)	.74	Sleep	4.51****
Feeds infant	3.49***		
Stimulates feeding	3.42***		
Burps infant	3.28***	.	
Rocks infant	1.08		
Higher at 3 months:		*Higher at 3 months:*	
Attends infant	5.15****	Awake active	2.47**
Affectionate contact	2.50**	Awake passive	5.22****
Stresses musculature	3.42***	Supine	1.75*
Stimulates/arouses infant	2.63**	Eyes on mother	3.21***
Imitates infant	4.26****	Vocalizes	3.56***
Looks at infant	.38	Infant smiles	6.84****
Talks to infant	2.67**	Mouths	3.69***
Smiles at infant	4.79****		

*$p < .10$ **$p < .05$ ***$p < .01$ ****$p < .001$

are a number of marked shifts in behavior from 3 weeks to 3 months, since the early months of life are characterized by enormous growth and change. The maternal variables that show the greatest decrement are those involving feeding behaviors and close physical contact. It is of interest that the decrease in close contact is paralleled by an equally pronounced increase in attending behavior, so that the net amount of maternal contact remains similar for the 3-week and 3-month observations. The main difference was that the mothers, for the later observation, tended to hold their infants less but spent considerably more time near them, in what usually was a vis-à-vis posture, while interacting and ministering to their needs. Along with this shift, the mothers showed a marked increase in affectionate behavior toward the older infant, positioned him more so that he was required to make active use of his muscles, presented him with a greater amount of stimulation and finally, she exhibited more social behavior (imitated, smiled, and talked) toward the older child.

The changes in maternal behavior from 3 weeks to 3 months probably are largely a function of the maturation of various characteristics of the infant. However, the increased confidence of the mother, her greater familiarity with her infant, and her developing attachment toward him will also account for some of the changes that occurred over this period of time.

By 3 months of age the infant is crying less and awake more. Moreover, he is becoming an interesting and responsive person. There are substantial increases in the total time spent by him in smiling, vocalizing, and looking at the mother's face, so that the greater amount of social-type behavior he manifested at three months parallels the increments shown in the mothers' social responsiveness toward him over this same period The increase with age in the time the infant is kept in a supine position also should facilitate his participation in vis-à-vis interactions with the mother as well as provide him with greater opportunity for varied visual experiences.

Table 3 presents the correlations between the 3-week and the 3-month observations for the maternal and infant behaviors we studied. These findings further reflect the relative instability of the mother-infant system over the first few months of life. Moderate correlation coefficients were obtained only for the class of maternal variables concerning affectionate-social responses. It thus may be that these behaviors are more sensitive indicators of enduring maternal attitudes than

Table 3. Correlations between Observations at 3 Weeks and at 3 Months ($N = 26$)

Maternal Variables	$r =$	Infant Variables	$r =$
Holds infant close	.23	Cry	.28
Holds infant distant	.04	Fuss	.42**
Total holds	.18	Irritable (cry and fuss)	.37*
Attends infant	.36*	Awake active	.25
Maternal contact		Awake passive	.26
(holds and attends)	.25	Drowsy	.44**
Feeds infant	.21	Sleep	.24
Stimulates feeding	.37*	Supine	.29
Burps infant	.20	Eyes on mother	−.12
Affectionate contact	.64****	Vocalizes	.41**
Rocks infant	.29	Infant smiles	.32
Stresses musculature	.06	Mouths	−.17
Stimulates/arouses infant	.23		
Imitates infant	.45**		
Looks at infant	.37*		
Talks to infant	.58***		
Smiles at infant	.66****		

$*p<.10$ $**p<.05$ $***p<.01$ $****p<.001$

the absolute amount of time the mother devoted to such activities as feeding and physical contact. The few infant variables that show some stability are, with the exception of vocalizing, those concerning the state of the organism. Even though some of the behaviors are moderately stable from three weeks to three months, the overall magnitude of the correlations reported in Table 3 seem quite low considering that they represent repeated measures of the same individual over a relatively short period.

Table 4 presents t-values based on comparisons between the sexes for the 3-week and 3-month observations. A number of statistically significant differences were obtained with, in most instances, the boys having higher mean scores than the girls. The sex differences are most pronounced at 3 weeks for both maternal and infant variables. By 3 months the boys and girls are no longer as clearly differentiated on the

Table 4. Sex Differences in Frequency of Maternal and Infant Behaviors at 3 Weeks and 3 Months

Maternal Variables	t-values		Infant Variables	t-values	
	3 Weeks	3 Months		3 Weeks	3 Months
Male higher:			*Male higher:*		
Holds infant close	1.42	1.52	Cry	1.68	1.11
Holds infant distant	2.64**		Fuss	2.48**	3.47***
Total holds	1.65	1.12	Irritable (cry		
Attends infant	2.66**	1.10	and fuss)	2.23**	2.68**
Maternal contact			Awake active	1.66	.57
(holds and attends)	2.09**	1.57	Awake passive	2.94***	1.77*
Feeds infant	.06	.27	Drowsy		.41
Burps infant	1.67	.69	Supine	2.30**	1.07
Affectionate contact	.90	1.00	Eyes on mother	1.99*	.75
Rocks infant	1.21		Mouths	.64	
Stresses musculature	2.48**	1.67			
Stimulates/arouses					
infant	2.20**	1.53			
Looks at infant	1.97*	1.36			
Talks to infant	1.02	.79			
Smiles at infant	.57				
Female higher:			*Female higher:*		
Holds infant distant		.05	Drowsy	.03	
Stimulates feeding	.62	1.47	Sleep	3.15***	2.87***
Rocks infant		.82	Vocalizes	1.34	.23
Imitates infant	.80	1.76*	Infant smiles	.02	.08
Smiles at infant		.44	Mouths		2.57**

*$p<.10$ **$p<.05$ ***$p<.01$

49

maternal variables although the trend persists for the males to tend to have higher mean scores. On the other hand, the findings for the infant variables concerning state remain relatively similar at 3 weeks and 3 months. Thus, the sex differences are relatively stable for the two observations even though the stability coefficients for the total sample are low (in terms of our variables).

In general, these results indicate that much more was happening with the male infants than with the female infants. Males slept less and cried more during both observations and these behaviors probably contributed to the more extensive and stimulating interaction the boys experienced with the mother, particularly for the 3-week observation. In order to determine the effect of state we selected the 15 variables, excluding those dealing with state, where the sex differences were most marked and did an analysis of covariance with these variables, controlling for irritability and another analysis of covariance controlling for sleep. These results are presented in Table 5. When the state of the

Table 5. Sex Differences after Controlling for Irritability and Sleep Time through Analysis of Covariance[a]

Maternal or Infant Behaviors	Sleep Time Controlled for		Sex with Higher Mean Score	Irritability Controlled for		Sex with Higher Mean Score
	3 Weeks	3 Months		3 Weeks	3 Months	
Variables	t	t		t	t	
Holds infant close	.30	1.22		.64	1.70	
Holds infant distant	.59	−.20		.92	−.20	
Total holds	.43	.88		.86	1.08	
Attends infant	1.12	1.36		1.91*	.94	Males
Maternal contact (holds and attends)	.62	1.04		1.20	1.12	
Stimulates feeding	.55	−1.12		−.09	−1.06	
Affectionate contact	−.46	.91		.56	1.27	
Rocks	.35	−.70		.44	−1.44	
Stresses musculature	1.84*	.71	Males	1.97*	1.40	
Stimulates/arouses infant	2.09**	1.82*	Males	2.43**	2.31**	Males
Imitates infant	−.91	−2.73**	Females	−.63	−2.14**	Females
Looks at Infant	.58	1.35		1.17	1.02	
Talks to infant	−.48	.24		.70	.59	
Infant supine	.82	−.03		1.36	.69	
Eyes on mother	.37	.58		1.76*	−.37	Males

*$p<.10$ **$p<.05$
[a] A positive t-value indicates that males had the higher mean score, and a negative t-value indicates a higher mean score for females.

infant was controlled for, most of the sex differences were no longer statistically significant. The exceptions were that the t-values were greater, after controlling for state, for the variables "mother stimulates/arouses infant" and "mother imitates infant." The higher score for "stimulates/arouse" was obtained for the males and the higher score for "imitates" by the females. The variable "imitates" involves repeating vocalizations made by the child, and it is interesting that mothers exhibited more of this behavior with the girls. This response could be viewed as the reinforcement of verbal behavior, and the evidence presented here suggests that the mothers differentially reinforce this behavior on the basis of the sex of the child.

In order to further clarify the relation between infant state and maternal treatment, product-moment correlations were computed relating the infant irritability score with the degree of maternal contact. The maternal contact variable is based on the sum of the holding and attending scores with the time devoted to feeding behaviors subtracted out. These correlations were computed for the 3-week and 3-month observations for the male and female samples combined and separate. At 3 weeks a correlation of .52 ($p<.01$) was obtained between irritability and maternal contact for the total sample. However, for the female subsample this correlation was .68 ($p<.02$) and for males only .20 (non. sig.). Furthermore, a somewhat similar pattern occurred for the correlations between maternal contact and infant irritability for the 3-month observation. At this age the correlation is .37 ($p<.10$ level) for the combined sample and .54 ($p<.05$ level) for females and $-.47$ ($p<.10$ level) for males. A statistically significant difference was obtained ($t=2.40$, $p<.05$ level) in a test comparing the difference between the female and male correlations for the 3-month observation. In other words maternal contact and irritability positively covaried for females at both ages; whereas for males, there was no relationship at 3 weeks, and by 3 months the mothers tended to spend less time with the more irritable male babies. It should be emphasized that these correlations reflect within group patterns, and that when we combine the female and male samples positive correlations still emerge for both ages. Since the males had substantially higher scores for irritability and maternal contact than the females, the correlation for the male subjects does not strongly attentuate the correlations derived for the total sample, even when the males within group covariation seems random or negative. That is, in terms of the total sample, the patterning of the males scores is still consistent with a positive relationship between irritability and maternal contact.

From these findings it is difficult to posit a causal relationship. However, it seems most plausible that it is the infant's cry that is determining the maternal behavior. Mothers describe the cry as a signal that the infant needs attention and they often report their nurturant actions in response to the cry. Furthermore, the cry is a noxious and often painful stimulus that probably has biological utility for the infant, propelling the mother into action for her own comfort as well as out of concern for the infant. Ethological reports confirm the proposition that the cry functions as a "releaser" of maternal behavior (Bowlby, 1958; Hinde et al., 1964; Hoffman et al., 1966). Bowlby (1958) states:

> It is my belief that both of them (crying and smiling), act as social releasers of instinctual responses in mothers. As regards crying, there is plentiful evidence from the animal world that this is so .... It seems to me clear that similar impulses are also evoked in the human mother ....

Thus, we are adopting the hypothesis that the correlations we have obtained reflect a causal sequence whereby the cry acts to instigate maternal intervention. Certainly there are other important determinants of maternal contact, and it is evident that mothers exhibit considerable variability concerning how responsive they are to the stimulus signal of the cry. Yet it seems that the effect of the cry is sufficient to account at least partially for the structure of the mother-infant relationship. We further maintain the thesis that the infant's cry shapes maternal behavior even for the instance where the negative correlation was noted at 3 months for the males. The effect is still present, but in this case the more irritable infants were responded to *less* by the mothers. Our speculation for explaining this relationship and the fact that, conversely, a positive correlation was obtained for the female infants is that the mothers probably were negatively reinforced for responding to a number of the boys but tended to be positively reinforced for their responses toward the girls. That is, mothers of the more irritable boys may have learned that they could not be successful in quieting boys whereas the girls were more uniformly responsive (quieted by) to maternal handling. There is not much present in our data to bear out this contention, with the exception that the males were significantly more irritable than the girls for both observations. However, evidence that suggests males are more subject to inconsolable states comes from studies (Serr & Ismajovich, 1963; McDonald, Gynther, & Christakos, 1963; Stechler, 1964) which indicate that males have less well organized physiological reactions and are more vulnerable to adverse conditions than females. The relatively more efficient functioning of the female organism should thus contribute to their responding more favorably to maternal intervention.

In summary, we propose that maternal behavior initially tends to be under the control of the stimulus and reinforcing conditions provided by the young infant. As the infant gets older, the mother, if she behaved contingently toward his signals, gradually acquires reinforcement value which in turn increases her efficacy in regulating infant behaviors. Concurrently, the earlier control asserted by the infant becomes less functional and diminishes. In a sense, the point where the infant's control over the mother declines and the mother's reinforcement value emerges could be regarded as the first manifestation of socialization, or at least represents the initial conditions favoring social learning. Thus, at first the mother is shaped by the infant and this later facilitates her shaping the behavior of the infant. We would therefore say, that the infant, through his own temperament or signal system contributes to establishing the stimulus and reinforcement value eventually associated with the mother. According to this reasoning, the more irritable infants (who can be soothed) whose mothers respond in a contingent manner to their signals should become most amenable to the effects of social reinforcement and manifest a higher degree of attachment behavior. The fact that the mothers responded more contingently toward the female infants should maximize the ease with which females learn social responses.

This statement is consistent with data on older children which indicate that girls learn social responses earlier and with greater facility than boys (Becker, 1964). Previously we argued that the mothers learned to be more contingent toward the girls because they probably were more responsive to maternal intervention. An alternative explanation is that mothers respond contingently to the girls and not to the boys as a form of differential reinforcement, whereby, in keeping with cultural expectations, the mother is initiating a pattern that contributes to males being more aggressive or assertive, and less responsive to socialization. Indeed, these two explanations are not inconsistent with one another since the mother who is unable to sooth an upset male infant may eventually come to classify this intractable irritability as an expression of "maleness."

There are certain environmental settings where noncontingent caretaking is more likely and these situations should impede social learning and result in weaker attachment responses. Lennenberg (1965) found that deaf parents tended not to respond to the infant's cry. One would have to assume that it was more than the inability to hear the infant that influenced their behavior, since even when they observed their crying infants these parents tended not to make any effort to quiet them. The function of the cry as a noxious stimulus or "releaser" of maternal behavior did not pertain under these unusual circumstances. Infants in institutions also are more likely to be cared for in terms of some arbitrary schedule with little opportunity for them to shape caretakers in accordance with their own behavioral vicissitudes.

Although we have shown that there is a covariation between maternal contact and infant irritability and have attempted to develop some theoretical implications concerning this relationship, considerable variability remains as to how responsive different mothers are to their infants' crying behavior. This variability probably reflects differences in maternal attitudes. Women who express positive feelings about babies and who consider the well-being of the infant to be of essential importance should tend to be more responsive to signals of distress from the infant than women who exhibit negative maternal attitudes. In order to test this assumption, we first derived a score for measuring maternal responsiveness. This score was obtained through a regression analysis where we determined the amount of maternal contact that would be expected for each mother by controlling for her infant's irritability score. The expected maternal contact score was then subtracted from the mother's actual contact score and this difference was used as the measure of maternal responsivity. The maternal responsivity scores were obtained separately for the 3-week and the 3-month observations. The parents of 23 of the infants in our sample were interviewed for a project investigating marital careers, approximately 2 years prior to the birth of their child, and these interviews provided us with the unusual opportunity of having antecedent data relevant to prospective parental functioning. A number of variables from this material were rated and two of them, "acceptance of nurturant role," and the "degree that the baby is seen in a positive sense" were correlated with the scores on the maternal responsivity measure.[1] Annotated definitions of these interview variables are as follows:

"Acceptance of nurturant role" concerns the degree to which the subject is invested in caring for others and in acquiring domestic and homemaking skills such as cooking, sewing, and cleaning house. Evidence for a high rating would be describing the care of infants and children with much pleasure and satisfaction even when this involves subordinating her own needs.

The interview variable concerning the "degree that the baby is seen in a positive sense" assesses the extent to which the subject views a baby as gratifying, pleasant and non-burdensome. In discussing what she imagines infants to be like she stresses the warmer, more personal, and rewarding aspects of the baby and anticipates these qualities as primary.

Correlations of .40 ($p<.10$ level) and .48 ($p<.05$ level) were obtained between the ratings on "acceptance of nurturant role" and the maternal responsivity scores for the 3-week and 3-month observations, respectively. The "degree that the baby is seen in a positive sense" correlated .38 ($p<.10$ level) and .44 ($p<.05$ level) with maternal responsivity for the two ages. However, the two interview variables were so highly intercorrelated ($r=.93$) that they clearly involve the same dimension. Thus, the psychological status of the mother, assessed substantially before the birth of her infant, as well as the infant's state, are predictive of her maternal behavior. Schaffer and Emerson (1964) found that maternal responsiveness to the cry was associated with the attachment behavior of infants. Extrapolating from our findings, we now have some basis for assuming that the early attitudes of the mother represent antecedent conditions for facilitating the attachment behavior observed by Schaffer and Emerson. . . .

1 Dr. Kenneth Robson collaborated in developing these variables, and made the ratings.

References

Becker, W. C.
1964 "Consequences of different kinds of parental discipline." Pp. 169–208 in M. L. Hoffman and Lois W. Hoffman (eds.), Review of Child Development Research: I. New York: Russell Sage Foundation.

Bowlby, J.
1958 "The nature of a child's tie to this mother." International Journal of Psychoanalysis 39:350–373.

Bridger, W. H.
1965 "Psychophysiological measurement of the roles of state in the human neonate." Paper presented at the Society for Research in Child Development, Minneapolis, April.

Brown, Janet L.
1964 "States in newborn infants." Merrill-Palmer Quarterly 10:313–327.

Escalona, Sibylle K.
1962 "The study of individual differences and the problem of state." Journal of Child Psychiatry 1:11–37.

Hinde, R. A.; T. E. Rowell; and Y. Spencer-Booth.
1964 "Behavior of living rhesus monkeys in their first six months." Proceedings of the Zoological Society, London 143:609–649.

Hoffman, H. et al.
1966 "Enhanced distress vocalization through selective reinforcement." Science 151:354–356.

Lennenberg, E. H.; Freda G. Rebelsky; and I. A. Nichols.
1965 "The vocalizations of infants born to deaf and to hearing parents." Vita Humana 8:23–37.

Levy, D. M.
1958 Behavioral Analysis. Springfield, Illinois: Charles C. Thomas.

McDonald, R. L.; M. D. Gynther; and A. C. Christakos.
1963 "Relations between maternal anxiety and obstetric complications." Psychosomatic Medicine 25:357–362.

Schaffer, H. R., and Peggy E. Emerson.
1964 "The development of social attachments in infancy." Monographs of the Society for Research in Child Development 29 (No. 3). Serial No. 94.

Serr, D. M., and B. Ismajovich.
1963 "Determination of the primary sex ratio from human abortions." American Journal of Obstetrics and Gynecology 87:63–65.

Stechler, G. A.
1964 "A longitudinal follow-up of neonatal apnea." Child Development 35:333–348.

Wolff, P. H.
1959 "Observations on newborn infants." Psychosomatic Medicine 21:110–118.

Part II
Sex and Personality

Popular stereotypes of males and females suggest that a variety of psychological differences exist between the sexes. Objective measurements sometimes support these stereotypes and sometimes not. The brief review of evidence below is meant to separate some of the hearsay from fact and so provide some background for the discussion of cultural and physiological factors in sex differences that follow in Chapters 4 and 5. Theories about the development of sex identification are not discussed here, but reviews of these theories are provided by Kagan (1964), Kohlberg (1966), Biller and Borstelmann (1967), and Mischel (1970).

Sex Differences in Psychological Characteristics

No significant difference in overall intelligence exists between the sexes. However, females compared with males, on the average have somewhat greater verbal ability and somewhat lesser numerical and spatial abilities (Maccoby, 1966). Also, females tend to be less analytical in their perception and thinking (Witkin, 1967). The difference in verbal ability is evident from early childhood; the other differences in intellectual functioning develop during the school years.

Males are more assertive and aggressive than females (Kagan, 1964; Mischel, 1970). In fact, according to Kagan (1964:140), "It is difficult to find a sound study of preschool or school-age children in which aggressive behavior was not more frequent among boys than among girls." This ubiquitous difference may have a genetic basis. Males show higher levels of irritability so early as apparently to preclude environmental determination (Chapter 3), and what appears as irritability in infancy may be identified as aggressiveness later on. Also, recent evidence indicates that aggressiveness is closely linked to male hormone levels (Chapter 5). The possibility of an innate difference does not imply that sex differences in aggression are entirely a function of genes, however. Moss and Kagan (1964) found evidence of a substantial socialization effect as well, and even hormone levels can be affected by social experiences (Chapter 5).

Females are supposed to be more conforming than males, and research studies tend to support this, but not consistently (Kagan, 1964; Mischel, 1970). Some studies also have found females to be relatively passive and noninventive when confronted with problems (e.g., Straus & Straus, 1968; Goldberg & Lewis, 1969). Growing evidence suggests that some of these differences actually do not reflect a basic difference between the sexes in conformity, passivity, or dependency but rather are a product of differential responses by the sexes to different situations. For example, Sistrunk and McDavid (1971) found that females are more conforming than males when confronted with typical issues of masculine interest but that males are more conforming than females when confronted with issues of feminine interest. Similarly, French and Lesser (1964) showed that women who valued their feminine identity did not respond much to the usual achievement situations involving men and intellectual competition but that they did become achievement oriented in response to situations involving women and female problems.

Self-report questionnaires and cross-cultural reports of dreams and daydreams indicate that men tend to be interested in aggressive, sexual, and economic pursuits whereas females tend to be involved more with clothes, personal attractiveness, and affiliative relationships (Gough, 1952; Harris, 1959; Colby, 1963; Wagman, 1967). Aesthetically, men seem to prefer active, angular and boldly structured works in contrast to females' preferences for more static, rounded, and internally complex items (Franck & Rosen, 1949). Such differences in interests and values generally are fairly substantial, and they have been exploited to create a variety of sex-identification tests (see Biller & Borstelmann, 1967). Even on measures of sex identification, however, there is a fair amount of gender overlap. For example, Bezdek and Strodtbeck (1970) reported that as many as 40 percent of the persons in their samples displayed cross-sex preferences on a particular sex-identification measure.

With respect to morality, females tend to be more religious than males (Elkind, 1966), and females with a coherent feminine identity have been found to take an idealistic, moral orientation toward issues whereas males with an integrated masculine identity tend toward a pragmatic, instrumental orientation (Bezdek & Strodtbeck, 1970). At the behavioral level, males are far more likely than females to be the perpetrators of crime and acts of violence (Cressey, 1961; National Commission on the Causes and Prevention of Violence, 1969:22) and to engage in sexual deviations (Gebhard et al., 1965:9). On the other hand, females more than males are prone toward deviancy "in the areas where they have greater opportunity for deviancy or with acts that have some acceptance as being part of femininity even if they are deviant" (Heise, 1968:83), e.g., shoplifting and appointment-breaking. Females condemn most deviant acts more than males do (Christensen, 1962; Wright & Cox, 1967; Heise, 1968), but differences between the sexes in deviant activity cannot be explained entirely in terms of the sexes' different attitudes toward deviancy (Heise, 1968). In particular, the higher crime rate for males probably also is a function of males' greater aggressiveness and pragmatism and the greater social freedom accorded males.

When direct measurements of anxiety are made, females sometimes are found to be more anxious than males; in other cases no difference is evident (Oetzel, 1966:332–333). Mental health surveys often reveal a somewhat higher rate of maladjustment among females (Srole et al., 1962; Leighton et al., 1963), but the issue is complicated by the fact that the pattern is reversed within some categories (e.g., never-married adults) and the fact that females complain of more symptoms than do males with the same physical disorder so that they may give an impression of being worse off than they are (Phillips & Segal, 1969). In any case the differences are sufficiently small that neither sex seems to have much of a natural advantage over the other in overall mental health.

Differences in Developmental Mechanisms

A scattering of findings from twin studies suggest that female growth and personality development may be determined more by heredity than is the case for males (Thompson, 1968), and this seems to be corroborated by some studies that find more trait stability among females than among males (e.g., Kagan, 1969). Actually the full range of evidence suggests that heritabilities and trait stabilities are higher for girls on some traits and higher for boys on others (Bayley, 1964; Vandenberg, 1967; Vandenberg & Stafford, 1967). Such findings could mean that the sexes differ in the degree of genetic determination of particular traits, but this is not necessarily so. An alternative interpretation is that one sex is free to develop its genetic potentials while the genetic propensities of the other sex are stifled by counteracting socialization. This interpretation is to be favored especially when sex-typed traits are found to decline with age in one sex (e.g., Moss & Kagan, 1964; Bayley, 1968).

Boys and girls seem not to respond to all socialization forces in the same way. For example, Bayley (1964) found that boys' childhood personality is generally more correlated with levels of maternal love than is the case for girls. Moss and Kagan (1964) report that adult achievement orientations are negatively correlated with mother's hostility at infancy for males but that the correlation is positive for females; also that maternal protectiveness during infancy predicts the growth of intellectual needs in males but the relative absence of such needs in females. Complications like this could mean that separate socialization theories are required for males and females, but again this is not necessarily so. For example, the finding that maternal love is generally more important for boys than for girls might only reflect greater variations in maternal affection for boys than for girls. The relations of early love and protection with adult achievement and intellectual needs may simply mean that loving, protective mothers have an early impact on the development of sex-typed traits whereas hostile, neglectful mothers do not.

It is too early to determine whether it would be useful to develop separate theories of development for males and females. However, it is clear at this point that generalizations about development cannot be made too readily across the sexes. For various reasons, the socialization experiences of the sexes are different right from infancy (Chapter 3). And the life opportunities of the sexes, as well as their hormonal states, are so different (see Chapters 4 and 5) that even the same influence might have divergent consequences.

References

Bayley, Nancy.
  1964   "Consistency of maternal and child behaviors in the Berkeley Growth Study." Vita Humana 7:73-95.
  1968   "Behavioral correlates of mental growth: Birth to thirty-six years." American Psychologist 23:1-17.

Bezdek, William, and Fred L. Strodtbeck.
  1970   "Sex-role identity and pragmatic action." American Sociological Review 35:491-502.

Biller, Henry B., and Lloyd J. Borstelmann.
  1967   "Masculine development: An integrative review." Merrill-Palmer Quarterly 13:254-294.

Christensen, Harold T.
  1962   "A cross-cultural comparison of attitudes toward marital infidelity." International Journal of Comparative Sociology 3:124-137.

Colby, Kenneth M.
  1963   "Sex differences in dreams of primitive tribes." American Anthropologist 65:1116-1122.

Cressey, Donald R.
  1961   "Crime." Pp. 21-76 in R. K. Merton and R. A. Nisbet (eds.), Contemporary Social Problems. New York: Harcourt, Brace and World.

Elkind, David.
1966 "The developmental psychology of religion." Pp. 193–225 in A. E. Kidd and J. L. Rivoire (eds.), Perceptual Development in Children. New York: International Universities Press.

Franck, K., and E. Rosen.
1949 "A projective test of masculinity-femininity." Journal of Consulting Psychology 13:247–256.

French, Elizabeth G., and G. D. Lesser.
1964 "Some characteristics of the achievement motive in women." Journal of Abnormal and Social Psychology 68:119–128.

Gebhard, Paul H.; J. H. Gagnon; W. B. Pomeroy; and C. V. Christenson.
1965 Sex Offenders: An Analysis of Types. New York: Harper and Row.

Goldberg, Susan, and Michael Lewis.
1969 "Play behavior in the year-old infant; early sex differences." Child Development 40:21–31.

Gough, H.
1952 "Identifying psychological femininity." Educational and Psychological Measurement 12:427–439.

Harris, D. B.
1959 "Sex differences in the life problems and interests of adolescents, 1935 and 1957." Child Development 30:453-459.

Heise, D. R.
1968 "Norms and individual patterns in student deviancy." Social Problems 16:78–92.

Kagan, Jerome.
1964 "Acquisition and significance of sex typing and sex role identity." Pp. 137-167 in M. L. Hoffman and L. W. Hoffman (eds.), Review of Child Development Research. Volume I. New York: Russell Sage Foundation.
1969 "Continuity in cognitive development during the first year." Merrill-Palmer Quarterly 15:101-119.

Kohlberg, Lawrence.
1966 "A cognitive-developmental analysis of children's sex-role concepts and attitudes." Pp. 82-173 in E. E. Maccoby (ed.), The Development of Sex Differences. Stanford, California: Stanford University Press.

Leighton, Dorothea C.; J. S. Harding; D. B. Macklin; A. M. Macmillan; and A. H. Leighton.
1963 The Character of Danger: Psychiatric Symptoms in Selected Communities. New York: Basic Books.

Maccoby, Eleanor E.
1966 "Sex differences in intellectual functioning." Pp. 25–55 in E. E. Maccoby (ed.), The Development of Sex Differences. Stanford, California: Stanford University Press.

Mischel, Walter.
1970 "Sex-typing and socialization." Pp. 3–72 in P. H. Mussen (ed.) Carmichael's Manual of Child Psychology. Volume 2. New York: Wiley.

Moss, H. A., and Jerome Kagan.
1964　"Report on personality consistency and change from the Fels longitudinal study." Vita Humana 7:127–138.

National Commission on the Causes and Prevention of Violence.
1969　To Establish Justice, To Insure Domestic Tranquility. New York: Award Books.

Oetzel, Roberta M.
1966　"Annotated bibliography." Pp. 223–321 in E. E. Maccoby (ed.), The Development of Sex Differences. Stanford, California: Stanford University Press.

Phillips, Derek L., and Bernard E. Segal.
1969　"Sexual status and psychiatric symptoms." American Sociological Review, 34:58–72.

Sistrunk, Frank, and John W. McDavid.
1971　"Sex variable in conforming behavior." Journal of Personality and Social Psychology 17:200–207.

Srole, Leo; T. S. Langner; S. T. Michael; M. K. Opler; and T. A. C. Rennie.
1962　Mental Health in the Metropolis: The Midtown Manhattan Study. New York: McGraw-Hill.

Straus, Jacqueline, and Murray A. Straus.
1968　"Family roles and sex differences in creativity of children in Bombay and Minneapolis." Journal of Marriage and the Family 30:46–53.

Thompson, W. R.
1968　"Genetics and personality." Pp. 161–174, in E. Norbeck, D. Price-Williams, and W. McCord (eds.), The Study of Personality: An Interdisciplinary Appraisal. New York: Holt, Rinehart and Winston.

Vandenberg, Steven G.
1967　"Hereditary factors in normal personality traits (as measured by inventories)." Recent Advances in Biological Psychiatry 9:65–104.

Vandenberg, S. G., and R. R. Stafford.
1967　"Hereditary influences on vocational preferences as shown by scores of twins on the Minnesota vocational interest inventory." Journal of Applied Psychology 51:17–19.

Wagman, Morton.
1967　"Sex differences in types of daydreams." Journal of Personality and Social Psychology 7:329–332.

Witkin, H. A.
1967　"A cognitive-style approach to cross-cultural research." International Journal of Psychology 2:233–250.

Wright, Derek, and Edwin Cox.
1967　"A study of the relationship between moral judgment and religious belief in a sample of English adolescents." Journal of Social Psychology 72:135–144.

4

This chapter offers the thesis that differences engendered by specialized environments ultimately may become the basis of general, cultural roles. In particular, D'Andrade hypothesizes that males typically dominate the centers of society when the basic subsistence activity demands heavy labor because males, with their biological potentials for developing musculature and for maintaining a high level of energy output, inevitably control the highest priority functions in such situations. Once the subsistence activity has led to a sex-based division of labor, differences in sex roles tend to be elaborated and then perpetuated through socialization practices. D'Andrade's essay also provides insight into the cross-cultural universality of various sex-linked distinctions in roles and personality.

Sex Differences
and Cultural Institutions
Roy G. D'Andrade

Psychology tends to consider sex differences as differences in personal characteristics. Anthropology, on the other hand, generally conceives of sex differences as social and cultural institutions. From this point of view sex differences are not simply characteristics of individuals; they are also culturally transmitted patterns of behavior determined in part by the functioning of society. Some of the ways in which sex differences have been culturally institutionalized will be reviewed in this chapter. Cross-cultural trends for male-female differences in the performance of daily activities, in the ascription of social statuses, in interpersonal behavior, in gender identity, and in fantasy productions will be presented. Also an attempt will be made to explain some of these empirically observed behavioral sex differences.

Anthropology, like astronomy, is a natural science in which experimentation is rarely possible. Unfortunately, under such conditions good descriptions are easier to construct than good explanations. At present there is even considerable disagreement within anthropology about what constitutes a proper or possible explanation of cultural phenomena. The four major types of explanation currently in use are: the *historical* (a particular custom exists because it was invented at some previous time, and then transmitted from generation to generation, or from society to society, to its present location in time and

Abridged from "Sex Differences and Cultural Institutions" by Roy G. D'Andrade, in *The Development of Sex Differences,* edited by Eleanor E. Maccoby, with the permission of the publishers, Stanford University Press. ©1966 by the Board of Trustees of the Leland Stanford Junior University. Reprinted in the British Commonwealth market excluding Canada, by permission of Tavistock Publications Ltd., publishers.

space); the *structural* (a particular custom exists as an expression of some more basic or underlying cultural or social condition, and can only be understood as a manifestation of this more basic condition); the *functional* (a particular custom exists because it maintains or integrates social life in some beneficial way); and the *reductionistic* (a particular custom exists because of the operation of some psychological or physiological mechanism). While all of these types of explanation carry some information and can be used predictively, in this review the primary emphasis will be on reductionistic explanations.

Physical Differences

A comprehensive review of cross-cultural findings about physical sex differences will not be attempted here. However, some of these physical differences should be mentioned since they are basic to many of the explanations of behavioral sex differences. In all known human populations, males and females differ in primary sex characteristics and in many secondary characteristics as well. These secondary characteristics include, for the male, greater height, a higher muscle-to-fat ratio, a more massive skeleton, more body hair, etc. However, most of these differences in secondary sex characteristics are not absolute; they hold true only for a particular population. Furthermore, the average differences between the sexes vary from population to population. In height, for example, the mean difference between males and females is less than two inches for the Klamath, approximately six inches for the Nootka (both American Indian groups from the Northwest coast), and almost eight inches for the Shilluk (an African Negro group from the Eastern Sudan). As a result of the variance in population means, it is generally impossible to sex-type accurately on the basis of secondary sex characteristics alone unless population parameters are known. (Very probably this holds true not only for sex-linked physical characteristics, but also for behavioral characteristics as well.)

Secondary sex characteristics are not completely under genetic control, and can be affected by cultural and environmental factors. For example, cultural heightening of genetic secondary sex characteristics occurs frequently with regard to physical strength. The genetically determined greater size and more muscular body composition of the male results in a fairly large difference in physical strength between the sexes. This difference is often increased, however, by the tendency for males in most societies to perform those activities requiring rapid and extreme exertion. In Bali, where males do little heavy lifting work, preferring instead light, steady, many-handed labor, both males and females have slender somatypes. However, Balinese men who work as dock coolies under European supervision develop the heavy musculature more typical of males (Mead, 1949).

Generally biological differences in primary and secondary sex characteristics are considered major factors in explaining universal cultural patterning of sex-typed roles. The family has been said to be "a biological phenomenon, . . . as rooted in organic and physiological structures as insect societies" (LaBarre, 1954:104). Thus LaBarre argues that the human mother-child relationship is based on the mutual gratifications involved in long-term breast feeding, and the husband-wife relationship on the permanent sexuality of the female. However, most anthropological explanations of regularities in sex differences are not based on biological differences alone, but on the complex interactions of biological differences with environmental and technological factors.

The Division of Labor

One well-documented finding about behavioral sex differences is that men and women not only tend to perform different activities in every culture, but that men tend to perform particular types of activities and women to perform others. This division of labor is especially sharp for subsistence and other economic activities. The following table, adapted from one of Murdock's early cross-cultural studies, presents the frequencies with which 224 societies have a sex-based division of labor with respect to activities dealing mainly with food production and collection (Murdock, 1937).

The sex differences in Table 1 are quite strong for all activities except dairy operation, soil preparation, fowl tending, and shelter erection. Generally the male activities appear to involve behavior which is strenuous, cooperative, and which may require long periods of travel. The female activities, on the other hand, are more likely to involve the physically easier, more solitary, and less mobile activities. These differences appear to be more or less the direct result of physical male-female differences.

However, not all sex-specialized activities can be explained by phys-

Table 1. Cross-Cultural Data from 224 Societies on Subsistence Activities
and Division of Labor by Sex

| Activity | Number of Societies in Which Activity is Performed by | | | | |
	Men always	Men usually	Either sex	Women usually	Women always
Pursuit of sea mammals	34	1	0	0	0
Hunting	166	13	0	0	0
Trapping small animals	128	13	4	1	2
Herding	38	8	4	0	5
Fishing	98	34	19	3	4
Clearing land for agriculture	73	22	17	5	13
Dairy operations	17	4	3	1	13
Preparing and planting soil	31	23	33	20	37
Erecting and dismantling shelter	14	2	5	6	22
Tending fowl and small animals	21	4	8	1	39
Tending and harvesting crops	10	15	35	39	44
Gathering shellfish	9	4	8	7	25
Making and tending fires	18	6	25	22	62
Bearing burdens	12	6	35	20	57
Preparing drinks and narcotics	20	1	13	8	57
Gathering fruits, berries, nuts	12	3	15	13	63
Gathering fuel	22	1	10	19	89
Preservation of meat and fish	8	2	10	14	74
Gatherings herbs, roots, seeds	8	1	11	7	74
Cooking	5	1	9	28	158
Carrying water	7	0	5	7	119
Grinding grain	2	4	5	13	114

ical differences. Most of the results in Table 2, which presents data on sex differences in the manufacture of objects, cannot be so explained. Weapon making, for example, is predominantly a male activity, even though it does not necessarily require more physical strength than the manufacture and repair of clothing. One possible explanation for the sex differences found in the manufacture of objects is that the objects being made are intended for use in activities that are directly related to physical differences. Thus weapon making is anticipatory to activities that do involve physically strenuous and mobile behavior.

The thesis here, to be considered in more detail below, is that the division of labor by sex comes about as a result of generalization from activities directly related to physical sex differences to activities only indirectly related to these differences; that is, from behaviors which are differentially reinforced as a result of physical differences to behaviors which are anticipatory or similar to such directly conditioned activities.

Table 2. Cross-Cultural Data on the Manufacture of Objects and
Division of Labor by Sex

Activity	Number of Societies in Which Activity is Performed by				
	Men always	Men usually	Either sex	Women usually	Women always
Metalworking	78	0	0	0	0
Weapon making	121	1	0	0	0
Boat building	91	4	4	0	1
Manufacture of musical instruments	45	2	0	0	1
Work in wood and bark	113	9	5	1	1
Work in stone	68	3	2	0	2
Work in bone, horn, shell	67	4	3	0	3
Manufacture of ceremonial objects	37	1	13	0	1
House building	86	32	25	3	14
Net making	44	6	4	2	11
Manufacture of ornaments	24	3	40	6	18
Manufacture of leather products	29	3	9	3	32
Hide preparation	31	2	4	4	49
Manufacture of nontextile fabrics	14	0	9	2	32
Manufacture of thread and cordage	23	2	11	10	73
Basket making	25	3	10	6	82
Mat making	16	2	6	4	61
Weaving	19	2	2	6	67
Pottery making	13	2	6	8	77
Manufacture and repair of clothing	12	3	8	9	95

Perhaps the complexity and strength of the factors that bring about and maintain the division of labor by sex can be illustrated by the following excerpt from M. E. Spiro's (1956) study of an Israeli Kibbutz.

The social structure of the Kibbutz is responsible for a problem of . . . serious proportions—"the problem of the woman. . . ." With the exception of politics, nothing occupies so much attention in the Kibbutz. . . . It is no exaggeration to say that if Kiryat Yedidim should ever disintegrate, the "problem of the woman" will be one of the main contributing factors.

In a society in which the equality of the sexes is a fundamental premise, and in which the emancipation of women is a major goal, the fact that there is a "problem of the woman" requires analysis. . . . The Youth Movement from which many Kibbutz values are derived was strongly feminist in orientation. The woman in bourgeois society, it is believed, was subjected to the male and tied to her home and family. This "biological tragedy of woman" forced her into menial roles, such as house cleaning, cooking, and other domestic duties, and prevented her from taking her place beside the man in the fields, the workshop, the laboratory, and the lecture hall.

In the new society all this was to be changed. The woman would be relieved of her domestic burdens by means of the various institutions of collective living, and she could then take her place as man's equal in all the activities of life. The communal dining room would free her from the burden of cooking; the communal nurseries, from the responsibilities of raising children; the small rooms, from the job of cleaning.

In a formal sense, the Kibbutz has been successful in this task. . . . In spite of "emancipation" which they have experienced in the Kibbutz, there is considerable sentiment among the women . . . that they would prefer not to have been "emancipated." Almost every couple who has left the Kibbutz has done so because of the unhappiness of the woman. . . . At a town meeting devoted to the "problem of the woman," one of the most respected women in Kiryat Yedidim—the wife of a leader of the Kibbutz movement—publicly proclaimed that the Kibbutz women had not achieved what they had originally hoped for; as for herself, after thirty years in Kiryat Yedidim she could pronounce her life a disappointment.

One source of the woman's poor morale is that many women are dissatisfied with their economic roles. . . . When the vattikim [original settlers] first settled on the land, there was no sexual division of labor. Women, like men, worked in the fields and drove tractors; men, like women, worked in the kitchen and in the laundry. Men and women, it was assumed, were equal and could perform their jobs equally well. It was soon discovered, however, that men and women were not equal. For obvious biological reasons, women could not undertake many of the physical tasks of which men were capable; tractor driving, harvesting, and other heavy labor proved too difficult for them. Moreover, women were compelled at times to take temporary leave from that physical labor of which they were capable. A pregnant woman, for example, could not work too long, even in the vegetable garden, and a nursing mother had to work near the Infants House in order to be able to feed her child.

Hence, as the Kibbutz grew older and the birth rate increased, more and more women were forced to leave the "productive" branches of the economy and enter its "service" branches. But as they left the "productive" branches, it was necessary that their places be filled, and they were filled by men. The result was that the women found themselves in the same jobs from which they were supposed to have been emanicipated—*cooking, cleaning, laundering, teaching, caring for children,* etc.

... What has been substituted for the traditional routine of housekeeping ... is more housekeeping—and a restricted and narrow kind of housekeeping at that. Instead of cooking and sewing and baking and cleaning and laundering and caring for children, the woman in Kiryat Yedidim cooks *or* sews *or* launders *or* takes care of children for eight hours a day.... This new housekeeping is more boring and less rewarding than the traditional type. It is small wonder, then, given this combination of low prestige, difficult working conditions, and monotony, that the chavera [female member of the Kibbutz] has found little happiness in her economic activities.[1]

The outcome of this attempt to alter radically the sexual basis of the division of labor appears to have been a tragedy. Margaret Mead (1949:77) has pointed out that "envy of the male role can come as much from an undervaluation of the role of wife and mother as from an overvaluation of the public aspects of achievement that have been reserved for men." Apparently a cultural undervaluation of women cannot be corrected by abolishing the female role.

It is of interest that the Kibbutz had to alter the organization of the family in order to free women to perform previously male activities, especially in light of the anthropologist's argument that the formation of the family depends not only on biological differences and sexual alliance, but on the division of labor as well.....

Sex Distinctions in Social Structure

The general notion that forms of social organization are related to sex

---

1 Excerpt reprinted from Melford E. Spiro, *Kibbutz: Venture in Utopia* (Cambridge, Mass.: Harvard University Press, 1956), pp. 221-230, with permission of the publisher and the author.

differences in subsistence activities can be partially investigated by an examination of the cross-cultural data.

First, with respect to the variety of forms of social organization found cross-culturally, it should be pointed out that the distinction of gender is basic to understanding many of these forms. That is, the distinction of gender is used not only as a basis for assigning activities, as in the division of labor, but also as a basis for transmitting rights and duties in the proper allocation of social statuses. Thus in the marital rules of residence, in the permitted forms of multiple marriage, in the criteria for membership in descent groups, and in kinship terminology, gender is used to decide who will live where, who can marry whom, who will belong to which group, and so on.

Furthermore, there tends to be a general cross-cultural bias concerning the use of gender as social criteria. The majority of societies organize their social institutions around males rather than females. For example, certain types of rules of residence group together spatially a core of kin-related males, while other rules of residence group together a core of kin-related females. In Murdock's World Ethnographic Sample of 565 societies, 376 societies are labeled as predominantly patrilocal (i.e., sons after marriage reside with or near their parental family), while only 84 are rated predominantly matrilocal (i.e., daughters after marriage tend to live with or near their parental family). With respect to descent groups, the ratio is roughly four to one in favor of membership being transmitted patrilineally through a line of males rather than matrilineally through females. For forms of multiple marriage the sex ratio is even more biased. Of the 431 societies that permit polygamous marriage, 427 permit men to have more than one wife, but only four permit women to have more than one husband.

Returning to the relation between subsistence activities and forms of social organization, it is possible, using only the categories of residence and descent group, to construct a simple typology of nine types of social organization that will account for over 95 percent of the societies in Murdock's World Ethnographic Sample (see Table 3). These nine types of social organization are:

1. No descent group—neolocal residence.
2. No descent group—biolocal residence.
3. No descent group—patrilocal residence.
4. No descent group—matrilocal residence.

5. Matrilineal descent group—matrilocal residence.
6. Matrilineal descent group—avunculocal residence.
7. Matrilineal descent group—patrilocal residence.
8. Patrilineal descent group—patrilocal residence.
9. Both matrilineal and patrilineal descent group—patrilocal residence.

Both the dominant form of subsistence activity and the degree of sex difference in the division of labor appear to affect which of these nine types of social organization will occur. Table 4 presents these data taken from a subsample of Murdock's World Ethnographic Sample (1957).

The results indicate that there is a complete network of relationships between division of labor by sex, subsistence activities, and types of social organization. Generally those subsistence activities which require predominantly male effort and which involve the use of economic capital, such as *animal husbandry* and *agriculture with cattle,* are likely to be both patrilineal and patrilocal. There are a large number of neo-local societies without descent groups that have *agriculture with cattle* subsistence economies, but this is perhaps because most of these societies belong to the Western European tradition in which industrial manufacture rather than agriculture is actually the predominant form of economic activity.

In contrast to *agriculture with cattle* and *animal husbandry, agriculture without cattle,* which frequently involves both slash-and-burn

Table 3. Cross-Cultural Data on the Association between Rules of Residence and Descent Group for 428 Societies

| Rules of Residence | Descent Group | | | | |
	Patri-lineal	Matri-lineal	Mat. & Pat.	None	Total
Patrilocal	**177**	**9**	**17**	**78**	281
Matrilocal	0	**32**	2	**30**	64
Avunculocal	0	**15**	1	1	17
Bilocal	3	1	1	**33**	38
Neolocal	1	1	0	**26**	28
Total	181	58	21	168	428

NOTE: Boldface indicates social organizations listed in typology presented above.

Table 4. Cross-Cultural Data on Sex Division of Labor (by Subsistence Activity) and Type of Social Organization (by Descent Group and Residence)

Sex Division of Labor	No Descent Group				Matrilineal			Patrilineal	Mat. & Pat.	Total
	Neo-local	Bi-local	Patri-local	Matri-local	Matri-local	Avuncu-local	Patri-local	Patri-local	Patri-local	
Agriculture with cattle										
Men do most	11	6	6	1	1	0	1	34	1	61
Both do	6	2	9	3	4	1	0	40	2	67
Women do most	0	0	0	1	0	0	1	12	2	16
Total	17	8	15	5	5	1	2	86	5	144
Animal husbandry										
Men do most	0	0	2	0	0	0	1	14	0	17
Both do	1	0	2	0	0	1	0	10	1	15
Women do most	0	0	0	0	0	0	0	0	0	0
Total	1	0	4	0	0	1	1	24	1	32
Agriculture without cattle										
Men do most	3	5	13	2	6	0	1	5	0	35
Both do	0	2	0	4	5	10	1	27	2	51
Women do most	2	4	9	4	5	2	1	14	2	43
Total	5	11	22	10	16	12	3	46	4	129
Fishing										
Men do most	1	4	11	0	2	0	1	3	1	23
Both do	0	1	0	2	0	0	1	2	0	6
Women do most	0	0	1	0	0	0	0	0	0	1
Total	1	5	12	2	2	0	2	5	1	30
Hunting and gathering										
Men do most	0	1	7	3	0	0	0	2	0	13
Both do	1	8	10	6	1	0	1	6	6	39
Women do most	0	0	0	0	0	0	0	0	0	0
Total	1	9	17	9	1	0	1	8	6	52
Total	25	33	70	26	24	14	9	169	17	387

techniques of farming and root crops rather than cereal grains, is more likely to depend on a greater proportion of female labor, and to occur with matrilineal descent groupings and matrilocal or avunculocal residence. Avunculocal residence, in which a man moves with his wife at marriage to live with his mother's brother or a classificatory equivalent, groups together a core of males who are matrilineally related. Such a rule of residence is thought to be a result of factors that operate to produce patrilocal residence acting on a previously matrilineal-matrilocal system (Murdock, 1949). It is interesting that avunculocal residence most often occurs in societies that have a fairly balanced division of labor by sex. Aberle (1961), using Murdock's sample, found that avunculocal residence is also more likely to occur in societies with a hereditary aristocracy.

Hunting and gathering and *fishing* apparently only rarely create the kind of capital that is utilized in corporate descent groups; both sets of subsistence activities have few matrilineal or patrilineal groups, despite the fact that *fishing* and *hunting* are predominantly male activities with a high frequency of patrilocal residence.

The overall results suggest that both economic capital and sex bias in the use and control of this capital are important in forming corporate descent groups and in determining rules of residence. Although sex differences in who does the work appear to help determine which sex controls the economic capital, the evidence does not indicate that sex bias in the division of labor by itself can determine the type of residence or the formation of kinship groups.

Sexual Behavior

In general males appear to be more sexually active, females more sexually restricted. The evidence also suggests not only that sexual restrictions are more typically applied to females, but that females tend to be more inhibited by sexual restrictions than males (mutuality in sexual activity appears only in societies that are permissive rather than restrictive). The result of both these factors — greater sexual restrictiveness applied to women and greater ease of inhibiting female sexuality — would tend to create greater sex differences in the amount and kind of sexual activity in those societies that have more severe sex restrictions, with the males being much more active than the females and the females much less responsive than the males.

At present, two major social correlates of sexual restrictiveness have been found in cross-cultural research. One of these correlates, discussed by William Stephens (1963), involves the effect of "civilization" and the "autocratic political state" on sexual activity. Stephens presents data taken from ethnographies and interviews with ethnographers which indicate that culturally permitted premarital and extramarital liaisons occur more frequently in noncivilized communities (24 out of 31 cases), and less frequently in civilized communities (2 out of 18 cases). Civilized communities, which are defined as communities belonging to "a society that embraces cities," are thought to have less sexual freedom because of their association with the autocratic state.

A second social correlate that has been found to be related to sexual restrictiveness is the form of family organization. For example, of the nine societies surveyed by Ford and Beach (1951) in which females but not males are sexually restricted in childhood and adolescence, eight are strongly polygynous. Of the 26 sexually permissive societies for which information is available, only nine are strongly polygynous. Sexual restrictiveness, as measured by the Whiting and Child rating of the severity of socialization of sexual behavior, has also been found to be significantly related to polygyny (Whiting & Child, 1953; Whiting, 1961.

The reason for the relationship between polygyny and sexual restrictiveness (especially toward the female) is not obvious. Perhaps restrictiveness is needed because strong female sexuality on the part of adult women poses too great a threat for the husband of many wives; strong female sexuality may also pose a threat to the polygynously married mother who must control the sexual behavior of her male children with only diluted support from her husband. Or perhaps because both polygyny and autocratic states create or rely on unequal distributions of authority and deference, mutuality in sexual behavior, which tends to establish intimacy and equality, is discouraged.

Authority and Deference

A second dimension of interpersonal behavior that has been investigated cross-culturally with respect to sex differences involves authority and respect relationships. Stephens, in a systematic study of authority and deference between husband and wife, finds that in 21 of the 31 societies in his sample there is clear evidence that the husband exercises "considerable" authority over his wife; in six societies the husbands are "mildly" dominant over wives, and in five societies there is fairly equal sharing of authority. In six other cases there appear to be separate spheres of authority for husband and wife. In only four societies from this sample does it appear that women may have more de facto authority in the family than males: the people of Modjokuta, Java, the Tchambuli of New Guinea, the Jivarvo of South America, and the Berbers of North Africa. However, if power over groups larger than the family is considered, it is very likely all societies would be found to be male controlled (Stephens, 1963).

In deference between husband and wife, Stephens finds a similar male bias. By deference, Stephens means the ritualistic acknowledgement of power, measured by the presence or absence of such behaviors as bowing or kneeling before another, having special speech etiquette, not joking, not contradicting, not being positionally higher than the other person, and so on. In only one society out of four is the wife not required to observe some of these customs with respect to her husband. Very rarely does the husband make any kind of deference to his wife —with the exception of the chivalrous males of Western European cultures, for whom this order is reversed.

Stephens finds the degree of deference between husband and wife to be strongly correlated with the degree of deference between father and son. Deference within the family, like sexual restrictiveness, correlates with an autocratic political state rather than a "tribal" political system.

Another variable that appears to affect the distribution of authority and deference between the sexes is the degree to which men rather than women control and mediate property; and this in turn, it has been argued above, is affected by the division of labor and the cultural capacity to create capital. Support for this hypothesis is found in Gouldner and Peterson's correlation and factor-analytic study of cross-cultural data (Gouldner and Peterson, 1962). The actual data were collected by Leo Simmons (1945), who scored 71 primarily nonliterate societies on 99 culture traits by means of a four-point scale of importance-unimportance. Fifty-nine of these traits were subjected to a factor analysis by Gouldner and Peterson. The following tabulation presents the correlation coefficients for culture traits that are significantly related to patripotestal family authority and the subjection or inferiority of women.

	Subjection or Inferiority of Women	Patripotestal Family Authority
Patrilineal inheritance	.58	.65
Patrilineal succession	.51	.57
Patrilineal descent	.44	.66
Patrilocal residence	.25	.38
Herding	.21	.26
Matrilineal residence	−.24	−.23
Matrilineal descent	−.34	−.39
Matrilineal inheritance	−.41	−.63
Subjection or inferiority of women	−	.41

Generally we find that societies in which inheritance, succession, and descent-group membership are through males rather than females are more likely to concentrate power and respect in the hands of men. However, these structural variables do not always tell us which sex actually controls scarce resources and holds authority. Murdock presents the example of the Lovedu, one of the Bantu-speaking tribes of South Africa, as a culture which, despite its patrilineal, patrilocal, and polygynous structure, has granted a relatively high status to women (Murdock, 1959). Among the Lovedu, polygynous women form strong coalitions against their husbands, forcing them to treat each wife with strict fairness. The Lovedu women's high status is partly the result of a matrilateral cross-cousin marriage system — a system in which a man marries his mother's brother's daughter or some woman from his mother's patrilineage. In such a system a woman holds an advantage in negotiating marriages; the Lovedu women, for example, have gained control of the bride prices, which involve considerable amounts of cattle.

It is interesting that the Tchambuli (the New Guinea tribe studied by Margaret Mead) also have a patrilineal system with matrilateral (mother's brother's daughter) cross-cousin marriage and female control of important property. Women appear to be the actual holders of power and to have the more practical and instrumental type of temperament. Marriage conditions parallel those of the Lovedu; the application of the matrilateral cross-cousin marriage rule results in a polygynously married Tchambuli man having wives who are clan sisters and who typically form strong coalitions against him (Mead, 1935).

Similar in many ways to the authority dimension of interpersonal behavior is the instrumental-expressive dimension of role behavior. Zelditch (1955) found consistent cross-cultural regularities among almost all societies having the husband-father role described as more instrumental, and the wife-mother role as more expressive. Whether this differentiation is based on factors external to the nuclear family or on the universal requirements of the family as a social system is not clear, although both kinds of factors may be involved.

Aggression, Conflict, and Responsibility

A detailed and systematic cross-cultural study of sex differences in interpersonal behavior has been carried out by the Six Culture Socialization project, directed by J. Whiting, I. Child, W. Lambert, and B. Whiting. (See B. Whiting, 1963, for ethnographic descriptions of these cultures.) In this study 24 children (aged three to ten) from each of the six cultures were observed by trained fieldworkers for 20 five-minute periods. Each child's behavior was then systematically recorded and coded. The initial results indicate that boys are more likely than girls to engage in physical aggression in all six cultures, while girls are more likely to act affectionately and responsibly. In five of the six cultures, girls are more likely to act sociably and succorantly; but in one cultural group, a Mixtecan Indian barrio in Oaxaca, Mexico, boys are significantly more sociable and succorant than girls (J. Whiting, personal communication).

Although the differences recorded above may be due to differential child-training practices rather than to innate sex-linked behavioral tendencies, the fact that the largest sex differences occur in the younger (three to six) rather than in the older (seven to ten) group gives less weight to the training hypothesis, which would predict the opposite result.

A second systematic investigation of the interpersonal behavior of children has been made by Melford Spiro (1958) in his study of children reared in an Israeli Kibbutz. These children were reared in peer groups primarily by female nurses in a culture in which sex differences are deliberately played down in accordance with the norms of Kibbutz ideology. Thus the effects on the child's behavior of different-sex socializers and cultural sex stereotypes are to some extent absent in this study. The children in the sample range in age from one to five years. Twenty-four boys and twenty-three girls were observed. In the area of interpersonal behavior, Spiro compares the frequencies of child-to-child interaction for the categories of integrative behavior, conflict behavior, and aggressive behavior by sex of initiator and sex of object. He summarizes his findings as follows:

> In all (age) groups girls are more integrative (give aid, share, act affectionate, cooperate, etc.) than boys, and boys more disintegrative. In all groups boys engage in more acts of conflict (seizure of another child's possessions) than girls, and in all but one group the boys engage in more acts of aggression (disobedience, hitting, insulting, etc.) than the girls. Boys, moreover, are the recipients of the girls' excess integrations — boys are integrated more than the girls — but the girls are recipients of only part of the boys' excess disintegration. For though girls are the more frequent victims of conflict, boys are the more frequent victims of aggression.
>
> Though more integrative than boys, girls also display more frequent symptoms of regression than boys. In all groups but one, for example, girls have a higher incidence of thumbsucking, and in the two groups for which there are data, girls exhibit more regressive play than do boys.[2]

For each observed sex difference, Spiro speculates on whether the difference is due to innate causes or to the child's attempt to model sex-linked adult behaviors. In many cases, both these factors seem to be present. However, it is Spiro's general conclusion that in this particular culture many of the sex differences observed are most reasonably accounted for by the innate sex-linked behavior hypothesis. Also, insofar as Spiro's categories of aggression and integration are similar to the Whitings' categories of physical aggression and responsibility, the sex differences in the Kibbutz study are in the same direction as in the six-culture study.

Even though some sex differences in interpersonal behavior may be biologically influenced, there is considerable evidence that the interpersonal behaviors of boys and girls are socialized quite differently. Barry, Bacon, and Child (1957), in a cross-cultural survey based on ethnographic reports for 110 societies, found very consistent sex differences in the socialization of children aged four or older. In general

2 Excerpt reprinted from Melford E. Spiro, *Children of the Kibbutz* (Cambridge, Mass.: Harvard University Press, 1958), pp. 247–248, with permission of the publisher and the author.

they found that boys are trained to be self-reliant and to achieve, while girls are trained to be nurturant, responsible, and obedient. . . .

. . . Using Murdock's World Ethnographic Sample, Barry et al. tested the relationship between the extent of sex differences in socialization and other cultural variables such as residence rules, forms of marriage, and degree of political integration. Out of 40 comparisons, six significant associations were found. These were: (1) Grain rather than root crops grown. (2) Large or milk-producing animals rather than small animals kept. (3) Nomadic rather than sedentary residence. (4) Large animals hunted. (5) Fishing unimportant or absent. (6) Polygyny rather than monogamy.

Of these six variables, four deal directly with subsistence activities, and another, nomadism, is closely related to subsistence activities. Barry, Bacon, and Child (1957:330) conclude from these results that large sex differences will occur in "an economy that places a high premium on the superior strength and superior development of motor skills requiring strength, which characterize the male." The correlation between large sex differences in socialization and polygyny, however, is thought to be due to the effect of larger family units, which permit sharper sex differentiation than an isolated nuclear family in which the illness, death, or absence of one parent forces the other to take over some of the missing parent's activities. Romney, in a re-analysis of these data, suggests that the correlation between the types of subsistence activity that involve food accumulation and a child-training emphasis on compliance rather than assertion may be confounded with type of family organization. Thus, societies that rely primarily on food accumulation are also very likely to have father-absent families. If the sex of the socializing parent affects the way the child is socialized, the correlation between types of economy and child-rearing might then be the result of their relationship to type of family organization (Romney, 1965).

Identity

In the beginning of this review, it was emphasized that in all cultures biological sex differences are recognized as distinct social statuses for men and women. On the individual level these social statuses become psychological identities involving evaluative discriminations about one's own self and behavior. A male or female identity can be a product both of direct tuition (the child is taught to call and perceive himself as male or female) and of indirect tuition (the child is responded to or taught to behave in sex-specific ways, and so comes to respond to himself as others respond to him) . . . .

Thus almost everyone in every society learns his sex status and the role behaviors appropriate to it (Linton, 1942). Even the biological hermaphrodite can apparently learn one or the other of its possible sex statuses without great difficulty if one status is firmly assigned and not switched (Hampson, 1965). Nevertheless, not everyone wishes to occupy only his or her actual sex status. . . .

One of the ways in which a culture can institutionalize the potential discrepancy between assigned and optative identities is to permit certain persons to take on many of the role behaviors of the opposite sex, as, for example, in the institution of the berdache. Such transvestism often, but not always, involves homosexual behavior. Unlike transvestism, which is an open and overt expression of the wish to assume a feminine status, institutions such as the couvade and male initiation rites are thought to express a disguised and less conscious cross-sex optative identity. The couvade is a set of customs in which a husband participates ritually in the birth of his child by adopting some of the behavior and taboos of his wife, sometimes actually experiencing labor pains and postpartum fatigue.

Initiation ceremonies also appear to express an envy of the female role. For example, the initiation is often culturally perceived as a rebirth ritual in which men take a child and bring about his birth as a man by magical techniques stolen long ago from women. These techniques would lose their magical efficacy if women were ever to observe them. The need for the initiate to prove his manhood by bearing extreme fatigue and pain without complaint appears to indicate some uncertainty in sex identity.

Working with cross-cultural data, Whiting and his associates have come to similar conclusions concerning the role of status and envy and cross-sex identification in the functioning of initiation rites and in the couvade. Whiting distinguishes two sets of conditions: the first pertains to the persons who surround the infant and young child, those persons who presumably create the child's "primary" optative identity; the second pertains to the child's experiences in later childhood and adolescence, which create a "secondary," and sometimes conflicting, optative identity. The first set of conditions appears to involve mainly the presence versus the absence of the father in the household, with the expectation that "in the exclusive mother-infant case the mother should be seen as all powerful, all important, and insofar as she sometimes withholds resources, the person to be envied; and we predict the infant will covertly practice her role, and his optative identity will be female" (Burton and Whiting 1961:88).

In fact, this hypothesis has empirical support; societies that have exclusive mother-infant sleeping arrangements (in which the father sleeps in either a different hut or different bed while the mother and infant sleep together) are significantly more likely to have male initiation rites and couvade than societies without such exclusive arrangements (Whiting, 1962).

Whether the males who form a primary cross-sex optative identity express their envy of, and identification with, females in couvade or male initiation rites appears to be determined by a second set of conditions. Thus male initiation rites occur more frequently in patrilocal societies, while couvade is more likely to be practiced in matrilocal societies. It appears that in societies with exclusive mother-infant arrangements, later patrilocal residence, in which kin-related males are grouped together, creates a conflicting secondary optative identity for the young boy. This conflict in primary and secondary identities appears to be resolved in part by initiation rites, which symbolically remove the young boy's clinging femininity and reward masculine behavior. In matrilocal societies, on the other hand, no such conflict is created, so that the male envy of women is more directly acted out in an imitation of female childbearing. (See Young, 1962, for a contrary view of the functions of male initiation ceremonies.)

In order to test some of these hypotheses more directly, Whiting and his students have begun research in specific cultures that present internal contrasts relevant to identification theories. These studies have found the composition of the family in which the infant and young child is reared to be related to a number of variables, including math-verbal differences (Carlsmith, 1964), individual participation in the ritual of couvade (Munroe, 1964), interpersonal behavior (Longabaugh, 1962), and psychological tests of sex identity (D'Andrade, 1962). Generally the results of these studies are congruent with the hypothesis that optative identity and related behaviors are influenced by identification with significant others, and that the person with whom the child identifies is strongly influenced by the physical presence or absence of family members.

Sex Differences in Fantasy and Cognition

Perhaps the most complete cross-cultural investigation of sex difference in fantasy is Colby's (1963) study of dreams. From a collection of 1,853 reported dreams from 75 "tribal" societies, Colby selected one dream from each subject (366 males and 183 females), and coded each dream for the presence or absence of nineteen "qualities." For example, the quality "wife" was scored as present if the dream contained either the words "my wife" or "his wife" or "brother's wife" or "Felicia" when it was known that Felicia was the dreamer's wife. Table 5 presents the results of this study.

Colby's initial hypothesis, based on work with American subjects, was that males would dream more about qualities associated with "female mating choice" and "intensified penetration of space," while females would dream more about "male mating choice objects."

Table 5. Sex Differences in Fantasy: Dream Qualities Reported by Subjects from 75 Tribal Societies

	Male Preferred Qualities			Female Preferred Qualities		
Quality	Total No. of dreams	M/F ratio		Quality	Total No. of dreams	F/M ratio
grass	11	5.0[a]		husband	25	10.5
coitus	23	3.3		clothes	21	2.7
wife	37	2.6		mother	37	1.9
weapon	60	2.0		father	40	1.7
animal	179	1.6		child	61	1.6
death	121	1.5		home	52	1.6
red	16	1.5		female figure	198	1.3
vehicle	83	1.4		cry	29	1.1
hit	70	1.4		male figure	317	1.01
ineffectual attempt	14	1.2				

SOURCE: Reproduced from K. M. Colby, "Sex differences in dreams of primitive tribes." *American Anthropologist*, 65 (1963): 1116–1121, with permission of the author and the American Anthropological Association.

[a] That is, the quality "grass" appeared in five times as many men's dreams as women's. Since there were twice as many men as women in the sample, we had to double the number of women's dreams to obtain true ratios.

Generally, cross-cultural results support this hypothesis, although some modification in the definition of these categories was necessary.

One question with respect to these findings is whether these male-female differences in visual images are due to the expression of "body imagery" or to the fact that these visual images are reinforced in the daily performance of sex-typed activities. In other words, as a result of the division of labor, are males more likely to have higher frequencies of rewarding activities relating to such objects as dead animals, weapons, wives, and females more likely to have rewarding activities relating to clothes, husbands, children, and the like? The fact that male-female differences in dreams correspond roughly to these differences in daily activities could then be the result of simple contiguity. However, to the extent that psychological sex differences affect the reinforcement values of external events, sex differences in fantasy (or any other behavior) would be found despite identical external environmental conditions. This double confounding of stimulus conditions, in which males and females inhabit somewhat different internal *and* external environments, makes ambiguous the interpretation of many sex differences in fantasy productions.

References

Aberle, D. F.
1961 "Matrilineal descent in cross-cutting perspective," in D. M. Schneider and Kathleen Gough (eds.), Matrilineal Kinship. Berkeley: University of California Press.

Barry, Herbert III; Margaret K. Bacon; and I. I. Child.
1957 "A cross-cultural survey of some sex differences in socialization." Journal of Abnormal and Social Psychology 55:327-332.

Carlsmith, Lyn.
1964 "Effect of early father absence on scholastic aptitude." Harvard Educational Review 34:3-21.

Colby, K. M.
1963 "Sex differences in dreams of primitive tribes." American Anthropologist 65:1116-1121.

D'Andrade, R. G.
1962 "Paternal absence and cross-sex indentification." Ph.D. Dissertation, Harvard University (unpublished).

Ford, C. S., and F. A. Beach.
1951 Patterns of Sexual Behavior. New York: Harper.

Gouldner, A. W., and R. A. Peterson.
1962   Notes on Technology and the Moral Order. Indianapolis: Bobbs-Merrill.

Hampson, J. L.
1965   "Determinants of psychosexual orientation," in Frank Beach (ed.), Sex and Behavior. New York: Wiley.

LaBarre, Weston.
1954   The Human Animal. Chicago: University of Chicago Press.

Linton, Ralph.
1942   "Age and sex categories." American Sociological Review 7:589–603.

Longabaugh, R. H. W.
1962   "The description of mother-child interaction." Ed. D. thesis, Harvard University.

Mead, Margaret.
1935   Sex and Temperament. New York: William Morrow.
1949   Male and Female. New York: William Morrow.

Munroe, R. L.
1964   "Couvade practices of the Black Carib: A psychological study." Ph.D. Dissertation, Harvard University (unpublished).

Murdock, G. P.
1937   "Comparative data on the division of labor by sex." Social Forces 15:551–553.
1949   Social Structure. New York: Macmillan.
1957   "World ethnographic sample." American Anthropologist 59:664–687.
1959   Africa: Its Peoples and Their Culture History. New York: McGraw-Hill.

Romney, A. K.
1965   "Variations in household structure as determinants of sex-typed behavior," in Frank Beach (ed.), Sex and Behavior. New York: Wiley.

Simmons, Leo W.
1945   The Role of the Aged in Primitive Society. New Haven: Yale University Press.

Spiro, M. E.
1956   Kibbutz: Venture in Utopia. Cambridge: Harvard University Press.
1958   Children of the Kibbutz. Cambridge: Harvard University Press.

Stephens, W. N.
1963   The Family in Cross-Cultural Perspective. New York: Holt, Rinehart and Winston.

Whiting, Beatrice B. (ed.)
1963   Six Cultures: Studies of Child Rearing. New York: Wiley.

Whiting, J. W. M.
1961   "Socialization process and personality," in F. K. Hsu (ed.), Psychological Anthropology. Homewood, Illinois: Dorsey Press.

Whiting, J. W. M., and I. I. Child.
1953   Child Training and Personality Development. New Haven: Yale University Press.

Zelditch, Morris, Jr.
1955   "Role differentiation in the nuclear family: A comparative study," in Talcott Parsons and R. F. Bales (eds.), Family, Socialization and Interaction Process. Glencoe, Illinois: Free Press.

5

This article, by a free-lance writer interested in psychology and psychiatry, achieves an up-to-date review of some rapidly moving research by integrating interviews with scientists with information available from published sources. From the evidence thus assembled, it is clear that sex hormones and behavior interact in complex ways. Some of the most significant hormone effects already have been implemented at the time of birth in that the hormones affect prenatal neural development and thereby affect basic dispositions toward masculinity or femininity. Adult levels of male hormone correlate with levels of libido and aggressiveness, and this finding provides some insight into typical male-female psychological differences. Finally, the relationship between stress and hormone levels, as it occurs in both ordinary adults and pregnant women, suggests paths by which sociocultural systems may influence the physiological basis of sex differences.

He and She: Sex Hormones and Behavior

Maggie Scarf

Freud always maintained that human psychology had, as one of its components, some unknown biological "bedrock." He thought that we all, male and female alike, were captives of our physiology: that inborn propensities and tendencies exerted a profound effect upon behavior—and that these inner propensities were different in the two sexes. (Hence his now-infamous remark: "Anatomy is Destiny.") This belief is, however, not popular in the present, more "environmentalist" intellectual climate. The common assumption nowadays appears to be that where male behavior and female behavior are different they are so because of acculturation: that the display of either "masculinity" or "femininity" is by and large the result of social training.

Recent research on the sex hormones suggests that it is Freud's ideas which may be the more valid approximation of the reality. Endocrine studies have now established the critical role played by the sex hormones during prenatal life: These hormones are not only crucial to differentiation of the (male or female) sexual organs; but they "program" the brain, during fetal development, for the later display of either masculine or feminine behavior.

The word *hormone,* in the Greek, means "to arouse"—and this is what hormones do. They are chemical substances, secreted first in one

Reprinted from Maggie Scarf, "He and She: Sex Hormones and Behavior," *The New York Times Magazine,* May 7, 1972, ©1972 by The New York Times Company. Reprinted by permission of the publisher and the author.

place (usually, but not always, a gland or organ), then released into the bloodstream to move through the body and exert their ultimate effects elsewhere—on other "target" organs. The hormones and hormone-producing glands are part of an interrelated chemical system, as intricately balanced as the body's "electrical" system (brain, spinal cord, nerves, sense organs). Hormones must be present in order for the initiation—or in some cases, inhibition—of a multitude of complex chemical processes. They are involved, for example, in the vital maintenance of correct blood sugar in the body; of the overall rate of metabolism; in the regulation of water retention, of growth, of body responses to stress; and in the mediation of reproductive behavior.

The major sex hormones are secreted either in the testes in males (testosterone) or in the ovaries of females (progesterone and the estrogens, the important ones being 17 *beta*-estradiol and estrone). The adrenals, small yellowish organs lying just above each kidney, also secrete some sex hormones, including small amounts of testosterone and larger amounts of the weaker male hormone androstenedione (AD)—as well as a variety of other important hormones, including cortisol, cortisone and the "fight-or-flight" epinephrine (adrenalin).

Both sexes produce hormones of the opposite sex. In fact, men produce as much of the potent 17 *beta*-estradiol as adult women early in their menstrual cycle (when estrogen levels are at a low ebb). Men also have as much, or more, 17 *beta*-estradiol and estrone in their bloodstreams as do most postmenopausal women.

It is not the lack of estrogens which make a male a male, but the far higher levels of testosterone, antagonizing and nullifying the biological effects of the female hormones. An interesting little example of this is the recent finding that women after puberty have a greater sensitivity to odors than do men; and that this sensitivity is lost if male hormones are administered. (It is also lost when women are deprived of estrogen; and regained if the estrogen is replaced.)

In both males *and females*, testosterone appears to be the hormone which most strongly influences levels of libido. Incongruous as this idea might seem in the case of the female, it is now well supported by documentation from many sources. Studies of women who have had their adrenals (where most of the male hormones produced by females are secreted) removed indicate that these women suffer a dramatic loss in sexual desire; women who have had their ovaries removed rarely respond to loss of estrogens with loss of sex drive. In a report on a group of women who had had both operations (adrenalectomy and ovariectomy) it was found that virtually all were affected postoperatively, some merely reducing the frequency of intercourse, some losing interest in sex entirely. A subgroup of the same patients, who had the ovariectomy earlier in a separate and prior operation, reported experiencing no change in sexual interest or desire at that point.

Studies of women receiving testosterone injections also confirm the current hypothesis that male hormone mediates libidinal drive in the female. In one survey of a group of women receiving massive male hormone dosages (in the treatment of breast cancer), it was found that 99 percent of the patients were experiencing a marked surge in sexual desire. In another study, more than 100 women were treated with male hormone for such symptoms as frigidity, dysmenorrhea, etc. More than three-fourths of these women responded with a reported rise in libido: some even complained that their sex drives had become excessive. (A small group of the same patients, treated for a period of time with estrogens, experienced no apparent change in libido whatsoever.)

In the male, testosterone has sometimes been used as a"maleness-bolstering" medication. Doctors have attempted to treat a variety of problems, including impotence, decreasing libido in aging men, and homosexuality with extracts of this most potent of male hormones. However, the efficacy of such treatments remains unclear. A massive review of efforts to counteract impotence with male hormones, published in 1947, concluded that physically healthy men did not respond to stepped-up dosages of testosterone; the problem was psychological. Where sexual performance did improve after male hormone injections, it was suggested, the improvement came from the easing of psychological anxieties.

A more recent (1970) research report suggests, however, that adding testosterone may after all have more than a placebo effect. In the study described, two groups of male patients with problems of impotence were compared: The men in the first group, receiving a placebo, showed improved sexual performance among less than half of their number. The second group, receiving real medication in the form of oral testosterone doses, responded with more adequate sexual functioning among more than three-quarters of the men taking part.

As to whether or not testosterone is useful in combating the sag in sexual drive sometimes experienced by aging males, the answer, simply, is not known—information on the results of such treatment is largely anecdotal and not, it should be added, particularly optimistic. Attempts to overcome homosexuality with added male hormones have, of course, been doomed: Testosterone influences libido strength in both sexes, but has nothing to do with determining the sex of the individual toward whom heightened sexual interest will be directed.

Puberty is a time when the sex hormones are said to be "awakening." The pituitary or "master gland" (an organ just under the brain, not much larger than a small pea) now begins sending increasing amounts of hormones called gonadotropins into the bloodstream. These are chemical messengers which, in the case of the male, stimulate sperm production and the secretion of testosterone by the cells of the testes. In the female the same gonadotropins (chemically identical to those of the male) are released by the pituitary; but in females they appear in sequence, rather than simultaneously. The first of these hormones stimulates the growth of the egg and its nest cells within the ovary, with an accompanying rise in estrogen secretion. The second gonadotropin, appearing slightly later in the cycle, subserves the production of progesterone, the female hormone which prepares the uterine lining to receive the fertilized egg. The sex hormones bring about, in their turn, the onset of secondary sexual characteristics—breast development in girls, growth of facial hair in boys, etc.—as well as the behavioral changes seen in adolescence.

Puberty, however, it now appears, does not constitute an "awakening" so much as it does a *reawakening*. Research during the past several decades has demonstrated that the sex hormones are, in fact, present during prenatal development. The concentrations in which they appear in utero are crucial not only to sexual differentiation (to produce a male or a female) but, it now appears, to differentiation of central nervous system tissues which will mediate masculine or feminine behavior during adult life.

The primitive gonad, it should be mentioned here, is sexually bipotential: it contains everything necessary for the fetus to develop either as male or female. There is a "rind," capable of becoming an ovary; a "core" which can develop as a testis; and two sets of internal duct systems, male and female. (One of them will become vestigial during sexual differentiation.) The "genital tubercle" grows into either a clitoris or a penis; the tissue above the urogenital groove either fuses, in the male, to become a scrotum or remains separate as the lips of the vagina.

What makes the embryonic gonad move toward differentiation as male or female? Surely it is genetic sex which sets a "direction"—and, it used to be assumed, determined everything that followed. But a series of brilliant experiments begun in the late forties by the French physiologist Alfred Jost gave definitive proof that it was in fact the prenatal hormones which played the decisive role in sexual differentiation of the developing fetus.

Jost, using surgical methods so delicate that they have been difficult for other investigators to imitate, castrated a male rabbit in utero. The infant male, when it was born, had completely *female* external genitalia: It appeared that in the absence of the testes (and therefore, testosterone) a genetic XY male fetus had developed in a female direction.

What would happen, then, to an ovariectomized female fetus? Jost removed the ovaries of a developing female rabbit fetus: At birth, she had normal female internal ducts and external genitalia. It seemed that the ovaries—and therefore, prenatal estrogens—were not vital to the female in order to ensure her normal differentiation. Indeed, given that no interference (such as the presence of testosterone) occurred, the fetus would always develop along female lines. Jost's work suggested that Nature had some fundamental bias in favor of producing females. Femaleness thus could not be—as Freud had suggested—some state of incompleted maleness; it appeared to be the basic form of life. Maleness was itself the correction: to achieve it, something had to be added on—male hormones.

(One psychoendocrinologist tells a story of how he explained to a very religious friend that the Adam and Eve story in Genesis was unlikely—that all biological evidence now available suggested that if one sex arose from the side of the other, it would have had to have been Adam who came from Eve. "Isn't God wonderful?" retorted his friend. "When He created the sexes, He even did it the hard way!")

Later work of Jost's, and a variety of other studies, have now demonstrated that testosterone must not only be present in utero in order for normal male differentiation to occur; it must be present during a sensitive "critical period." A male rabbit fetus, castrated by the 19th day after conception, will develop a completely female internal duct system and female genitalia. If castrated on day 24, however, when the crucial phase is over, its development will be completely male.

Similarly, a male rat castrated in utero (this can now be done using chemical methods) will differentiate in a female direction—with a vaginal pouch, unfused scrotal tissues and a miniaturized penis which is indistinguishable from a clitoris. If castration is delayed until the critical period has passed, however—in this species, several days before birth—the rat will be irreversibly male.

In females, the presence of testosterone during the sensitive phase is as dramatic as its absence in males: A female rat receiving injections of male hormone during the critical period will become virilized, develop male-appearing genitalia, grow at an increased (male-type) rate, lose her reproductive cycle and become sterile. The same hormone doses, given 10 days after birth, will achieve none of these effects.

Hormones—the right concentrations at the right times—are decisive to normal sexual differentiation. In the middle fifties, the group of researchers working with the great pioneer in hormones and behavior, Dr. William C. Young (who died in 1965), began to wonder: Was it possible that fetal hormones also had some determining effect upon the type of sexual behavior that would be shown much later on, at puberty? What actually caused males to show masculine sexual responses during mating, and females to display feminine responses? It had always been assumed that the reason, in each case, was genetic. A genetic male simply looked like a male and was expected to behave like one.

But if prenatal hormones could feminize his genitalia, and masculinize those of the female, could they also affect the two, complementary sets of behavior and the type of sexual responses each would show?

In a now-classic experiment, Young and his colleagues demonstrated that a female guinea pig which had been virilized during prenatal life (through testosterone shots to the mother) would, when given male hormones at puberty, respond with startling amounts of male behavior. In subsequent work, Dr. Arnold A. Gerall showed that such females would not only mount other females and display pelvic thrusting, but (granted that genital development had been sufficiently anomalous) even intromission and ejaculation. In contrast, even when given high doses of estrogens, the capacity for showing normal female behavior— such as the "lordotic" response, typical in female rats and guinea pigs, in which the back is deeply arched and the genitals raised and presented to the male—was dramatically diminished. It was as if, during the period of prenatal life, some inner behavioral dial had been set at "male."

Experimental studies of the past 10 years have now established that, at least in lower animals, there are sensitive neural tissues which (like the primitive gonad) are bisexual in potential. These tissues, located in the hypothalamic region at the base of the brain, differentiate during fetal development to produce an unequivocally "male" or "female" brain; that is, they become imprinted during prenatal life to mediate either masculine or feminine mating behavior at puberty. Again, the key to what happens is testosterone. If it is present, the "female" pattern will be suppressed and the "male" tissues will become organized for the steady release of gonadotropins at puberty, and for male sexual responses during reproductive behavior. If, on the other hand, testosterone is absent in uterine life, the sensitive brain areas will differentiate as "female." They will become programed for the cyclical release of pituitary hormones at puberty, and for female sexual responses during mating.

Might homosexuality in the male be tied to a less-than-adequate supply of testosterone during the cirtical period when brain tissues are differentiating and becoming "programed" for the display of later sexual behavior? A number of researchers, intrigued by a vast animal literature on the subject, have recently begun looking for a possible correlation between homosexual behavior and the actions of fetal hormones.

In a British report, published last fall, it was found that a group of homosexual males had lower levels of testosterone in their urine than did a comparison group of heterosexual males; and that a group of lesbian women had higher testosterone in urinary samples than did a control group of female heterosexuals.

This past year, in an investigation carried out at the Masters and Johnson research institute in St. Louis, the blood plasma testosterone values and sperm counts of 30 young homosexual college students were carefully analyzed. It was found that among the 15 men in the group who were totally, or almost totally, homosexual, testosterone readings were much lower than they were among the other half of the men, who had definite heterosexual proclivities also. Sperm scores were also astonishingly lower among exclusively homosexual males. There appeared, interestingly enough, to be no great difference either in hormone levels or sperm counts when the bi-sexual males were compared with a "control" group of heterosexuals. According to the director of this research project, Dr. Robert C. Kolodny, the important question to be studied now is whether diminished testosterone supply is somehow a *result* of homosexual behavior—or whether it reflects an endocrine makeup that is simply different from that of heterosexuals in the first place.

A fascinating addendum to the recent research on human homosexuality—and, certainly, food for speculation—is the work of Dr. Ingeborg Ward of Villanova University. In an experiment reported in *Science,* Dr. Ward demonstrated that severe stress to a mother rat during pregnancy can block the normal behavioral development of her male offspring—and in effect, demasculinize them.

Dr. Ward, trained as a psychologist, proceeded in this experiment by placing the rat mothers-to-be, periodically, into clear plastic tubes. The tubes, from which it was impossible to escape, were then illuminated from above by implacable, glaring lights. The animals responded with every sign of distress: urination, defecation, hair standing on end. (Rats fear these lights so greatly that, initially, when they were too bright, several of the animals died.) Other pregant females, kept in a nearby vivarium, were not placed under stress, and served as control animals.

After birth, some of the male "pups" from the stressed mothers, and some from the unstressed mothers, were subjected to further adversities—they were placed in icecube trays which were shaken periodically on a vibrating metal rack. When the male offspring all reached the age of puberty (90 days in the rat), they were paired with females in heat.

Those males which had been stressed prenatally showed low degrees of masculine response, and little sexual interest (as did males which were both prenatally and postnatally stressed). They mated far less frequently than did the group which had been subjected to stress only after birth, or those which had not been stressed at all.

All of the rats were then castrated. Some 10 days later they were given injections of estrogen, which were followed up with shots of progesterone. The males were then paired with "stud" male partners. In this situation, those pups which had been stressed in utero displayed striking amounts of female sexual behavior, including the lordotic arch. The same high degree of feminine receptivity could not be elicited from males stressed after birth, or those not stressed at all.

It is Dr. Ward's belief that the nonmasculine behavior shown by the prenatally stressed pups resulted from abnormal neural tissue-imprinting during the cirtical period of fetal development. "In response to high degrees of environmental stress," she explains, "the pituitary began stimulating increased production of the adrenal 'stress' hormones. Included among these is a weak male sex hormone, androstenedione (AD). As a side effect of this situation, the testes also slowed down their production and release of the far more potent testosterone."

The weaker but more plentiful AD then competed with the more powerful testosterone, theorizes Dr. Ward, for control of the same chemical resting sites within the sensitive neural tissues—and the weaker AD won out. "The net result was that testosterone was unable to do its normal job of programing the brain," she says. "The tissues developed under the influence of the weaker hormone, and thus the animals were unable to differentiate as normally functioning males."

Dr. Ward is now trying to determine whether male rats will become feminized simply by being given large doses of AD prenatally. But at present the ingenious experiment described above stands as the sole demonstration that, by manipulating the prenatal environment, one can obtain exactly the same awesome alterations in male and female behavior as have been obtained previously only through direct manipulations of the fetal hormones.

One cannot of course generalize from rats to humans. (And the psychoendocrinological journals are as full of cautions about this temptation as the old temperance tracts once were about the dangers of drink.) Nevertheless, as one researcher remarked privately: "We do, in fact, work with the implicit assumption that what is found to be true in one species will hold true up and down the phylogenetic scale. It's usually an exception when one discovers a physiological mechanism in one species and then finds it absent—or totally reversed—in others. After all, aren't we making the same sorts of assumptions when we test out our drugs on rats?"

The presumption is, then, that the higher animals including monkeys, apes and human beings are, like the rat and the guinea pig, *not* psychosexually neutral at birth: That they are, even before the onset of learning and social experience, "programed" or predisposed by early hormonal influences to acquire specific, either masculine or feminine, patterns of behavior. In a study carried out in the late nineteen-sixties by Dr. Robert W. Goy, it was demonstrated that female rhesus monkeys, exposed to male sex hormones during prenatal development, would later behave in more malelike, than femalelike, fashion. Dr. Goy, working at the Oregon Regional Primate Research Center, injected a group of expectant monkey mothers with periodic doses of testosterone. The result was, not surprisingly, a generation of female offspring whose genitalia were male in appearance. These female "pseudohermaphrodites" were separated from their mothers at birth, and henceforth socialized only with their agemates.

Goy carefully studied the behavior of the virilized females as they grew into childhood. It had already been well established, through the famous monkey studies of Dr. Harry Harlow and others, that the play behavior of juvenile male monkeys was measurably different from that of the young females (and that these differences were not "taught" by the parent monkeys, because they manifested themselves even when the juveniles had no contact whatsoever with the older generation). The young males, for example, showed much more social threat behavior; they initiated play more often than did the young females; and they engaged in rough-and-tumble and pursuit play to a far greater degree. The males also withdrew less from threats and approaches made by others; and they engaged in more sexual play, including the frequent mounting which was in effect a "game" in which the future sexual role was being rehearsed.

The impressive thing about Goy's experimentally masculinized females was that they too behaved in all of these ways. They displayed the elevated levels of energy and activity commonly seen in young male monkeys. In fact their play behavior was much more similar to that of the male than to anything normally encountered in the behavior of the juvenile female.

In a 1967 study carried out at the Psychohormonal Research Unit of Johns Hopkins Medical School, the same unusually high levels of energy and activity were found in a group of 10 young girls who had been accidentally masculinized in utero. This research investigation was carried out by Dr. Anke Ehrhardt, working in collaboration with the Psychohormonal Unit's well-known director, Dr. John Money. The 10 young females taking part had all been virilized as a result of what was essentially a medical mishap: Their mothers were given progestin, a synthetic hormone, during pregnancy (in order to prevent unwanted abortion). It was not known at the time—during the 1950s—that certain progestins have a masculinizing effect on the developing female fetus. Nine of the 10 girls had been born with malelike genitalia, including an enlarged clitoris and a fused, empty scrotum. They received surgical correction early in life, and development proceeded normally from that point onward; psychosexual development, carefully evaluated by Dr. Ehrhardt in extensive tests and interviews, was certainly within the normal female range also. But it did seem to point toward some interesting questions about what the influence of those masculinizing fetal hormones had been.

Of the 10 girls, ranging in age from almost 4 to almost 15, nine were out-and-out tomboys. They preferred trucks, guns and other boys' toys to dolls. They loved being outdoors, climbing trees, playing football and baseball. They preferred being with boys to being with other girls; they wore boys' clothing styles and were more or less indifferent—some were actively opposed—to skirts and more feminine modes of dress. All displayed a high frequency of self-assertion and self-reliance, some of them to such an extent that their mothers were concerned about their behavior. "My daughter acts like a boy," complained one woman. "It might be because of the hormones. She is the opposite from me. I was the dainty type." Another family was having problems because their fetally virilized daughter was far better in sports than was her older brother.

Says Dr. Ehrhardt, who is now an assistant research professor of pediatrics and psychiatry at the New York State University at Buffalo: "The girls were consistently less interested in doll-playing than were a 'control' group of 10 girls, who were matched with them in every possible way—age, race, socioeconomic level, I.Q., etc. Also, the 'control' girls did a great deal of bride-fantasying, and involved themselves frequently in those sorts of games which are actually childhood rehearsals of the future maternal and wifely roles. In contrast, the fetally masculinized girls tended to fantasize about future careers."

In studies which she and Dr. Money have done on girls suffering from adrenogenital syndrome, notes Dr. Ehrhardt, the same tomboyish element and high-energy level regularly appear. Adrenogenital syndrome is a genetically transmitted condition which causes masculinization of the female fetus during prenatal development. The condition is due, briefly, to an error in metabolism which causes the adrenals to become overactive and produce too many hormones, including too many male hormones. It is now possible to stabilize this dysfunction with cortisone, so that overproduction of male hormones in the adrenogenital girl can be stopped postnatally, and her genitals can be surgically feminized. Still, psychosexual development of these girls, similarly to the progestin-induced masculinized girls, is toward the more "malelike" end of the normal female spectrum—high degrees of activity expressed in more masculine kinds of behavior.

In assessing which behaviors were to be called "masculine" and which were to be called "feminine," Drs. Ehrhardt and Money relied on criteria such as energy expenditures (much higher in boys), toy and sports preferences, career ambitions, maternalism (girls are usually fascinated by infants and infant care; boys are usually not) and several other items, including body image, clothing choice, etc. In statistical analyses of responses of large groups of boys and girls, sex-related "male" and "female" clusters about these items do reliably emerge.

"Nevertheless, isn't it possible," I asked Dr. Ehrhardt, who is a fair-haired, pretty German-born woman in her early 30's, "that these 'sex differences' are merely artifacts of our culture? Most psychiatrists and psychologists (and of course, most Women's Liberationists) believe that they result primarily from social experience. That is, a small female child is taught very early, or learns by imitation, those 'feminine' ways in which she is expected to behave—and responds by doing it."

"I would agree," she answered, "that the most powerful factors in the shaping of gender identity are probably experiential and social. In other words the primary thing is whether a person is called and thought of (and calls himself or herself) male or female. This is of course fundamental to identity. But within the broad spectrums of behavior which we call either masculine or feminine, there are certainly very wide variations. You can have, on the one hand, a woman who is totally domestic and maternal; and on the other, a person who is uninterested in children and wants only a career. My speculation would be that there is a fetal hormonal history, in both these cases, disposing the individual in one direction or the other. In other words, what I'm suggesting is that there may very well be normal female hormone correlates to the variations of normal female behavior.

"The main message of most of this work, both with animals and with humans," she added, "is that hormones before birth may have an organizing effect upon behavior that will appear only much later—that social environment is the mold in which basic tendencies, already present, will be shaped and formed. The idea is that testosterone, by its presence or absence, sets some kind of behavioral potential; and that postnatal experiences are actually acting upon a physiologically biased substrate."

One very strange factor emerging from Dr. Ehrhardt's study of the

10 progestin-virilized girls was that their I.Q.'s were all unusually high. Six of them had I.Q.'s above 130; thus, in a random sample in which one would normally expect to see this elevated value in 2.2 percent of cases, it appeared in 60 percent. In an earlier study of 70 adrenogenital girls and boys carried out by Drs. Money and V. Lewis, the same peculiar incidence of high I.Q. was encountered. In a group where, it would have been expected, 25 percent of those tested would have I.Q.'s above 110, it was found that there was an actual observed frequency of 60 percent having I.Q.'s above that value.

"Does this make you think," I asked Dr. Ehrhardt, "that boys, who are normally exposed to more masculinizing hormones in utero, would be expected to be ipso facto brighter than girls?"

"I don't think boys are brighter," she answered quickly. "But again, female and male intelligences do tend to cluster, statistically, around different sets of abilities. Boys appear to do better in mathematics and more abstract kinds of intellectual functioning, while girls score much higher in verbal capabilities." She paused: "I would be willing to allow that chemical influences in prenatal life might increase the level of energy and activity; and that they might have some enhancing effect upon intellectual capacities."

In a recent British publication, "Antenatal Progesterone and Intelligence," by Dr. Katherina Dalton, the very same phenomenon appeared. Dr. Dalton studied a group of boys and girls whose mothers had been given progesterone during pregnancy. (Progestorone, a female hormone, is similar to the progestins, but has no masculinizing side-effects.) All of the progesterone offspring studied by Dr. Dalton, both male and female, progressed better and faster than a comparison control group of children. They stood earlier, walked earlier, received significantly better grades in academic subjects, verbal reasoning, English, etc. Moreover, the more of the hormone their mothers had received, the earlier they walked and the better they did in school.

Thus, according to Dr. Ehrhardt, the intelligence-enhancing effect, if it proves to be definitely there, may have nothing to do with the masculinizing effect: "The kids in Dr. Dalton's study showed an increase in I.Q. without becoming virilized. So what we're seeing may just be due to some general chemical influence of these hormones. As far as I'm concerned, the whole question of the connection between intelligence and prenatal hormones is definitely a wide-open one."

Stress, Aggression, and Male Hormones

Numerous animal studies have confirmed that there is a curious link between the male hormone, testosterone, and levels of ongoing aggression. In the mouse, for example, fighting among males commences with the onset of puberty, when hormone levels are rising abruptly. Female mice fight only rarely, as is the case for males which have been castrated. When male mouse castrates are given testosterone injections, however, they display normal male adult fighting behavior within a matter of hours.

Does high testosterone level in the male bear a direct, one-to-one relationship to high levels of displayed aggression? In a study published last year, Dr. Robert Rose of the Boston University School of Medicine used new hormone assay techniques to take precise readings of male hormone levels in the bloodstreams of 34 male rhesus monkeys. At the same time, Rose, working with colleagues Irwin Bernstein and John Holaday, measured the frequency with which each monkey became involved in aggressive interactions with other members of the colony; and also assessed the dominance rank of each rhesus within the entire group.

Rose and his coworkers found that there was a high correlation between the levels of the animals' testosterone and the position which each held within the dominance hierarchy. The higher a monkey's male hormone concentration was, the higher his position in the "pecking order" tended to be. Those monkeys who were the more dominant were those who were more aggressive. And testosterone levels related, with almost startling simplicity, to levels of displayed aggression: The five animals showing the greatest degree of threat and confrontation behavior were the five with the highest hormonal level. If a clear-cut principle can be said to have emerged from the Rose study it was that, at least among male rhesus monkeys, Testosterone Rules.

Dr. Rose, 35, who trained as both a physician and a psychiatrist, is chief of the department of Psychosomatic Medicine at Boston University Medical School. He is currently, he notes, trying to investigate some of the questions raised by last year's male rhesus study. For example, was the superior status of the more dominant monkeys predicated on the fact that their male hormone levels were high in the first place? Or had testosterone levels risen as a *result* of dominance? Or both: Had raised hormonal levels meant more aggressiveness, which in turn lent itself to higher dominance position, which in turn had the effect of raising testosterone level—a question of the rich getting richer?

Rose and his colleagues, in order to test these possibilities, took several of the male monkeys and placed them, individually, into new colonies consisting only of females (13 or more). The lone male, in each instance, assumed the highest dominance position immediately. He had frequent copulations and, says Rose, had "what appeared to be a fairly blissful existence. After several weeks in these paradisiacal circumstances, we tested each male for levels of testosterone circulating in his bloodstream. We found that, across the board, the levels had risen—something like a fourfold increase."

It seemed that male hormone levels were not set and fixed within the body; they could be "turned up" as a consequence of environmental stimuli. The next question was, would the reverse also hold true? The researchers took each of their experimental monkeys and introduced them into new and far different groups—colonies of strange males in which the dominance hierarchy was already well established. In this situation, each lone "new boy" in the colony was set upon by the other males, outnumbered and subjected to total defeat. After a mere half-hour of such treatment, the monkeys were rescued from their respective fields of disgrace, and testosterone measurements were taken once more. In all cases, hormone levels had fallen sharply.

"Defeat was associated with behavioral withdrawal. The monkeys all did, after their experience with the strange males, show every sign of real depression," says Rose. "And that withdrawal involved a concomitant drop in sexual levels." Rose is now interested in finding out what happens to a male rhesus's level of displayed aggressiveness, and to his position within the social hierarchy, when testosterone levels are manipulated upward or downward by adding or removing fixed amounts of male hormone.

Is the human male, like the male rhesus monkey, likely to behave more aggressively if his male hormone levels are high? In a study of a young criminal population at a Southern prison, Dr. Robert Rose, working with Dr. Leo Kreuz, attempted to correlate degrees of expressed aggression (threats, refusals to obey orders, fights, etc.) among a group of young male prisoners with the levels of testosterone measured in their bloodstreams. He could not find, in this group of human males, the same direct relationship that had appeared in an earlier male rhesus study. The only link between high testosterone and aggressive behavior appeared to be the odd fact that those men with the highest male hormone values were the ones who had committed more violent crimes during adolescence: Indeed, the higher a prisoner's testosterone level was in adulthood, the earlier in life he had tended to commit a violent crime.

Rose's fairly negative results are, however, at variance with the findings of a slightly earlier study (1971) of young college men, carried out by Dr. Harold Persky at the Albert Einstein Medical Center in Philadelphia. Persky and his coworkers measured testosterone production rates in a group of 18 healthy males; at the same time, they administered a battery of psychological tests to their subjects designed to indicate degrees of hostility. In comparing results of endocrine and psychological measurements, the Persky researchers found a positive and direct correlation. In fact they found that those men with the highest testosterone production per unit of time were the very men whose sums of aggressive responses added up to the highest scores.

One of the great problems demonstrated by the conflicting results of the Rose and Persky research projects is—how does one define aggression? Is it observable outward acts, as specified in the Rose study; or is it negative aggressive *feelings* as defined by Persky? One writer, trying to sort out what is meant by "aggressive behavior," has suggested that there are at least nine different kinds, including fear-induced, territorial, intermale, etc.

A further complication for the researcher trying to correlate hormone levels and aggression in humans is that the human male, unlike the male rhesus monkey, has learned to have a variety of complex feelings about showing aggressiveness—and has also a far greater awareness of the consequences that can follow. Thus, behaving aggressively may in itself be a stressor—and stress is another variable which, as further work of Rose's has demonstrated, appears to affect testosterone production in both monkeys and men.

In a study published in 1971, Rose and a group of five colleagues (which included the eminent Dr. John Mason) compared testosterone concentrations in urine samples of three disparate groups of men: The first were Vietnam soldiers awaiting an imminent attack; the second were infantrymen undergoing a stressful basic training period; and the third was a "control group" of Army volunteers—men working at routine jobs, and undergoing no stress at all. Rose and his coworkers found that the testosterone levels of the men under great stress were dramatically lower than the testosterone levels of the men in the unstressed group. In fact, male hormone readings for the Vietnam soldiers and basic-training groups were similar to the lowest testosterone values reported in studies of normal male subjects.

In a subsequent research effort, Rose studied a group of men in Officer's Candidate School, as they passed through the first 12 emotional, stressful weeks of training. He found that during this initial period, when anxiety about failure was intense, testosterone levels predictably dropped. Later on, in a subsequent, more relaxed phase of training, when it was clear to the remaining candidates that they had "made it," male hormone levels rose once more—and so did levels of reported libido. "Stress seems to have an inhibiting effect on hormone secretion," remarks Rose. "It almost looks like a see-saw relationship: as the stress goes up the testosterone goes down. In fact," he adds with a smile, "it's my hunch that, where those Vietnam soldiers were concerned, you couldn't even *give* away a copy of Playboy!"

Suggested Readings

Dalton, Katharina.
   1968   "Ante-natal progesterone and intelligence." British Journal of Psychiatry 114:1377–1382.

Edwards, David A.
   1969   "Early androgen stimulation and aggressive behavior in male and female mice." Pp. 333–338 in Physiology and Behavior. Volume 4. Oxford, England: Pergamon Press.

Ehrhardt, Anke A.
   1971   "Maternalism in fetal hormonal and related syndromes." Paper presented as part of the symposium on Critical Issues in Contemporary Sexual Behavior at the 61st annual meeting of the American Psychopathological Association, New York, February 5.

Ehrhardt, Anke A.; Ralph Epstein; and John Money.
   1968   "Fetal androgens and female gender identity in the early-treated adrenogenital syndrome." The Johns Hopkins Medical Journal 122 (March):165–167.

Ehrhardt, Anke A., and John Money.
   1967   "Progestin-induced hermaphroditism: I.Q. and psychosexual identity in a study of ten girls." Journal of Sex Research 3(February):83–100.

Gadpaille, Warren J.
   1972   "Research into the physiology of maleness and femaleness: Its contributions to the etiology and psychodynamics of homosexuality." Archives of General Psychiatry 26(March):193–206.

Gerall, Arnold A.; Shelton E. Hendricks; Larry L. Johnson; and Thomas W. Bounds.
1967   "Effects of early castration in male rats on adult sexual behavior." Journal of Comparative and Physiological Psychology 64(No. 2):206–212.

Goy, Robert W.
1970   "Early hormonal influences on the development of sexual and sex-related behavior." Pp. 196–207 in Francis O. Schmitt (ed.), The Neurosciences: Second Study Program. New York: Rockefeller University Press.

Grady, Kenneth L.; Charles H. Phoenix; and William C. Young.
1965   "Roll of the developing rat testis in differentiation of the neural tissues mediating mating behavior." Journal of Comparative and Physiological Psychology 59(No. 2):176–182.

Keruz, Leo E.; Robert M. Rose; and J. Richard Jennings.
1972   "Suppression of plasma testosterone levels and psychological stress: A longitudinal study of young men in officer candidate school." Archives of General Psychiatry 26(May):479–482.

Masica, Daniel N.; John Money; Anke A. Ehrhardt; and Viola G. Lewis.
1969   "IQ, fetal sex hormones and cognitive patterns: Studies in the testicular feminizing syndrome of androgen insensitivity." The Johns Hopkins Medical Journal 124(January):34–43.

Moyer, K. E.
1968   "Kinds of aggression and their physiological basis." Communications in Behavioral Biology 2:65–87.

Netter, Frank H.
1965   "Differentiation of gonads," in The Ciba Collection of Medical Illustrations. Volume 4, Endocrine Systems. Summit, New Jersey: Ciba Pharmaceutical Company.

Neumann, F.; H. Steinbeck; and J. D. Hahn.
1970   "Hormones and brain differentiation," in M. Motta and F. Fraschini (eds.), The Hypothalamus. New York: Academic Press.

Rose, Robert M.; Peter G. Bourne; Richard O. Poe; Edward H. Mougey; David R. Collins; and John W. Mason.
1969   "Androgen responses to stress. II. Excretion of testosterone, epitestosterone, androsterone and etiocholanolone during basic combat training and under threat of attack." Psychosomatic Medicine 31(No. 5):418–436.

Rose, Robert M.; John W. Holaday; Irwin S. Bernstein.
1971   "Plasma testosterone, dominance rank and aggressive behaviour in male rhesus monkeys." Nature 231(June 11):366–368.

Stoller, Robert J.
1972   "The 'bedrock' of masculinity and feminity: Bisexuality." Archives of General Psychiatry 26(March):207–212.

Part III
Race and Mental Functioning

Intelligence tests were administered to large segments of the United States population in a massive testing program during World War I, and it was discovered that on the average blacks scored lower than whites. The average black-white difference of about 15 I.Q. points has been replicated many times up to the present (e.g., see reviews by Tyler, 1965; Spuhler & Lindzey, 1967; Baughman, 1971), and the discovery of this difference, perhaps more than any other fact, has set the tenor of studies on racial psychology. The difference documents separate trends in the psychology of American blacks and whites; the difference is large relative to those usually found in psychological research; and it involves an important psychological variable or at least one highly valued in contemporary society as a predictor of success. But the most consequential aspect of the difference is that it has been readily adapted to make invidious comparisons between racial groups (George, 1962), seemingly rationalizing the existing system of racial discrimination and buttressing the continuation of an American caste system giving superior privilege and power to whites.

Thus one of the first systematic observations in the area of empirical racial psychology seemed to support widely held prejudices about races in America (Harding et al., 1969) and resonated with the kind of "racial psychology" involved in the Nazi attempt at Jewish genocide. The field of racial psychology still reels in confusion from the emotionality of the intelligence issue (e.g., see Harvard College, 1969), and even after more than fifty years of research, little real knowledge is solidly established concerning racial differences in psychological functioning.

The view that truths exist in a pristine state waiting for men to discover them has been discarded, and it is understood today that knowledge consists of agreements about facts and interpretations among groups of informed humans (Kuhn, 1962). This perspective makes clear that knowledge is a form of culture, and creating knowledge inevitably requires value judgments shaped by the goals of knowledge seeking. The values come into play in deciding which observable facts to discount and which to emphasize as well as in interpreting the facts that finally are assembled.

From this perspective, it can be surmised that the lack of scientific progress in racial psychology is rooted in conflicts over societies' use of racial differences to control the distribution of power and privileges. In the United States, for example, sociologists have demonstrated conclusively that blacks have not had equal opportunities for occupational success (Duncan & Duncan, 1968), and as late as 1972 the Supreme Court held that it is constitutionally valid for private clubs to allocate their recreational privileges on the basis of race (The New York Times, June 13, 1972). Those who want to keep this system of racial stratification the way it is, possibly out of material interests (Glenn, 1968), sometimes seek knowledge to justify the social structure's racial girding; those who wish to allocate privileges on other bases seek to remove any scientific rationalization for racial discrimination; and these political motives define conflicting purposes for assembling knowledge on racial psychology. Because the field of racial psychology has received much of its impetus from political currents, it has come to be stuck in the vortex of a societal whirlpool.

Race and Evolution

Human races developed in the course of biological evolution, and evolutionary theory provides an objective perspective for developing a science of racial psychology. The evolutionary perspective (e.g., see Gottesman, 1968) reveals that some of the most embattled issues at present are of limited scientific import; it raises new questions addressed to more general human concerns than those associated with the social structure of a particular society at a particular time; and it suggests new methods of research for studying some of the issues in racial psychology. The implications of the evolutionary perspective are best seen by outlining the basic factors involved in the genetic differentiation of a species into separate races. The points below are drawn primarily from a text on biological evolution by Stebbins (1971).

The development of races begins when a population separates into different geographic locations sufficiently remote from one another so that the different groups are isolated for extremely long periods of time. Races cannot develop when all parts of the species' population are mingling with one another and exchanging genes every generation or every few generations, since in this case any genetic modifications will be incorporated into the gene pool for the species as a whole and will not produce racial differentiation. Furthermore, specialization of the gene pool is a process requiring dozens of generations; therefore, in the case of humans the isolation must continue for hundreds of years at least, thousands of years most probably.

Random division of a population and isolation of groups do not alone produce races. One or several evolutionary mechanisms must operate if the subpopulations' gene pools are to diverge.

The founder principle. A small population of humans with idiosyncratic genes may form a band and the special gene pool of the founders may be perpetuated as long as the band is isolated from the parent group. If the group grows it may come to be recognized as a somewhat distinct race. Differentiation of this kind probably is a factor in the occurrence of local races and microraces (Gottesman, 1968) and may account also for some differences among major geographical races since the world was populated by migrations, and the founders on different continents may have had somewhat different characteristics. However, whenever the founder principle alone is employed to account for a genetic distinction between populations, it is being assumed that the parent population contained the multiple "races" as part of its original natural variation, that this population divided for some reason into the groups that were racially distinct, and that the migrating founder group was both genetically distinct and sufficiently large to survive and grow. Thus one would have to adopt an implausible set of assumptions to employ this principle in accounting for the full range of racial diversity among humans, and the other two mechanisms discussed below necessarily are involved.

Mutations. Ordinarily the genes that one transmits to offspring are identical to genes that were received from one's own parents. Occasionally, though, a gene is transmitted that has changed character, or mutated, because of exposure to radiation or some unusual biochemical agent. Mutations usually are degenerative, and offspring with mutated genes typically abort or die at an early age (Stebbins, 1971: 24). However, a small proportion of mutations are not lethal; in such cases the person carrying the new mutated gene may enter it into the population gene pool in the course of further reproduction. Mutated genes, of course, could lead to the ultimate appearance of idiosyncratic characteristics in an isolated population and be at least partly involved in the development of a distinct race.

Random mutation, like the founder principle, might account for some divergencies between races but not the full range of differences. Successful mutations are quite rare, and once in the gene pool they, like all other genes, are subject to the powerful forces of natural selection. Stebbins (1971:31) states: "Mutations could have a direct influence on the rate and direction of evolution only if they occurred on an essentially uniform genetic background. . . . [But] populations of sexually reproducing and cross-fertilizing organisms are never genetically homogeneous." Thus mutations are unlikely to contribute to racial distinctions in a purely random way; they have their effect by interacting with processes of natural selection.

Natural Selection

Mainly races begin developing when different geographic locations impose significantly different environments on isolated populations, and the individuals in the species that are more adapted to one environment survive in that environment while other individuals do not. In other words, major races are created by the demands of different environments, and differences among major races must be explained ultimately in terms of their histories in different environments.

However, because natural selection operates strictly as a function of the survival of individuals, environmental demands are relevant to the development of racial differences only if they are matters affecting life, death, and reproduction. Natural selection causes change in a population because individuals who are more adapted to a particular environment live to reproduce and continue their specific genes in the gene pool while other individuals who are not adapted fail to make this contribution. So development of races requires not just isolation, not just different environments, but also profound interactions between genetic dispositions and environmental demands such that individual variations in the species that are benign in one environment are genetically *lethal* in another. Physiological characteristics are most directly tied to life, death, and reproduction, and so it is physiological differences that are most likely to be different in different races. Thus, equatorial races develop a dark skin to protect against the traumatic and sometimes cancerous effects of a tropical sun (Gottesman, 1968), and many Africans carry a gene that provides protection against malaria (Gottesman, 1969; Stebbins, 1971:77). Factors that have a more roundabout effect on biological survival and reproduction might also come to differentiate races, but the differentiation ordinarily would be less complete or it would require far longer periods of isolation in order to develop completeness.

Because of the mechanism of natural selection, each genotypic difference between major races is most likely associated with some difference in capacity for survival in different environments. However, it does not follow that each observable feature distinguishing a race was environmentally selected because the presence of a single gene may be correlated with the development of multiple phenotypic characteristics, both physical and behavioral. For example a gene might be selected because it provides physiological protection against a disease, but at the same time it could be associated with the development of an unrelated psychological trait, and so selection on the gene would cause racial specialization in both disease resistance and the psychological trait.

Actually spurious selection of this kind should be rare in the case of general psychological characteristics, because general psychological traits are genetically complex if they are genetically determined at all.[1] Studies of the number of genes causing differences in a particular psychological characteristic are still in the exploratory stage but, for example, Jinks and Fulker (1970) estimated that a minimum of 22 genes control variations in intelligence, acting in an essentially additive manner, and the number most likely is nearer 100. Such polygenetic determination of psychological differences means that a gene selected to enhance physical survival is unlikely to produce significant but spurious psychological differentiations between races. Suppose that some particular gene did increase vulnerability to a regionally isolated disease and at the same time was one of the genes contributing to individual differences in intelligence. A race that developed in that particular geographical location might have that gene deleted from its gene pool, and this conceivably could be a detriment in the development of the race's average intelligence as compared to other races. However, because intellectual variations are additively dependent on at least 21 other genes and more likely on scores of other genes, this particular deficit

---

1 Some specific psychological capacities, like the capacity for color vision, are linked to one gene or just a few genes, and racial differences on a number of such traits have been documented (Tyler, 1965; Spuhler & Lindzey, 1967).

would be small, perhaps unnoticeable in magnitude. Only if many of the genes involved in the development of differential intelligence also were implicated in matters of physical survival in a given environment would there be a pronounced effect on racial intelligence; genetically this is a most improbable circumstance. Thus, if general psychological differences between races exist and do have a genetic base, then these differences most likely have developed because of their varying adaptive value in different environments and not merely because they are correlated with aspects of biological adaptation.

Gains from the Evolutionary Perspective

Following the evolutionary perspective, the key question in studying racial psychology is not, Can we interpret certain aspects of social differentiation in terms of racial and genetic potentials? Rather, the question is, How can genetically induced personality differences between races, if any, be interpreted in terms of the different evolutionary histories of the races? A racial explanation of differential psychology is never complete nor finally validated until some appropriate evolutionary process of differentiation has been specified; usually this means accounting for how the trait came to be a matter affecting life, death, or reproduction in an isolated population of humans adapting to a particular environment. Ultimately the answers to the two questions above might communicate, although it should be clear by now that this would be nearly accidental. There seems little *a priori* reason to suppose that the ''biological values'' determining natural selection in various earth habitats over many millenia have much relationship to the social values dominating technological societies developed in the last century.

Racial psychology is a neonate among sciences and has labored through a birth period attended by political midwives and disrupted by traumas of racism. No doubt findings in the area will continue to be abused politically and socially, but this should not discourage us so that we fail to see the value of real knowledge on the topic. Through studying race in an evolutionary perspective we can gain a more detailed understanding about how different environments and events interact with psychological potentials to yield survival or disaster, thereby glimmering some knowledge about the directionality of our species in the context of its new, man-created world.

Research Problems in Racial Psychology

Most of the available research on racial psychology is methodologically inadequate to provide definitive answers about the relative contribution of genes versus environment, and it rarely directs itself to evolutionary issues. However, it is worth reviewing some of the main features of present research if only to point out what kind of research needs to be done.[2]

Nearly everywhere race and social circumstances are correlated to the point that it is a scientific challenge to assess the relative impact of biological and environmental factors on racial differences in psychology. The central populations of each major race tend to be divergent not only in their gene pools but in their national and cultural traditions as well. And when races do co-occur in a single society, they frequently accommodate by cultural separatism, as with the urban Chinese in America, or by a caste system such as that involved in South Africa's (or to a lesser extent, America's) black-white distinctions. In all such cases, races differ in both genes and environmental circumstances, so it is difficult to decide which factor is the cause of psychological differences.

The nature-nurture problem is typically involved in the controversy over black-white intelligence differences. Here it is well known that persons in the less-privileged lower strata tend to display lower levels of intelligence (Spuhler & Lindzey, 1967; Gottesman, 1968), therefore the argument always can be made that blacks in America, for example, score lower in I.Q. not because of their genes but because they occupy the least-privileged strata in society and are deprived of the

2   The focus here is on the problems arising in psychological and ecological analyses. In addition, difficult biometric problems arise in determining the race of an individual (e.g., see Spuhler & Lindzey, 1967; Gottesman, 1968).

physiological and psychological nourishments required for mental growth. One way of weighing the plausibility of the argument is to assume an 80 percent heritability for intelligence (see Chapter 1) and on this basis state the implications of the strictly genetic and the strictly environmental positions. A strictly genetic interpretation of the usual 15-point I.Q. difference would imply that about 84 percent of the whites have greater genetic potential than the average black while all relevant factors in their environments are the same. On the other hand, a strictly environmental interpretation would imply that genetic potentials are the same across races but that about 98 percent of the whites live in a more nurturant environment than the average black experiences. With such guidelines, some people find a mere visit to a black ghetto enough to maintain the credibility of the environmental position (although a misperception of blacks' life circumstances may be involved in the judgment).

One might try to resolve the issue objectively by finding samples of ''typical'' blacks and ''typical'' whites who are completely equivalent in terms of their environmental backgrounds, thereby eliminating environmental factors as a possible contributing factor. Many attempts have been made to do this by controlling socioeconomic status, i.e., by selecting and comparing whites and blacks who have attained equal occupational, educational, and monetary advantages. Such controls do reduce the average I.Q. difference a great deal although not entirely (Chapter 6), and the residual difference has been used as a basis for claiming that a difference in genetic capacity actually does exist. However, this claim, too, is vulnerable because it can be argued that even high-status blacks remain in a different caste and, therefore, being so easily identifiable, they still grow and live under conditions of discrimination and disadvantage. It is somewhat like trying to assess the genetic and environmental sources of sex role behavior by comparing male homosexuals with normal females under the assumption that we thereby have ''controlled'' for the factor of feminine identification. Obviously, in this case, the control is inadequate because even were a male to maintain an entirely feminine identification, there are many formative events in his life wherein he continues to be treated as a male and so he never has a chance to become a female in "all but biology." Similarly, it can be argued that blacks in America may obtain material advantages and yet, because of racial discrimination, they never have a chance to become whites in all but biology.

The study of racial psychology demands a near revolution in research technology before the nature-nurture questions begin receiving even fairly viable answers. The detrimental and enriching aspects of environments must be explicitly assessed, and numerous different levels of environment must be represented in future research studies. Attempts also must be made to sample groups representing mixed gene pools, using biometric techniques to assess the degree of gene mixture (e.g., see Gottesman, 1968). With designs elaborated in this way, there is some hope of assessing the relative contributions of genetic and environmental factors in racial differences in psychology through analyses of variance similar to those employed in heritability studies (Chapter 1). Designs employing multiple levels of environments and different degrees of race mixture also can be used to determine whether environmental effects interact with racial genotypes, thereby enriching our understanding of biological development and also, perhaps, our comprehension of the effects of the caste system. In addition, future research must expand its focus beyond racial differences that are merely of political interest and deal with a greater range of comparisons among black, brown, yellow, red, and white humans and do this within the context of variety of national cultures. Until such studies are done, we can have no confidence in statements that this or that psychological difference between races is genetically fixed.

Yet useful knowledge in racial psychology requires more than establishing facts about the genetic determination of racial differences. In addition we must provide logical accounts of how different genotypes have been selected in the course of each race's natural history. Without any credible account of how a psychological difference might have evolved, there is less reason to invest resources in trying to show that that psychological difference has a genetic source. And if a psychological difference is proven to be genetic in origin, this constitutes only an isolated fact until it is understood within an evolutionary perspective. Thus the science of racial psychology founders without the contributions of what might be called historical ecology—the study of particular populations over time to comprehend how human gene pools are affected by key ecological events.

A study by Stanley Elkins (1959) provides an approximate example of the kind of work that needs to be done in historical ecology. From historical documents he reconstructed the forced migration of millions of Africans to the Americas during the slave trade of the 1700s and 1800s. His research revealed that a third of the captive Africans died in forced marches to the sea, another third died in the holds of the slave ships during transport, and in the New World the survivors entered differing social systems that exercised different kinds of control over matters of life, death, and reproduction. Such facts provide circumstantial evidence that blacks in the New World have undergone a variety of "natural" selection processes that could reflect for at least a few generations in their biological and psychological characteristics.[3]

Studies in historical ecology must take account of continuously operating natural processes like climate, recurrent natural catastrophes like famine and disease, and social events with selective capability like wars and mass migrations. The focal question is always, How do such events act to discard some human variations and thereby specialize separated groups of humans into races?

3 Gottesman (1968), in an excellent review of race classifications, notes that blacks in America are distinguishable as a unique race if only because of their high degree of hybridization with whites. Elkins' account of various selection factors suggests that there might be additional bases for their having a distinct gene pool. However, a review of selective breeding studies indicates that a selection factor would have to operate a very long time before it finally crystallizes a new race; if the selection mechanism is removed too soon, the population gene pool returns to its original state within a few generations (Dobzhansky, 1972).

References

Baughman, E. Earl.
1971   Black Americans: A Psychological Analysis. New York: Academic Press.

Dobzhansky, Theodosius.
1972   "Genetics and the diversity of behavior." American Psychologist 27:523-530.

Duncan, Beverly, and Otis Dudley Duncan.
1968   "Minorities and the process of stratification." American Sociological Review 33:356-364.

Elkins, Stanley M.
1959   Slavery: A Problem in American Institutional and Intellectual Life. Chicago: University of Chicago Press. (Citation is to the Universal Library Edition, New York: Grosset & Dunlap, 1963.)

George, W. C.
1962   The Biology of the Race Problem. New York: National Putnam Letters Committee.

Glenn, Norval.
1966   "White gain from Negro subordination." Social Problems 14:159-178.

Gottesman, I. I.
1968   "Biogenetics of race and class." Chapter 1 in Martin Deutsch, I. Katz, and A. R. Jensen (eds.), Social Class, Race and Psychological Development. New York: Holt, Rinehart and Winston.

Harding, J.; Harold Proshansky; Bernard Kutner; and Isidor Chein.
1969   "Prejudice and ethnic relations." Chapter 37 in Gardner Lindzey and Elliot Aronson (eds.), The Handbook of Social Psychology. Second Edition, Volume 5. Reading, Massachusetts: Addison-Wesley.

Harvard College.
1969   Environment, Heredity, and Intelligence. Cambridge, Massachusetts: Harvard Educational Review Reprint Series, No. 2.

Jinks, J. L., and D. W. Fulker.
1970   "Comparison of the biometrical genetical, MAVA, and classical approaches to the analysis of human behavior." Psychological Bulletin 73:311-349.

Kuhn, Thomas S.
1962   The Structure of Scientific Revolutions. Chicago: University of Chicago Press.

Spuhler, James N., and Gardner Lindzey.
1967   "Racial differences in behavior." Chapter 19 in Jerry Hirsch (ed.), Behavior-Genetic Analysis. New York: McGraw-Hill.

Stebbins, G. Ledyard.
1971   Processes of Organic Evolution. Second Edition. Englewood Cliffs, New Jersey: Prentice-Hall.

Tyler, Leona E.
1965   "Race differences." Chapter 12 in The Psychology of Human Differences. Third Edition. New York: Appleton-Century-Crofts.

6

What is discovered when the intellectual abilities of different racial and ethnic groups are compared, with every effort being made to select samples with comparable distributions on socioeconomic status and to provide tests that are fair to all groups? The following brief summary of a research monograph provides some of the answers. Socioeconomic deprivation is found to have a general detrimental effect regardless of the specific kind of intellectual ability considered. On the other hand, differences in racial and ethnic background appear to be associated with different configurations of mental abilities. Of course, such research still says nothing about whether the group differences are genetic or environmental in origin since gene pools and ethnic subcultures still are confounded.

Mental Abilities of Children from Different Social-Class and Cultural Groups

Gerald S. Lesser
Gordon Fifer
Donald H. Clark

This study examined the patterns among various mental abilities in six- and seven-year-old children from different social-class and cultural backgrounds. The main intent was to extend the empirical analyses of the development of differential mental abilities in children, but the findings of this research also bear directly upon the problems of building valid and precise assessment instruments for children from different cultural groups.

Despite the considerable amount of work in the field of mental abilities in an attempt to create "culture-free" or "culture-fair" tests, little has been shown to yield consistent and valid results. The problem still remains of how to evaluate the intellectual potential of children whose backgrounds necessarily handicap them seriously on the usual tests of mental ability. This study focused on two major aspects of the problem: first, to devise tests that would be as free as possible of any direct class or cultural bias but still would be acceptable measures of intellectual traits and, second, to structure a testing situation that would enable each child to be evaluated under optimal conditions.

Reprinted in part from *Monographs of the Society for Research in Child Development,* 1965, 30(Ser. no. 102), pp. 1–93, with permission of The Society for Research in Child Development, Inc., and the authors. ©1965 by the Society for Research in Child Development, Inc. All rights reserved.

Hypotheses were tested regarding the effects of social-class and ethnic-group affiliation (and their interactions) upon both the level of each mental ability considered singly and the pattern among mental abilities considered in combination. Four mental abilities (Verbal ability, Reasoning, Number facility, and Space conceptualization) were studied in first-grade children from four ethnic groups (Chinese, Jewish, Negro, and Puerto Rican), with each ethnic group divided into middle- and lower-class groups.

The following specific predictions were made:

1. Significant differences will exist between the two *social-class* groups in the *level* of scores for each mental ability.
2. Significant differences will exist among the four *ethnic* groups in the *level* of scores for each mental ability.
3. *Social-class* and *ethnicity* will interact significantly in determining the *level* of scores for each mental ability.
4. Significant differences will exist between the two *social-class* groups in the *pattern* of scores from the four mental-ability scales.
5. Significant differences will exist among the four *ethnic* groups in the *pattern* of scores from the four mental-ability scales.
6. *Social-class* and *ethnicity* will interact significantly in determining the *pattern* of scores from the four mental-ability scales.

To test these hypotheses, a 4 × 2 × 2 analysis-of-covariance design (completely balanced randomized blocks) was used. The four ethnic groups (Chinese, Jewish, Negro, and Puerto Rican) were each divided into two social-class groups (middle and lower), each in turn divided into equal numbers of boys and girls. A total of 16 subgroups, each composed of 20 children, was represented. The total sample was thus composed of 320 first-grade children. Three test influences were controlled statistically in the analysis-of-covariance design: effort and persistence, persuasibility or responsiveness to the tester, and age of the subject.

The major findings were as follows:

1. Differences in *social-class* placement *do* produce significant differences in the absolute *level* of each mental ability but *do not* produce significant differences in the *patterns* among these abilities.

121

2. Differences in *ethnic-group* membership *do* produce significant differences in *both* the absolute *level* of each mental ability and the *patterns* among these abilities.

3. *Social-class* and *ethnicity do* interact to affect the absolute *level* of each mental ability but *do not* interact to affect the *patterns* among these abilities.

Thus, predictions 1, 2, 3, and 5 were strongly confirmed. No statistically significant support was found for predictions 4 and 6. The following other specific results were found:

1. Regarding social-class effects upon mental abilities, middle-class children are significantly superior to lower-class children on all scales and subtests.

2. Regarding ethnic-group effects upon mental abilities: (*a*) On Verbal ability, Jewish children ranked first (being significantly better than all other ethnic groups), Negroes ranked second and Chinese third (both being significantly better than Puerto Ricans), and Puerto Ricans fourth. (*b*) On Reasoning, the Chinese ranked first and Jews second (both being significantly better than Negroes and Puerto Ricans), Negroes third, and Puerto Ricans, fourth. (*c*) On Numerical ability, Jews ranked first and Chinese second (both being significantly better than Puerto Ricans and Negroes), Puerto Ricans third, and Negroes, fourth. (*d*) On Space, Chinese ranked first (being significantly better than Puerto Ricans and Negroes), Jews second, Puerto Ricans third, and Negroes, fourth.

3. Regarding sex differences, boys were significantly better than girls on the total Space scale, on the Picture Vocabulary subtest (but not on the total Verbal scale), and on the Jump Peg subtest (but not on the total Reasoning scale).

4. Regarding the interactions of social class and ethnicity, two effects combined to produce the statistically significant interaction effects upon each scale of mental ability: (*a*) On each mental-ability scale, social-class position produced more of a difference in the mental abilities of the Negro children than in the other groups. That is, the middle-class Negro children were more different in level of mental

abilities from the lower-class Negroes than, for example, the middle-class Chinese were from the lower-class Chinese. (*b*) On each mental-ability scale, the scores of the middle-class children from the various ethnic groups resembled each other to a greater extent than did the scores of the lower-class children from the various ethnic groups. That is, the middle-class Chinese, Jewish, Negro, and Puerto Rican children were more alike in their mental-ability scores than were the lower-class Chinese, Jewish, Negro, and Puerto Rican children.

5. Regarding the interactions of sex and ethnicity, the significant interactions for both Verbal and Space reflected the higher scores for boys than for girls in all ethnic groups, except for the Jewish children; Jewish girls were superior to Jewish boys for both Verbal and Space scales.

It was concluded that social-class and ethnic-group membership (and their interaction) have strong effects upon the level of each of four mental abilities (verbal ability, reasoning, numerical facility, and space conceptualization).

Ethnic-group affiliation also affects strongly the pattern or organization of mental abilities, but once the pattern specific to the ethnic group emerges, social-class variations within the ethnic group do not alter this basic organization. Apparently, different mediators are associated with social-class and ethnic-group conditions. The mediating variables associated with ethnic-group conditions do affect strongly the organization of abilities, while social-class status does not appear to modify further the basic pattern associated with ethnicity.

These findings allow a reassessment of the various proposed explanations of cultural influences upon intellectual performance. The importance of the mediators associated with ethnicity is to provide differential impacts upon the development of mental abilities, while the importance of the mediators associated with social class is to provide pervasive (and not differential) effects upon the various mental abilities. This conclusion allows selection among the several explanations offered to interpret cultural influences upon intellectual activity; the explanations based upon natural selection, differential reinforcement, motivation, problem-solving tactics, work habits, and so forth, were reexamined in the light of the present results.

In summary, the findings lend selective support to Anastasi's premise (1958:563) that "Groups differ in their relative standing on different functions. Each ... fosters the development of a different *pattern* of abilities." It seems true that social-class and ethnic groups do "differ in their relative standing on different functions." However, ethnic groups do "foster the development of a different pattern of abilities," while social-class differences do not modify these basic organizations associated with ethnic-group conditions.

The present effort to construct suitable testing procedures for studying children from culturally diverse groups must now incorporate the broader educational considerations of curriculum development, teacher training, and school organization. We have shown that several mental abilities are related to each other in ways that are culturally determined. We propose that the identification of relative intellectual strengths and weaknesses of members of different cultural groups must now become a basic and vital prerequisite to making enlightened decisions about education in urban areas.

Reference

Anastasi, Anne.
1958   Differential Psychology. New York: Macmillan.

7

Although this chapter is only an excerpt from a longer review, it clearly registers the immense interest of American social scientists in black-white psychological differences. The review does document the fact that many black-white differences on general personality traits have been discovered in American populations, but it also points out repeatedly that little is known about the sources of these differences. In particular, the authors emphasize that black-white psychological differences arise within a complex sociocultural system of statuses and interactions, therefore no simple inferences can be made about the genetic origins of the differences. The specification of dates in the title should serve as a reminder that the sociocultural matrix itself is changing rapidly; there can be no assurance that the differences discussed in the article still persist a decade later.

Comparative Psychological Studies of Negroes and Whites in the United States: 1959–1965

Ralph Mason Dreger

Kent S. Miller

This review covers the psychological studies comparing Negroes and whites in the United States for the most part from 1959 through 1965. Some earlier studies which were omitted from our last review (Dreger & Miller, 1960) have been included, as well as some articles which were published in 1966. We have been concerned primarily with direct psychological comparison of groups of Negroes and whites, although in some instances we have given attention to studies which did not involve a direct comparison, but which provided pertinent information for interpreting other studies. The literature covered in this review contains a larger proportion of studies which might be referred to as sociological than did the 1960 review.

We have been ambitious. We have attempted to cover much of human behavior. Consequently, this is not a complete bibliography.

Abridged from *Psychological Bulletin Monograph Supplement,* 70 (no. 3, pt. 2), 1968, pp. 1–58, by permission of the American Psychological Association and the authors.

The authors wish to express gratitude to the Graduate Research Council of Louisiana State University and to the Southern Regional Council for financial support in the preparation of this review.

Several hundred additional studies have been reviewed and excluded from this review and its accompanying references because in our judgment they were poorly designed or of limited significance. Perhaps we have judged incorrectly or have failed to uncover some important work. Our concern has been to identify the significant trends and what we considered to be the major research contributing to these trends.

We have made no attempt to define race and have accepted the authors' definitions of white and Negro. That we consider the usual failure, however, to delineate carefully the independent variable of "race" is made more explicit later. In some instances—particularly with respect to demographic characteristics—the statistics quoted have been based on the nonwhite population rather than the Negro population. This is a minor source of error. . . .

Ego Development

With the recognition that there has not been adequate theoretical, including methodological, basis for much of the study that has been done, we nevertheless go ahead to report what has been done. Unreported in our previous review is Ausubel's (1958) summary of research on ego development of Negro children in the segregated lower class in contrast to the ego development of the child in the typical middle-class family. Roughly, this summary suggests that in white suburbia the infant is highly valued and catered to in such a way as to lead to convictions of omnipotence. In the preschool years demands are placed upon the child growing out of infancy, in a manner such as to create a satellization about the parent and a derived status coming from identification with that parent. In turn, this satellization leads to a self-esteem. In this middle-class child true desatellization occurs with a substitution at the school period of school and peer groups.

However, in the Negro segregated child who is ordinarily of the lower class (though in the 1960s possibly not; cf. Moynihan, 1965), development occurs under the direction of early authoritarian parents who provide less of what Murray would call p Succorance. The parents, nevertheless, relax their supervision earlier than do parents of the middle class, a phenomenon leading to an earlier independence (of the nature suggested by Gray previously), with, however, the added impedimenta of broken homes, matriarchal dominance, and inferior caste status. These conditions lead to a lower self-esteem and more difficulty in satellization about the parents. In turn a rejection of group membership occurs which concomitantly and subsequently leads to serious self-rejection, until at last the racial membership must be acknowledged. Added to these processes are lower-class devaluing of parents and school, who and which offer little for the child in the way of a primary or derived status, and also a low level of aspiration in respect to education and vocation which are found in the home of the lower-class child. . . .

Although the expressed vocational level of aspiration may be high, as we point out later, the functional levels of striving of the lower-class child are low, and failure leads to loss of academic interest and a perception that the child cannot achieve because of his status. It follows, then, that failure comes in developing the "ego maturity" that is necessary for success. In addition, the fact of caste membership for the Negro child acts as an ultimate barrier, so that finally self-depreciation and primarily passive-aggressive retaliatory mechanisms develop.

According to Ausubel, the Negro in a heterogeneous racial situation competes more and develops more self-esteem. (On this matter the evidence, as we have suggested previously, is not conclusive.) The Negro in a segregated situation has few models of superior achievement or quality teaching. Further, in the white middle class, girls enjoy an immediate higher status in terms of the academic situation, but boys eventually achieve a higher status than do girls. In the Negro segregated community, however, girls enjoy a higher status both immediately and eventually. Of course, Ausubel suggests, individual differences are important in both the type of home and personal reactions which occur. The stigmatized racial membership can in part be cushioned by the home which helps to establish self-esteem.

Although one can recognize a psychoanalytic framework for the above analysis and some portions of it have less empirical justification than others, the overall picture is one to which we as clinicians are inclined to give assent. At least, if Ausubel's review and interpretation of the research data are not completely adequate, we are convinced that the complexities of the psychodynamics of "personality" development of the lower-class Negro child are fully as great as Ausubel maintains. The simple picture of the Negro child as only a child of the lower socioeconomic classes in general, or as only genetically determined in certain ways, is entirely too simple. That single most important fact of being a Negro adds what at this time are partly incommensurable but still grossly identifiable complicating facets to the already extremely complex process of developing and maturing in a complex civilization.[1]

Self-Concepts and Their Correlates

More specifically, in the period since Ausubel's review we have a study by Wylie (1963) in which boys expressed belief that they had higher class standing for themselves than did the girls. White children made such estimates more than Negro children, and upper level white children more than lower level white children. The guessed ability for college work generally found males making a greater estimate for such ability than females in the white group. But in the Negro group the curve of estimated ability for college work was an erratic one compared with the white curve. On both the estimated ability for college and the desire to go to college the white higher socioeconomic class was higher than the white lower class. In all the measures self-favorability showed up as a response bias.

Contrary to a thesis proposed by Ausubel that the presence of white children in the heterogeneous situation leads to improvement in both achievement and self-esteem on the part of the Negro child is the finding by Gregor and Armstrong (1964) that the Negro child at the impressionable age when he enters the desegregated school has conflict over his status in the desegregated school which leads to intrapsychic tension greater than the child has in a segregated school. Whether one accepts Gregor and Armstrong's contention or not, they are correct in saying that a desegregated school does not mean an integrated school, especially in the extraacademic realm. Most psychologists would not feel that Gregor and Armstrong have presented enough data to support their position of greater Negro tension in a desegregated school, although the position appears reasonable enough.

Tackling these difficult problems of self-concept and relating them to academic achievement, intelligence, interests, and manifest anxiety—probably an order too large to be handled with the tools utilized—Henton and Johnson (1964) sampled from the Negro elementary schools in a Louisiana parish and made comparisons of their findings

---

1   Riese (1962) finds the Negro child in a guidance clinic to be basically just a hurt, lonely, and frightened *child*. We agree. Yet, we must point out that in this case much, if not most, of the hurt, loneliness, and fright stem from his being a *Negro* child.

with those of Bledsoe and Garrison (1962) on white children. Low positive relations held in both groups between self-concepts and California Test of Mental Maturity intelligence and with some exceptions between self-concepts and achievement. Self-concepts and cultural interests, related in Bledsoe and Garrison's white group, were virtually unrelated in Negro children. Again, with one exception, Negro and white children did not differ on the Children's Manifest Anxiety Scale. However, a negative self-image appeared to be more characteristic of the Negro child than of the white child. . . .

That temperament patterns are related to performance on intelligence tests is suggested by the study of Roen (1960) who matched 50 white and 50 Negro Army personnel on 10 socioeconomic and demographic variables and compared the correlations among the various scores derived from the Army classification batteries combined (that is, pattern analysis, reading and vocabulary, and arithmetic reasoning), picture arrangement, the California Test of Personality, the Manifest Anxiety scale, and the Bernreuter Self-Confidence scale. Though closer correlations existed for Negroes, and Negro personnel achieved lower scores on intelligence and social class, both groups were approximately equivalent on the CTP and the MA scale. The general pattern appears to be that correlations among various scales are higher for the Negro group than for the white group. Although he recognizes that causality is not proved by his correlational study, Roen concludes that his study is further research on the proposition "that Negroes as a group . . . incorporate intellectually defeating personality traits that play a significant role in their ability to score on measures of intelligence" (Roen, 1960:150).

Temperament Measured by Objective Personality Inventories

Several studies involving the Minnesota Multiphasic Personality Inventory (MMPI) and similar assessment techniques are grouped together here. Palermo (1959) studied fourth-, fifth-, and sixth-graders in a southern Illinois school system utilizing the Children's Manifest Anxiety scale. Test-retest reliability with the CMA scale teacher-administered and a one-month interval is not entirely satisfactory, for several of the reliability coefficients are rather low (.59, .61, .63). White children generally tended to be more consistent than Negro children from test to retest. At all grade levels, unlike Henton and

Johnson's Louisiana subjects, Negroes were significantly higher than whites on the basic anxiety score. Girls were measurably more anxious than boys in both groups but not significantly so in several cases. The tendency in both groups was for the anxiety scores to go down as grade level went up. Anxiety scores with white boys dropped in the fifth grade but with Negro boys not until the sixth grade. The drop for girls was not different in pattern between the white and Negro children, but the sixth-grade Negro girls were relatively lower compared to their own fifth-graders than were the white girls in the sixth grade compared to their own fifth-grade group. We hesitate to point out once more that such a study as this is vitiated in part because it does not use the right statistics. The design is basically an analysis of variance design inasmuch as comparisons are made among the grade levels as well as between sexes and between races. In addition, the possibility is that the Negro children were older on the average than the white children so that some of the grade differences may be attributable to age differences.

In an MMPI study of the entire ninth grades in integrated schools in two Kentucky towns, Ball (1960) found initially that the white boys and girls averaged 10 points higher on an I.Q. test, lower in the percentage of broken homes, higher in social class status, higher in mean grade-point averages, and lower in the percentage of children who were educationally retarded (though this latter difference was not statistically significant). One is surprised, however, by the fact that these young adolescents did not show more differences on the MMPI. As it was, the Negro boys scored higher on the *Hs* scale, Negro girls higher than white girls on the *F*, *Sc*, and *Si* scales, and white girls higher than Negro girls on the *K* and *Hy* scales. It may be that with as many comparisons as are found in a study of this nature one or more of the significant differences could come by chance. If the differences can be taken at face value, however, it would seem that Negro adolescents tend to have more serious difficulty than white adolescents. Ball had an inordinately large number of invalid profiles, 11 out of 31 Negroes, and 13 out of 169 whites.

Results similar to Ball's have been reported by McDonald and Gynther (1962). They had the MMPI administered by school counselors to a relatively large number of Negro and white males and females in senior classes in segregated schools. White children were mainly in socioeconomic Classes 1 and 2 and Negroes in Classes 3 and

4, higher and lower statuses, respectively. The authors concluded that social class had no effect upon the scores, their results paralleling those reported in another article (McDonald & Gynther, 1963). They assumed that they had no invalid records and discarded none, even with high L or F scores, because "several studies (Gynther, 1961) have suggested that such configurations are not invalid, but are meaningfully related to personality traits such as hostility" (McDonald & Gynther, 1962:278). One can question the effects of including profiles with elevated L and F scales, even though configurations may be meaningful, since test-taking attitudes associated with these elevations may invalidate the clinical scales. If the other scale differences can be accepted, Negroes scored significantly ($p<.01$) higher than whites on scales $L, F, D, Mf, Sc,$ and $Ma.$ Contrary to expectations, however, Negro and white males show equivalent scores on the Pd scale. From their two reports, the authors suggest that their results parallel those of others, that Negroes score more highly than whites on clinical scales in the adolescent years. They set forth the hypothesis that racial differences on the MMPI are culturally determined. Inasmuch as this conclusion is a post hoc explanation which the authors recognize needs to be tested further, the cultural explanation may or may not be justified.

In respect to Negroes' being more markedly deviant on the clinical scales than whites, some of the same conclusions show up in the reports on veterans by Miller, Wertz, and Counts (1961) and by Hokanson and Calden (1960). . . .

Not content with previous studies which they regard as inadequate because age, sex, educational, and institutional differences in addition to socioeconomic level have not been well controlled, Butcher, Ball, and Ray (1964) tried to control for these variables. Their results indicate that some of the differences found previously, implying that Negroes are more disturbed in their responses than whites, are eliminated when social class is "controlled." Until other controlled studies are made to confirm or disconfirm these findings, we shall accept the conclusion that individual differences and possibly sex differences may be more important than race differences in MMPI-revealed temperament. However, the relative effects of socioeconomic differences are not clear. Dahlstrom and Welsh (1960) state that though socioeconomic status has an important bearing on MMPI responses, it is difficult to evaluate just what that bearing is.

One study is reported here utilizing the Edwards Personal Preference Schedule which presumably controls for "social desirability." The author (Brazziel, 1964) recognizes that EPPS social desirability values were obtained from white student samples. Since, however, EPPS is the only one available for measuring the Murray type of need variables in an objective manner, he risks making his comparison anyway between upper-South Negroes, lower-South Negroes, and the white norm group. Differences were found between the sexes and between middle- and lower-middle-income classes, as well as rural-urban differences in the lower-South Negro group. However, the main findings of interest here are ones which should be known from studies of white individuals:

> Negro students from the upper-South urban areas . . seem to be motivated by need structures which are more similar to their white liberal arts counterparts . . . the lower-South Negro college student [is seen] as a deferent, orderly, submissive, intraceptive, persistent person with low needs for heterosexuality and exhibition (Brazziel, 1964:49–50).

Inasmuch as the social desirability values have not been determined for Negro samples, methodological objections could be raised to Brazziel's conclusions. On the other hand, because these conclusions are in line with the results suggested earlier in connection with "personality development," his findings are rendered more credible. . . .

Self-Attitudes

Studies relating to self-concept and achievement were discussed in an earlier section.[2] The research reviewed in this section is somewhat heterogeneous and covers much broader areas.

The fact that racial awareness develops at an early age received additional support from the work of Morland (1958; 1966). In questioning Southern and Northern children about their willingness to

---

2   For the reader interested in a discussion of the relation between Negro self-concept and education, a general overview may be found in papers presented at a conference held at Tufts University in 1963 (Kvaraceus, Gibson, Patterson, Seasholes, & Grambs, 1965).

accept members of both races, their racial preferences, self-identification, and the ability to recognize race differences, he employed a series of black and white pictures as stimuli. He found that racial recognition ability progresses from age three through six, with the fastest rate of growth occurring during the fourth year of age. Children of both races preferred and identified with whites; Southern white children had the highest racial recognition ability, and Southern Negroes were the least likely group to identify with and prefer their own race. Further evidence that children show racial awareness as early as age two or three, and have some concern about skin color, is found in a report by Stevenson and Stevenson (1960), although their observations were based on a small number of children.

Gregor and McPherson (1966), reported one of the few studies in which young Negro children were found to favor their own race. In this instance, white children were found to have a stronger preference for their own race than did the Negroes; but the study as a whole is limited by the fact that comparisons were between middle-class whites and lower-class Negroes.

Clinical observations of conflict about skin color and preferences for white skin have been noted by Brody (1963). His conclusions were formed on the basis of interviews with groups of Negro and white boys brought to a clinic. These observations are only suggestive in that clinic patients represent a select group and all interviews were conducted by a white psychiatrist, but they are consistent with the literature as a whole. Other incidental findings associated with skin color include the report that darkened skin color is associated positively with high Negro identification (Kirkhart, 1960), and that Negro children with impaired self-esteem as measured by the California Test of Personality perceive themselves less accurately in terms of skin color (Butts, 1963). There are indications that a fair number of light-skinned Negroes totally reject their Negroidness by permanently passing as whites (Conyers & Kennedy, 1963; Kennedy & Conyers, 1964).

Racial comparisons of self-concept on a variety of personality measures support earlier findings of more negative responses among Negroes (Keller, 1963; Henton & Johnson, 1964; Bayton, Austin, & Burke, 1965; Deutsch, 1965). Only one study failing to report racial differences came to our attention; in this instance the measure of inadequacy and inferiority was self-drawings of a small sample of subjects (Gasser, 1962). Gaier and Wambach (1960) found a number of similarities between Negro and white college students in the self-reporting of personality assets and liabilities. Even in the face of objective evidence of equal mental ability, however, Negroes have been found to feel inadequate and to orient compliantly toward whites (Katz, Goldston, & Benjamin, 1958; Katz & Benjamin, 1960).

Several studies during this period relate to attitudes regarding internal versus external control in groups of whites and Negroes (Battle & Rotter, 1963; Lefcourt, 1965; Lefcourt & Ladwig, 1965a; 1965b). Negroes seem to feel and behave as if they have limited control of reinforcement, although this reaction probably relates to the type of situation being studied. For example, Lefcourt (1965) reports that in a pure chance situation his Negro subjects behaved in a more cautious, internal control fashion than did the whites.

With the recent heavy emphasis upon research on race and housing, it is not surprising to find attempts to relate segregated housing to self-concept. Works (1962) failed to find any relationship between scores on a self-concept check list and residence in integrated housing. Haggstrom (1963), employing an unvalidated happiness rating scale, found that Negroes living in desegregated housing had significantly higher self-esteem and less hostility toward whites than matched households which were segregated.

The relation between status and attitude has been strongly underscored by Parker and Kleiner (1964). On the basis of interviews with over 1,400 Philadelphia Negroes, they came to the following conclusions: Individuals in high status positions have values more similar to those of the white middle class, stronger desires to associate with whites, a relatively weaker ethnic identification, and more negative attitudes toward other Negroes than those in lower status positions.

Further confirmation of a relation between self-attitude and tolerance toward others is the report that high scores on self-acceptance are positively associated with favorable attitudes toward both Negroes and whites (Trent, 1957).

Considering the variety of measures which have been used and the range of subjects studied, the results have been surprisingly uniform in revealing comparatively negative self-attitudes in Negroes. As with many of the other areas covered in this review, this research is subject to considerable criticism. In many instances the measures employed have limited reliability and they have been applied to small and atypical samples which sharply curtail generalizability. There have been failures to control obviously significant variables such as socioeconomic status, a factor which could clearly outweigh any racial differences found.

Even with the recognition of deficiencies, however, there still seems to be little doubt that the American Negro holds relatively negative self-valuations. Further, research needs to be directed at exploring the manner in which specific situations and events affect self-concept, particularly over time. In several of the studies reviewed, there are suggestions that the Negro female has more positive self-attitudes than does the Negro male. Quantification of these differences could have broad implications. The rapidly changing status of the Negro provides a natural laboratory to assess the importance of external change in status on self-attitude.

In summarizing this section on temperament comparisons, the generalization may be hazarded that very early in life both white and Negro children develop attitudes toward themselves which are reflected in positive and negative self-valuations, respectively, and that these self-valuations in turn may be related to achievement and other performances even much later in life. Whether any connection exists, however, between these early developed self-concepts and some later revealed differences such as in Negroes' greater inclination toward deviancy on clinical scales, is not certain. Such a connection most likely does exist in relation to greater deference, submissiveness, and introception among those Negroes more subject to caste sanctions than are their brothers who live in freer situations. Differences found elsewhere in anxiety level between white and Negro children were not revealed in Louisiana; differential locations and degrees of segregation could be adduced to account for the discrepancy, but speculation could probably reveal other suggested explanations. . . .

Attitudes, Miscellaneous

In a shotgun fashion, investigators have been concerned with measuring the attitudes of Negroes and whites with respect to nearly every aspect of human behavior. Many of the reports mentioned in this section are time-bound, but nevertheless shed some light on current conditions.

Broom and Glenn (1966) used 32 questions asked on national opinion surveys between 1950 and 1960 as a basis for comparing Negro and white differences in attitudes. Although public opinion surveys contain some sampling errors, this report is an excellent example of a relatively inexpensive reworking of earlier data. Negro-white differences were found which could not be due to differences in education or region of residence. In general, Negro-white differences were smaller than differences between Southern and non-Southern whites and between low-education and high-education whites. By age, the response differentiation between Negroes and white was uneven, suggesting that cultural differences have not diminished much. The greatest differences between the two races were on questions relating to childbearing, domestic, political, and economic issues, and international affairs. The smallest differences were on authoritarianism and personal morality.

The causes of racial friction must seem to investigators to be generally obvious, for there have been few attempts to quantify these causes. Killian and Grigg (1961) tested a modified version of Myrdal's (1944) rank order of discrimination on a group of Jacksonville, Florida, Negroes and whites. The hypothesized inverse relation between the scales of the two groups was not found. Negroes ranked the chance to vote without restriction lower and segregation in public facilities higher than Myrdal postulated. Whites showed more resistance to equal job opportunities than predicted. These attitudes were measured over five years ago and some shifts could be expected on the basis of changes which have occurred within that period. Wolfe (1961) and Wolfe and Horn (1962) took a direct approach in attempting to identify the causes of racial friction in some 1,200 Negro and white native Southerners. Subjects were asked a series of questions relating to contact with the other race such as "When were you made the maddest in your life?" Negroes objected to "cursing, chewing out, nicknaming," whereas whites objected to "pilfering, careless work, reneging on debts and promises." No instance of racial friction was reported by 23 percent of the Negroes and 12 percent of the whites. The authors imply that there seem to be few grounds for hate between the races, but their methodology was such that serious errors of underreporting were likely.

Gross distortions regarding attitudes of the other race continue to exist among Negroes and whites. For example, in one large scale study only 22 percent of the whites interviewed recognized that most Negroes favored integration (Matthews & Prothro, 1962).

At least two reports confirm the well-established fact that prejudice and stereotypes are not restricted to any one region of the country or to a single race (McDaniel & Babchuk, 1960; Alsop & Quayle, 1963). Additional findings related to prejudice stem from comparisons of Negroes and Jews in a Northeastern city (Simpson, 1959). Negroes who regularly attended religious services were found to be more highly prejudiced than those who did not, but this same relation was not found among Jewish subjects. Negroes with high-status striving were found to have less prejudice.

Two studies on Florida populations have dealt with the relation between race and alienation and race and anomia. Middleton (1963) asked questions about six different types of alienation (five of which were highly intercorrelated) and found the Negro population scoring significantly higher than the white. Killian and Grigg (1962) cast some doubt on the traditional assumptions concerning the relation between urbanism and anomia. In the urban community, Negroes in general do not differ from whites in anomia, but white-collar Negroes who live in rural areas most frequently display high anomia. Thus it is position in the social structure rather than urban or rural residence, that is most likely to be associated with differences in anomia. Somewhat related to the overall issue of alienation is the finding that among a group of adolescents, Negro children were more negatively oriented to society than were Latin or Anglo-American subjects (Pierce-Jones, Reid, & King, 1959).

The marked increase in voter registration among Negroes has led to increased concern with political attitudes within this group. Overviews may be found in some of the general references given earlier in this paper. A general analysis of the role of the Negro voter has been provided by Gosnell and Martin (1963). Erskine (1962) summarized various attitudes as they have been measured by specific polls over a period of years. There is no question about increases in political activity among Negroes. One study of three cities revealed that Negroes of the same social class as whites are more likely to belong to political groups than are the whites (Orum, 1966). There is no question about the Negro preference for candidates of the Democratic Party (Erskine, 1962; Middleton, 1962; Brink & Harris, 1964; Killian & Grigg, 1964). With respect to Negro registration, it has been suggested that political factors are almost as important as socioeconomic ones. Local political organizations, like organizations in general, seem to thrive on opposition (Matthews & Prothro, 1963a; 1963b).

Middleton has been interested not only in the political behavior and alienation of the Negro, but also in his humor (Middleton, 1959; Middleton & Moland, 1959). On the basis of a survey of jokes told on a Negro campus and on a white campus, he found no differences in the extent of joking or in the telling of sexual jokes. To the surprise of no one, Negroes were found to react more favorably than whites to anti-white jokes. But Negroes saw the anti-Negro jokes to be just as funny as did whites. These two studies are typical of a number being reviewed in this section in that they are of some limited interest, but the scope is such that there are no significant generalizations or any general advance in the understanding of racial comparisons or of humor. They are too limited with respect to sample size and design; they stand alone. But for the reader who likes racial jokes, one further reference is given—that of Prange and Vitols (1963).

In contradistinction to the situation obtaining in research on intelligence, it is widely recognized that in ethnic attitude research the race of the experimenter or interviewer is a significant variable. No additional evidence of this fact should be necessary but it continues to accumulate (Athey, Coleman, Reitman, & Tang, 1960; Kraus, 1962; Vaughn, 1964; Freedman, 1965). Surprisingly enough, journal editors continue to accept reports in which this variable was not controlled or even acknowledged.

Additional studies of attitudes directly or indirectly have touched upon consumer motivations (Alexis, 1962; Bullock, 1961a, 1961b; Schwartz, 1963; Barban & Grunbaum, 1965); attitudes toward communism (Kosa & Nunn, 1964); and attitudes toward Jews (Heller & Pinkney, 1965). Specific differences and similarities by race are reported but they do not fall into easily summarized generalizations. . . .

The material reviewed in the preceding sections clearly suggests that there are reliable differences in perceptions and attitudes of Negroes and whites. But evidence continues to mount which indicates that much of the variance is due to factors such as place of residence, education, position in the social structure, and belief congruence. And, in many instances, similarities far outweigh differences—for example, with respect to anti-Negro and anti-white prejudice. . . .

Educational and Occupational
Aspirations and Expectations

The Negro revolution of the 1960s and the federal government's concern with the lower socioeconomic classes have resulted in a series of studies measuring educational and occupational hopes and plans. Subjects have been studied from the third grade through high school, and from all sections of the country. The general approach has been to administer questionnaires to large groups, occasionally in conjunction with individual interviews.

As with the other areas being reviewed in this paper, generalizations are difficult to make. Sexton (1963) has accurately summarized the major problems: Frequently there is a failure to distinguish between aspirations and expectations; none of the studies is national in scope; in most instances there has been no attempt to quantify the intensity of aspiration. Nevertheless, some cautious generalizations are attempted here.

Earlier research had suggested that the expressed educational and occupational aspirations of Negroes were higher than those of whites. Recent work indicates that the aspirations of Negroes are high, but expectations are less, and with increasing age, reality factors become more significant. The Negro continues to stress education as the main route to occupational advancement but there is a realistic outlook in terms of job expectancies.

One of the most comprehensive studies to be reviewed is that of Bowerman and Campbell (1965). The subjects were 16,000 high school students in four Southern states, covering urban and rural areas. The investigators found that the overwhelming majority of both races say they plan to graduate from high school, but fewer than one-half of the Negroes are absolutely sure about carrying out these plans, as contrasted with two-thirds of the whites. Negroes are as likely as whites to say that they definitely want to go to college. In general, the races are found to have very similar educational goals. The authors make the same statement in regard to the level of occupational aspirations and expectations, but there are differences in the kinds of jobs sought and expected. Both groups seek white-collar occupations; but Negroes are more likely to desire and expect blue-collar or military jobs and less likely to be interested in farming. Consistent with earlier findings,

Negro girls have a low interest in being housewives and they have higher educational hopes than do Negro boys.

Essentially the same findings are reported for a sample from three low-income rural counties in Florida (Youmans, Grigsby, & King, 1963). About half of both Negro and white youth planned to continue their education in some way after leaving high school, and equal proportions expected to go to college. Compared with Negro boys, about twice as many Negro girls actually entered college.

Florida Negroes see their greatest occupational opportunity as existing in the city, and approximately three-fourths of those questioned by Bowerman and Campbell (1965) in their four-state survey would prefer living outside of the South. These are the only two studies to be reported in this section which involved subjects from the deep South. Reports from other sections of the country generally support the trends mentioned above.

Reiss and Rhodes (1959) surveyed over 21,000 students in the Nashville area, about 15 percent of whom were Negro. They concluded that Negroes place a much greater emphasis upon education and are more achievement oriented than whites. The age, sex, I.Q. and socioeconomic status position of the Negro was found to be of lesser influence on behavior than race position when comparison was made with white adolescents. Negro high school seniors in Kentucky set occupational goals similar to those of whites with the exception that the Negro female has higher expectations (Lott & Lott, 1963). The Negro girls concentrated their occupational expectations among the professions and totally rejected the role of housewife. Out of a total of 52 Negro female subjects not a single one wanted to be a housewife, as contrasted with 24 percent of the white girls. Sprey (1962) studied ninth graders and reported an ambitious pattern of aspiration and expectation among Negro girls, with a much greater percentage of Negro girls than boys actually enrolled in college preparatory programs. Study of ninth-grade students in New Jersey revealed that Negroes had uniformly high aspirations but planned lower than whites and were less certain about their plans (Stephensen, 1957). Stephensen's study has the merit of distinguishing between aspirations and plans; he was able to conclude that occupational aspiration does not seem to be affected by class, whereas plans and expectations are more definitely class based. Working with ninth- and twelfth-grade pupils in Kansas City, Gist and Bennett (1963) found that there were no significant differences in occupational aspirations, but Negroes had higher educational aspirations. In contrast to the Stephensen study, Gist and Bennett found no differences in plans for education.

Antonovsky and Lerner (1959) interviewed a sample of lower-class youths in New York and found that the Negroes generally had a higher level of aspiration. They suggest that among many of the Negro families the poor model provided by the father might raise aspirations by the child's choosing not to be like the father. An additional sample of New York children of a lower social class also reflected greater educational and occupational aspirations among the Negroes (Smith & Abramson, 1962).

The related factors of social class mentioned at several points in the previous discussion also seem to apply at younger ages. Sixth- through eighth-grade students of the lower classes have been found to plan below the middle classes in both educational and occupational areas, regardless of race (Holloway & Berreman, 1959). They also plan below the level to which they aspire.

One final study reflecting the high educational aspirations of Negroes deserves mention. Rosen (1959) studied 427 pairs of mothers and sons from four Northeastern states. Of the Negro mothers 83 percent said that they intended that their sons go to college, although these aspirations were not significantly different from those of Jews, Protestants, and Greeks. Of seven ethnic groups studied, the Negro mother's vocational aspirations for her son were lower than all but one group.

In addition to asking direct questions regarding aspirations, a number of investigators have been interested in measuring generalized achievement motivation. The most popular approach has been to employ some variation of the McClelland method. But regardless of the technique employed, it appears that Negroes are less achievement oriented than whites (Rosen, 1959; Merbaum, 1962; Lott & Lott, 1963; Mingione, 1965). Note the contrast between the results of direct questioning indicated above and those derived from more indirect methods. We found only one study in which a significant racial difference was not reported; and even then, on the basis of another measure, the whites were said to have a greater achievement-oriented value system (Smith & Abramson, 1962). These results appear to hold up even when intelligence and social class status are controlled, and when the examiners are of the same race as the subject. The sex differences frequently mentioned in previous paragraphs also seem to operate in this area with the Negro female's achievement motivation exceeding that of the Negro male. The research reviewed here is consistent with the empirical studies relating to prestige criteria. Glenn (1963), in reviewing this literature, reports that for the Negro formal education is the most important determinant of prestige, whereas for whites occupation and income have been as important, if not more important.

Over the years education has been seen as the major route for advancement for Negroes, and Negro parents have held high aspirations for their children. Recent research continues to reveal high aspirations, but when concrete expectations and plans have been assessed, Negroes have been found to be much more pessimistic and realistic than whites. The expressed goals are similar for the two races but Negroes plan less and generally appear to be less achievement oriented. Once again, as with so many other areas of comparison, the probability of planning appears to be class linked.

It is important that racial comparisons be made by sex. With respect to both the occupational and educational areas, the Negro female has consistently higher aspirations, more achievement motivation, and she is more likely than the male to make plans and follow through with them. There are also differences among Negroes and whites in occupation preference. The most striking of these is Negro girls' almost total rejection of the role of housewife.

These conclusions have been based on large-scale studies from most regions of the country. In contrast with the work covered in our earlier review, most of the current reports are at least aware of the distinction between aspirations and expectations, although there have been few attempts to quantify their intensity. It will be interesting to observe changes in aspiration in view of the large-scale effort to modify the educational and occupational opportunities for Negroes.

Mental Illness

"Mental illness" has continued as a popular subject for comparative studies, with approximately 40 reports that deserve some mention appearing during the brief period covered by this review. The conclusions put forth contain few surprises and for the most part represent an extension of earlier findings. These reports are not of uniform quality. Naive papers continue to find their way into print, but they are less common. Most authors now recognize the pitfalls in attempting racial comparisons regarding the kinds of behavior labeled as mental illness (Pasamanick, 1963). The role of values is more readily recognized; the relative meaninglessness of conventional psychiatric diagnosis is more likely to be noted; rates are more frequently reported as age and sex specific; distinctions are made between incidence and prevalence figures. Comparisons based on hospital and treatment statistics are properly understood to reflect social and economic factors rather than incidence of illness. And finally, the use of psychological tests not standardized on Negroes has decreased.

Severe Illness

Admission rates to state mental hospitals continue to be higher for Negroes than for whites, usually on the order of 2:1 (Malzberg, 1959; 1963; Crawford, Rollins, & Sutherland, 1960; Kleiner, Tuckman, & Lavell, 1960; Locke, Kramer, & Pasamanick, 1960; Gorwitz, 1964). This finding has been consistent over a period of years and does not seem to be open to question. The ratio changes, however, when other public and private hospitals are considered. Jaco (1960) conducted a large scale investigation of the incidence of mental disorder in Texas, including public and private hospitals, and concluded that the hospitalization rate for whites was greater than that for Negroes regardless of the source of treatment. Prevalence rates for a non-institutionalized population in Baltimore yielded a considerably higher rate of psychosis among whites. The authors of this latter study, which has been reported in detail (Pasamanick, Roberts, Lemkau, & Krueger, 1959; Pasamanick, 1961; 1962), recognize a number of methodological problems which limit generalization from their data.

Recent field studies have consistently reported a high incidence of mental illness in the general population, but it becomes increasingly apparent that entrance to a mental hospital is a highly selective process. In particular, the relation between social class and service from state institutions has been extensively documented (Miller, 1966). Thus attempts to talk about the "true" incidences of mental disturbance among races on the basis of those in treatment are questionable even without considering the many definitional problems which exist.

It should be noted that with respect to hospital admission trends over time, Malzberg (1959) reported that the Negro rate is decreasing and

Ralph Mason Dreger and Kent S. Miller

suggested that this lowering may be due to economic and educational advancements.

In the face of massive evidence that current psychiatric diagnoses are so unreliable as to be relatively meaningless, comparisons of races are still being made on these bases (Kleiner, Tuckman, & Lavell, 1959; 1960; Malzberg, 1959; 1963; Pasamanick et al., 1959; Clausen, 1961; London & Myers, 1961; Pasamanick, 1962; Prange & Vitols, 1962; Simon, 1965). A detailed analysis of the comparisons will not be made but we will attempt some generalizations. Negroes are more likely to receive a diagnosis of schizophrenia, alcoholism, paresis, mental deficiency, drug addiction. The following diagnoses are more likely to occur among whites: senile psychosis, chronic brain syndrome, arteriosclerosis, psychophysiological and autonomic-visceral disorders, and the various depressive reactions. Again, these differences are associated with lower socioeconomic groups regardless of race and are consistent with earlier findings.

There have been some attempts to move beyond conventional diagnostic categories and examine some specific aspects of behavior. Raskin and Golob (1966) made racial comparisons as an incidental part of a research project concerned with outcome in schizophrenics. They studied factor scores on a rating scale (Inpatient Multidimensional Psychiatric Scale, Lorr, Klett, & McNair, 1963), and found that Negroes scored significantly higher than whites on Disorientation, Perceptual Distortion, and Motor Disturbance, and lower on Excitement and Grandiose Expansiveness. Since differences by social class were not found, the results were interpreted as reflecting ethnic and subcultural influences on the patient's symptom pattern during the acute phase of his illness. In another study employing rating scales, utilized on the first and third day of hospitalization, Negroes were described as more disturbed than whites (Schleifer, Derbyshire, & Brown, 1964).

A few of the studies previously mentioned contain some reference to relative rates of psychoneurosis; but such comparisons have very appropriately decreased, being obviously of limited value.

Migration and Mental Illness
Recent reports regarding the relation between migration and racial

differences in severe mental illness leave the reader confused. On the basis of New York State figures, Malzberg (1959; 1963) feels that migration accounts for the major differences between Negroes and whites. He reported that 60 percent of the Negroes in the state of New York were born elsewhere, as compared with only 14 percent of the whites. An analysis of first admissions to Ohio hospitals supports this contention in that adjusted rates are higher for both Negroes and whites born outside the state, with the highest rate for the nonwhites born outside the state (Locke, Kramer, & Pasamanick, 1960). On the other hand, well-designed studies in Pennsylvania and Texas suggest that interstate migration is not a significant factor in mental illness (Kleiner & Parker, 1959; Jaco, 1960). Keeler and Vitols (1963) studied Negro schizophrenics in the North Carolina hospital system and reported that 40 percent met their definition of migrants. Their failure to make direct comparisons with whites limits the value of this latter study for our purposes.

A review of these studies and related work on migration suggests that the stressful influence of migration per se is yet to be demonstrated. It probably is somewhat naive to expect equally global concepts such as migration and mental illness to be related to each other.

Suicide

Vital statistics relating to suicide continue to reflect a much higher rate among whites, another consistent finding over the years. White and Negro rates are similar in New England but approximately three times as great among whites in the Southern sections of the United States (Prange & Vitols, 1962). An interesting hypothesis to explain part of this differential has been suggested by Wolfgang (1959). He reasoned that some individuals commit suicide by provoking others to kill them. The circumstances surrounding 588 criminal homicides in Philadelphia between 1948–1952 were studied and 150 of these were judged to be precipitated by the victim. Of these homicides, 79 percent were Negro and 21 percent white, a ratio of 4:1. The racial composition of 890 orthodox suicides during this same period revealed 90 percent white and 10 percent Negro. There are some obvious limitations in the generalizations possible from these data, but the study certainly warrants replication and extension.

Attitudes Toward Mental Illness

In the last five years there has been a surprising lack of interest in measuring racial difference with respect to attitudes toward mental illness. In the one such study to be commented on here, Negroes were found to have a lower level of understanding of current theories of mental illness, a greater sympathetic understanding of children and of the aged, and a greater tendency to feel that the mentally ill person is responsible for his difficulties (Crawford, Rollins, & Sutherland, 1960). Earlier studies have shown these same attitudes to be associated with low education and social status. Evaluations of attitudes and tolerance of deviance among various subcultures could aid in developing a sociological classification of mental illness and would be helpful in explaining why Negroes appear to be more disturbed than whites at the time of admission to hospitals (Vitols, Waters, & Keeler, 1963; Schleifer et al., 1964). Arguments can be found to support both sides of the statement that Negroes are more tolerant of mental illness than whites or vice versa. Data on one population have been provided by Linn (1961). He analyzed the timing of hospitalization for over 500 patients at St. Elizabeths Hospital, finding that whites who lived with others than their immediate family tended to have a longer time period between onset of symptoms and hospitalization than Negroes in the same living conditions.

Treatment

There have been few attempts to evaluate racial differences in response to treatment. Negro patients who were more disturbed than whites at the time of hospitalization experienced the same recovery rates as the whites (Schleifer et al., 1964). Goldberg and Schooler (1964) reported that Negro and white schizophrenics respond similarly to drug treatment, but Negroes appear to show greater improvement under placebo treatment. The authors interpret this finding to mean that there are no racial differences in genetic loadings but that Negroes have higher loadings than whites on psychological and environmental stress factors. At least two additional articles during this period deal with the problems associated with Negroes in psychotherapy (Shane, 1960; Rosen & Frank, 1962). These studies do not present empirical data but an overview from a clinical viewpoint.

Miscellaneous

A report by Coles (1963) on the effects of stress on Negro children who integrate previously all-white schools is also based on clinical observations. Over a two-year period he interviewed Negro and white children, their parents, teachers, and related individuals in Atlanta and New Orleans. His sample was relatively small and the Negro students represented a select group, but he provides the only detailed observations available regarding this issue. In the face of the considerable stress of this situation, only one Negro child developed substantial emotional illness and no harmful effects were reported among the white children.

The importance of the race of the examiner or interviewer in many situations has been well documented. Questions continue to be raised about the perceptions of the middle-class psychiatrist as he examines Negro patients. Dorfman and Kleiner (1962) reported that race was irrelevant to diagnosis and recommendations, but their conclusion was based on the analysis of the records of only five psychiatrists (two Negro and three white). De Hayos and de Hayos (1965) reported that an analysis of case records in a mental hospital revealed that fewer symptoms are recorded for Negroes as compared with whites.

Conclusions Concerning Mental Illness

It continues to be impossible to draw meaningful conclusions regarding the relation between race and the incidence of mental disorder. Simple linear relationships in this area do not exist, in part because of the lack of reliability in our definition of abnormality. However, we have referred to some consistent differences between Negroes and whites. It is our opinion that the evidence over the last five years suggests that these differences are primarily related to class and caste. But the relation between social status and mental disorder is not an uncomplicated one either (Kleiner & Parker, 1963; Miller, 1966; Parker & Kleiner, 1966). And there has been little or no progress in evaluating the genetic contributions to mental disorder. There has been further documentation of the irrelevancy and inappropriateness of many conclusions from the not-too-distant past.

References

Alexis, M.
1962 "Some Negro-white differences in consumption." American Journal of Economics and Sociology 21:11–28.

Alsop, S., and O. Quayle.
1963 "What northerners really think of Negroes." Saturday Evening Post 236 (September 7):17–21.

Antonovsky, A., and M. J. Lerner.
1959 "Occupational aspirations of lower class Negro and white youth." Social Problems 7:132–138.

Athey, K. R.; J. E. Coleman; A. P. Reitman; and J. Tang.
1960 "Two experiments showing the effect of the interviewer's racial background on response to questionnaires concerning racial issues." Journal of Applied Psychology 44:224–246.

Ausubel, D. P.
1958 "Ego development among segregated Negro children." Mental Hygiene 42:362–369.

Ball, J. C.
1960 "Comparison of MMPI profile of differences among Negro-white adolescents." Journal of Clinical Psychology 16:304–307.

Barban, A. M., and G. A. Grunbaum.
1965 "A factor analytic study of Negro and white responses to advertising stimuli." Journal of Applied Psychology 49:274–280.

Battle, E., and J. B. Rotter.
1963 "Children's feeling of personal control as related to social class and ethnic group." Journal of Personality 31:482–490.

Bayton, J. A.; L. J. Austin; and K. R. Burke.
1965 "Negro perception of Negro and white personality traits." Journal of Personality and Social Psychology 1:250–253.

Bledsoe, J. C., and K. C. Garrison.
1962 "The self concepts of elementary school children in relation to their academic achievement, intelligence, interest, and manifest anxiety." Research Project No. 1008. Washington, D.C.:U.S. Office of Health, Education, and Welfare.

Bowerman, C. E., and E. Q. Campbell.
1965 "Aspiration of southern youth: A look at racial comparisons." Trans-action 2:24.

Brazziel, W.
1964 "Correlates of southern Negro personality." Journal of Social Issues 20:346–353.

Brink, W., and L. Harris.
1964 The Negro Revolution in America. New York:Simon and Schuster.

Brody, E. B.
1963 "Color and identity conflict in young boys: Observations on Negro mothers and sons in urban Baltimore." Psychiatry 26:188–201.

Broom, L., and N. D. Glenn.
1966 "Negro-white differences in reported attitudes and behavior." Sociology and Social Research 50:187–200.

Bullock, H. A.
1961a "Consumer motivations in black and white: Part I." Harvard Business Review 39:89–104.
1961b "Consumer motivations in black and white: Part II." Harvard Business Review 39:110–124.

Butcher, J.; B. Ball; and E. Ray.
1964 "Effects of socioeconomic level on MMPI differences in Negro-white college students." Journal of Counseling Psychology 11:83–87.

Butts, H. F.
1963 "Skin color perception and self-esteem." Journal of Negro Education 32:122–128.

Clausen, J. A.
1961 "Drug addiction," in R. K. Merton and R. A. Nisbet (eds.), Contemporary Social Problems. New York: Harcourt, Brace and World.

Coles, R.
1963 The Desegregation of Southern Schools: A Psychiatric Study. New York: Anti-Defamation League of B'nai B'rith.

Conyers, J. E., and T. H. Kennedy.
1963 "Negro passing: To pass or not to pass." Phylon 24:215–223.

Crawford, F. R.; G. W. Rollins; and R. L. Sutherland.
1960 "Variations between Negroes and whites in concepts of mental illness and its treatment." Annals of the New York Academy of Sciences 84:918–937.

Dahlstrom, W. G., and G. S. Welsh.
1960 An MMPI Handbook: A Guide to Use in Clinical Practice and Research. Minneapolis: University of Minnesota Press.

de Hayos, A., and G. de Hayos.
1965 "Symptomatology differentials between Negro and white schizophrenics." International Journal of Social Psychiatry 11:245–255.

Deutsch, M.
1965 "The role of social class in language development and cognition." American Journal of Orthopsychiatry 35:78–88.

Dorfman, E., and R. J. Kleiner.
1962 "Race of examiner and patient in psychosomatic diagnosis and recommendation." Journal of Consulting Psychology 26:393.

Dreger, R. M., and K. S. Miller.
1960 "Comparative psychological studies of Negroes and whites in the United States." Psychological Bulletin 57:361–402.

Erskine, H. G.
1962 "The polls: Race relations." Public Opinion Quarterly 26:137–148.

Freedman, P. I.
1965 "Race as a factor in persuasion." American Journal of Orthopsychiatry 35:268.

Gaier, E. L., and H. S. Wambach.
1960 "Self-evaluation of personality assets and liabilities of southern white and Negro students." Journal of Social Psychology 51:135–143.

Gasser, E. S.
   1962   "An investigation of the body image of boys as expressed in self-drawings: An intercultural study." Dissertation Abstracts 22:4425–4426. (Abstract)

Gist, N. P., and W. S. Bennett, Jr.
   1963   "Aspirations of Negro and white students." Social Forces 42:40–48.

Glenn, N. D.
   1963   "Negro prestige criteria: A case study in the bases of prestige." American Journal of Sociology 68:645–657.

Goldberg, S. C., and N. R. Schooler.
   1964   "Sex and race differences in schizophrenic prognosis." Paper presented at the meeting of the American Psychological Association, Los Angeles, September.

Gorwitz, K.
   1964   "The demography of mental illness in Maryland." Paper presented at the meeting of the Phipps Psychiatric Unit of Johns Hopkins Hospital, November.

Gosnell, H. F., and R. E. Martin.
   1963   "The Negro as voter and office holder." Journal of Negro Education 32:415–425.

Gregor, A. J., and C. D. Armstrong.
   1964   "Integrated schools and Negro character development." Psychiatry 27:69–72.

Gregor, A. J., and D. A. McPherson.
   1966   "Racial attitudes among white and Negro children in a deep-South standard metropolitan area." Journal of Social Psychology 68:95–106.

Gynther, M. D.
   1961   "The clinical utility of 'invalid' MMPI F scores." Journal of Consulting Psychology 25:540–542.

Haggstrom, W. C.
   1963   "Self-esteem and other characteristics of residentially desegregated Negroes." Dissertation Abstracts 23:3007–3008. (Abstract)

Heller, C. S., and A. Pinkney.
   1965   "The attitudes of Negroes toward Jews." Social Forces 43:364–369.

Henton, C. L., and E. E. Johnson.
   1964   "Relationship between self concepts of Negro elementary school children and their academic achievement, intelligence, interests, and manifest anxiety." Comparative Research Project No. 1592. Washington, D.C.: U.S. Office of Education.

Hokanson, J. E., and G. Calden.
   1960   "Negro-white differences on the MMPI." Journal of Clinical Psychology 16:32–33.

Holloway, R. G., and J. V. Berreman.
   1959   "The educational and occupational aspirations and plans of Negro and white male elementary school students." Pacific Sociological Review 2:56–60.

Jaco, E. G.
   1960   The Social Epidemiology of Mental Disorders. New York: Russell Sage Foundation.

Katz, I., and L. Benjamin.
   1960   "Effects of white authoritarianism in biracial work groups." Journal of Abnormal and Social Psychology 61:448–456.

Katz, I.; J. Goldston; and L. Benjamin.
1958   "Behavior and productivity in biracial work groups." Human Relations 11:123–141.

Keeler, M. H., and M. M. Vitols.
1963   "Migration and schizophrenia in North Carolina Negroes." American Journal of Orthopsychiatry 33:554–557.

Keller, S.
1963   "The social world of the urban slum child: Some early findings." American Journal of Orthopsychiatry 33:823–831.

Kennedy, T. H., and J. E. Conyers.
1964   "Reported knowledge Negro and white college students have of Negroes who have passed as white." Journal of Negro Education 33:454–460.

Killian, L. M., and C. M. Grigg.
1961   "Rank orders of discrimination of Negroes and whites in a southern city." Social Forces 39:235–239.
1962   "Urbanism, race, and anomia." American Journal of Sociology 67:661–665.
1964   "Negro perceptions of organizational effectiveness." Social Problems 11:380–388.

Kirkhart, R. O.
1960   "Psychological and social-psychological correlates of marginality in Negroes." Dissertation Abstracts 20:4173. (Abstract)

Kleiner, R. J., and S. Parker.
1959   "Migration and mental illness: A new look." American Sociological Review 24:687–690.
1963   "Goal-striving, social status, and mental disorder: A research review." American Sociological Review 28:189–203.

Kleiner, R. J.; J. Tuckman; and M. Lavell.
1959   "Mental disorder and status based on religious affiliation." Human Relations 12:273–276.
1960   "Mental disorder and status based on race." Psychiatry 23:271–274.

Kosa, J., and C. Z. Nunn.
1964   "Race, deprivation, and attitude." Phylon 25:337–346.

Kraus, S.
1962   "Modifying prejudice: Attitude change as a function of the race of the communicator." Audiovisual Communications Review 10:14–22.

Kvaraceus, W. C.; J. S. Gibson; F. Patterson; B. Seasholes; and J. D. Grambs.
1965   Negro Self-Concept: Implications for School and Citizenship. New York: McGraw-Hill.

Lefcourt, H. M.
1965   "Risk taking in Negro and white adults." Journal of Personality and Social Psychology 2:765–770.

Lefcourt, H. M., and G. Ladwig.
1965a "The American Negro: A problem in expectancies." Journal of Personality and Social Psychology 1:377–380.
1965b "The effect of reference group upon Negroes' task persistence in a biracial competitive game." Journal of Personality and Social Psychology 1:668–671.

Linn, E. L.
   1961   "Agents, timing, and events leading to mental hospitalization." Human Orga-
          nization 20:92–98.

Locke, B. Z.; M. Kramer; and B. Pasamanick.
   1960   "Immigration and insanity." Public Health Reports 75:301–304.

London, N. J., and J. K. Myers.
   1961   "Young offenders: Psychopathology and social factors." Archives of General
          Psychiatry 4:274–282.

Lorr, M.; C. J. Klett; and D. M. McNair.
   1963   Syndromes of Psychosis. Oxford, England: Pergamon Press.

Lott, A. J., and B. E. Lott.
   1963   Negro and White Youth: A Psychological Study in a Border State Community.
          New York: Holt, Rinehart and Winston.

McDaniel, P. A., and N. Babchuk.
   1960   "Negro conceptions of white people in a northeastern city." Phylon 21:7–19.

McDonald, R. L., and M. D. Gynther.
   1962   "MMPI norms for southern adolescent Negroes." Journal of Social Psychology
          58:277–282.
   1963   "MMPI differences associated with sex, race, and class in two adolescent sam-
          ples." Journal of Consulting Psychology 27:112–116.

Malzberg, B.
   1959   "Mental disease among Negroes: An analysis of first admissions in New York
          State, 1949–51." Mental Hygiene 43:422–459.
   1963   The Mental Health of the Negro. Albany, New York: Research Foundation
          for Mental Hygiene, Inc.

Matthews, D. R., and J. W. Prothro.
   1962   "Southern racial attitudes: Conflict, awareness, and political change." Annals
          of the American Academy of Political and Social Science 344:108–121.
   1963a "Social and economic factors and Negro voter registration in the south."
          American Political Science Review 57:24–44.
   1963b "Political factors and Negro voter registration in the south." American Politi-
          cal Science Review 57:355–367.

Merbaum, A. D.
   1962   "Need for achievement in Negro and white children." Dissertation Abstracts
          23:693–694. (Abstract)

Middleton, R.
   1959   "Negro and white reactions to racial humor." Sociometry 22:175–183.
   1962   "The civil rights issue and presidential voting among southern Negroes and
          whites." Social Forces 40:209–215.
   1963   "Alienation, race and education." American Sociological Review 28:973–977.

Middleton, R., and J. Moland.
   1959   "Humor in Negro and white subcultures: A study of jokes among university
          students." American Sociological Review 24:61–69.

Miller, C.; C. Wertz; and S. Counts.
   1961   "Racial differences on the MMPI." Journal of Clinical Psychology 17:159–161.

Miller, K. S.
1966   "Mental health treatment and the lower socioeconomic classes," in K. S. Miller and C. M. Griff (eds.), Mental Health and the Lower Social Classes. Tallahassee: Florida State University.

Mingione, A. D.
1965   "Need for achievement in Negro and white children." Journal of Consulting Psychology 29:108-111.

Morland, J. K.
1958   "Racial recognition by nursery school children in Lynchburg, Virginia." Social Forces 37:132-137.
1966   "A comparison of race awareness of northern and southern children." American Journal of Orthopsychiatry 36:22-31.

Moynihan, D. P.
1965   The Negro Family. Washington, D.C.: Office of Policy Planning and Research, U.S. Department of Labor.

Myrdal, G.
1944   An American Dilemma: The Negro Problem and Modern Democracy. New York: Harper.

Orum, A. M.
1966   "A reappraisal of the social and political participation of Negroes." American Journal of Sociology 72:32-46.

Palermo, D. S.
1959   "Racial comparisons and additional normative data on the Children's Manifest Anxiety Scale." Child Development 30:53-57.

Parker, S., and R. J. Kleiner.
1964   "Status position, mobility and ethnic identifications of the Negro." Journal of Social Issues 20:85-102.
1966   Mental Illness in the Urban Negro Community. New York: Free Press.
Pasamanick, B.
1961   "A survey of mental disease in an urban population. IV: An approach to total prevalence rates." Archives of General Psychiatry 5:151-155.
1962   "A survey of mental disease in an urban population. VII: An approach to total prevalence by race." American Journal of Psychiatry 119:299-305.
1963   "Some misconceptions concerning differences in the racial prevalence of mental disease." American Journal of Orthopsychiatry 33:72-86.

Pasamanick, B.; D. W. Roberts; P. W. Lemkau; and D. B. Krueger.
1959   "A survey of mental disease in an urban population: Prevalence by race and income," in B. Pasamanick (ed.), Epidemiology of Mental Disorder (Publication No. 60). Washington, D. C.: American Association for the Advancement of Science.

Pierce-Jones, J.; J. B. Reid; and F. J. King.
1959   "Adolescent racial and ethnic group differences in social attitudes and adjustment." Psychological Reports 5:549-552.

Prange, A. J., Jr., and M. M. Vitols.
1962   "Cultural aspects of the relatively low incidence of depression in southern Negroes." International Journal of Social Psychiatry 8:104-112.
1963   Jokes among Southern Negroes: Revelation of conflict." Journal of Nervous and Mental Disease 136:162-167.

Raskin, A., and R. Golob.
  1966 "Occurrence of sex and social class differences in premorbid competence; Symptom and outcome measures in acute schizophrenics." Psychological Reports 18:11-22.

Reiss, A. J., Jr., and A. L. Rhodes.
  1959 "Are educational norms and goals of conforming, truant, and delinquent adolescents influenced by group position in American society?" Journal of Negro Education 28:252-267.

Riese, H.
  1962 Heal the Hurt Child. Chicago: University of Chicago Press.

Roen, S. R.
  1962 "Personality and Negro-white intelligence." Journal of Abnormal and Social Psychology 61:148-150.

Rosen, B. C.
  1959 "Race, ethnicity, and the achievement syndrome." American Sociological Review 24:47-60.

Rosen, H., and J. D. Frank.
  1962 "Negroes in psychotherapy." American Journal of Psychiatry 119:456-460.

Schleifer, C.; R. Derbyshire; and J. Brown.
  1964 "Symptoms and symptom change in hospitalized Negro and white mental patients." Journal of Human Relations 12:476-485.

Schwartz, J.
  1963 "Men's clothing and the Negro." Phylon 24:224-231.

Sexton, P.
  1963 "Negro career expectation." Merrill-Palmer Quarterly 9:303-316.

Shane, M.
  1960 "Some subcultural considerations in the psychotherapy of a Negro patient." Psychiatric Quarterly 34:9-27.

Simon, R. I.
  1965 "Involutional psychosis in Negroes." Archives of General Psychiatry 13:148-154.

Simpson, R. L.
  1959 "Negro-Jewish prejudice: Authoritarianism and some social variables as correlates." Social Problems 7:138-146.

Smith, H. P., and M. Abramson.
  1962 "Racial and family experience correlates of mobility aspiration." Journal of Negro Education 31:117-124.

Sprey, J.
  1962 "Sex differences in occupational choice patterns among Negro adolescents." Social problems 10:11-23.

Stephensen, R. M.
  1957 "Mobility orientation and stratification of 1,000 ninth graders." American Sociological Review 22:204-212.

Stevenson, H. W., and N. G. Stevenson.
  1960 "Social interaction in an interracial nursery school." Genetic Psychology Monographs 61:37-75.

Trent, R. D.
1957 "The relation between expressed self-acceptance and expressed attitudes toward Negroes and whites among Negro children." Journal of Genetic Psychology 91:25–31.

Vaughn, G. M.
1964 "The effect of the ethnic grouping of the experimenter upon children's responses to tests of an ethnic nature." British Journal of Social and Clinical Psychology 3:66–70.

Vitols, M. M.; H. G. Waters; and M. H. Keeler.
1963 "Hallucinations and delusions in white and Negro schizophrenics." American Journal of Psychiatry 120:472–476.

Wolfe, J. B.
1961 "Incidents of friction between Negroes and whites in southeastern U.S.A." Mankind Quarterly 2:122–127.

Wolfe, J. B., and P. Horn.
1962 "Racial friction in the deep south." Journal of Psychology 54:139–152.

Wolfgang, M. E.
1959 "Suicide by means of victim-precipitated homicide." Journal of Clinical Experimental Psychopathology 20:335–349.

Works, E.
1962 Residence in integrated and segregated housing and improvement in self-concepts of Negroes." Sociology and Social Research 46:294–301.

Wylie, R. C.
1963 "Children's estimates of their school work ability, as a function of sex, race, and socioeconomic level." Journal of Personality 31:203–224.

Youmans, E. G.; S. E. Grigsby; and H. C. King.
1963 "After high school what?" Gainesville: Cooperative Extension Service, University of Florida. (Mimeo)

Part IV
Age and Psychological Change

While a person's genes remain constant throughout life, the subset of genes that is operative at any particular time changes (Caspari, 1967) and determines the body types characteristic of infancy, childhood, adulthood, and old age. Every culture recognizes at least these four basic age distinctions, and in every society these different age identities are associated with contrasting roles and behavioral expectations (Linton, 1945:66). Thus, age constitutes a biosocial variable—that is, genetically induced physical differences linked to sociocultural distinctions. The unique aspects of age, as compared with sex or race, are that individuals change from one type to another, that they do this in a set sequence, and that over a full life-span a person assumes all the physical and social forms.

A person's competencies, interests, and behaviors rise and fall over the life-span roughly in correspondence with the different age phases (Frenkel-Brunswik, 1936). Because age is a biosocial variable, it has to be recognized that some of these psychological changes might be due to shifts in the operating genotypes, while other variations between age levels could be due to the different social experiences associated with the different age identities. Yet the unique aspect of age as a biosocial variable—its sequentiality—also must be taken into account in interpreting psychological differences between age levels. Psychological change can occur cumulatively, with characteristics developed in an earlier stage being retained and incremented during later stages. In addition, the competencies, interests, and behaviors acquired at an earlier age might exert a selective influence on what is acquired later.

Age thus is the most complicated of the biosocial variables, and interpreting psychological development with age requires use of several different explanatory models. Psychological differences between ages might be a function of cumulative growth, of biological differences, of differences in social position, or of old attainments taking on new meaning in later settings.

Sequential Accretion

The Growth of Intelligence

Adults can solve more complicated problems, using more intricate procedures and keeping more things in mind than infants and children can, and this fact is reflected in the higher scores that adults attain on intelligence tests. (The absolute score that a person obtains on an intelligence test is a reflection of overall mental capability; this "mental age" divided by chronological age yields the intelligence quotient or I.Q.). Since intelligence is genetically determined to a large degree, this suggests that neurophysiological changes supporting increased ability are occurring through infancy and childhood, and in fact there is evidence that neural tissue continues to become more and more differentiated at least through the middle teens (Thompson, 1968:154).

A more detailed picture of the growth of intelligence can be obtained by considering a group or cohort of children as they develop from birth to old age. Shortly after birth none of the children shows very developed intellectual capabilities; lacking both capacity and knowledge, they are capable of only the most elementary forms of problem-solving. By age 20 months, infants can be ranked in terms of their intellectual capacity, and these early rankings tend to predict similar ability rankings at a later age (Werner, Honzik, & Smith, 1968). This indicates that, even in infancy, intellectual capacities develop to some extent, enough to differentiate brighter children from the duller. As the cohort ages through childhood, its mean score on intelligence tests tends to rise higher and higher, indicating a higher level of mental age. Also, as the cohort ages, it becomes clearer who the brightest and who the dullest are (Bloom, 1964: chap. 3) possibly because the differences among the children are becoming greater. While individuals' ranks do not remain perfectly stable—for example, a child may move from second to third then back to first as time progresses—it nevertheless is true that, on the whole, the rankings are similar from one time period to another, and by late childhood the observed ranking of the children is very close to what it will be even in adulthood (Bloom, 1964).

During infancy and childhood, the rate of growth in intelligence is very rapid. As the children enter adolescence the rate of growth declines until, around the age of twenty, the rate of growth is nearly zero and persons in the cohort have achieved their adult level of intelligence (Bayley, 1970). For several decades, it was believed that intelligence levels declined after the early twenties. Recent research, studying the same individuals over time, indicates that this is not so, that intelligence tends to remain constant throughout adulthood and may even increase slightly until middle-age and beyond (Chapter 8; See also Owens, 1953; Riegel, Riegel, & Meyer, 1967; Bayley, 1970).

Two additional phenomena of interest make their appearance in late adulthood. First it appears that persons who have displayed lower levels of intelligence in the cohort are subject to higher levels of mortality so, as the cohort continues to age, they tend to be dropped from it (Slater & Scarr, 1964; Riegel & Riegel, 1972).[1]

Second, as the cohort moves into the upper age ranges—the sixties, seventies, and eighties—it becomes "normal" for a person to experience a sudden decline in intelligence. Such

1 Mortality rates correlate with a number of other psychological attributes as well: rigidity, dogmatism, negativism (Riegel, Riegel, & Meyer, 1967), and sociopathy (Robbins, 1966:91–92).

declines, however, appear to be predictors of death within a few years (Lieberman, 1965; Riegel & Riegel, 1972).

This picture of the development of intelligence over the life span has been constructed from a variety of sources, including some relatively recent discoveries; for this reason, there is no tested theoretical model to account for the full range of phenomena. The ideas outlined below constitute a plausible explanation for the growth of intelligence, and the theoretical model can be extended to a number of other traits whose development in some ways is similar to intelligence. These ideas are as yet untested, so the model's postulates and implications still are speculative. Other viewpoints on continuous growth processes are provided by Goulet and Baltes (1970) and Shock (1951).

A Theoretical Model

The development of most psychological traits is a function of both genetic influences and environmental influences, where these sources constitute blocks of variables rather than just single determinants (Roberts, 1967). For example, more than twenty genes are believed to be involved in the development of intelligence (Jinks & Fulker, 1970) and on the environmental side, the development of intelligence probably is affected by diet, by child-rearing practices, and by intellectual stimulation, among other things (Jensen, 1969:59–78). The block of genetic determinants is specially characterized by its essentially perfect stability over long periods of time (i.e., throughout the course of a particular operative genotype). Environmental factors usually are less stable: they show continuity over short periods of time but tend to be more variable when compared across years or decades.

A psychological attribute can be conceived as beginning with "zero development" sometime early in life (including the prenatal period), and genetic and environmental determinants can be thought of as building up or "depositing" the attribute by means of minute effects occurring repeatedly over time. Strictly speaking, it is probably the genetic factors that produce increments of biochemical change or tissue growth, and the environmental factors, when less than ideal, cause decrements or retardations. However, the distinction is not crucial: we can choose to think of the genetic factors as giving rise to an average state that is then either incremented or depressed by special environmental conditions. Genes and stable environmental forces give directionality to development because they make the same kinds of "deposits" and these deposits cumulate over time.

A psychological attribute possesses some degree of stability of its own. This stability allows the genetic and environmental influences to cumulate, new deposits building upon old, so that growth occurs. At the same time it is postulated that any tissue structure or biochemical state tends to atrophy over time unless restored or replaced by the same kinds of genetic and environmental effects that produced it in the first place and thus a psychological state tends to decay unless continuously bolstered. This tendency to atrophy establishes the conditions under which growth stops. While a structure is still small, its rate of atrophy is more than matched by the genetic-environmental deposits and growth occurs, but as the structure becomes more extensive, more atrophy occurs at any time and the deposits then merely serve to make up for what is lost. Thus when the growth process "stops," it is because a state of dynamic equilibrium has been reached where losses equal gains (Bertalanffy, 1968). The idea of maturity as a dynamic equilibrium implies that the neurological and/or biochemical changes involved in growth (of intelligence, for example) continue to occur throughout life but in maturity they are just counterbalanced by processes of atrophy. This provocative hypothesis is as yet untested.

A formula can be used to specify the level of a psychological trait at a particular time in terms of the trait's genetic and environmental determinants and the previously attained level of the trait (Werts & Linn, 1970). With the help of a computer, such a formula can be used to define the kinds of growth curves that would occur in a "sequential accretion" process as this has been described above. The writer has carried out such analyses, and some results are outlined below.

First, consider what happens if genes provide pressure for

growth of a capacity while environmental factors cause additional increments or decrements, acting independently of genes or the state of the trait itself. In this case, a cohort's mean level on the trait begins at zero, rises rapidly during early development, continues rising at a slower rate in later years, and ultimately levels off to a nearly constant value maintained thereafter. At the beginning of the process there is no differentiation among members of the cohort because all begin with zero development; but differentials in genetic potential and environmental conditions begin to produce variation soon after development begins. Variation grows rapidly at first, slower later on, and finally stabilizes to a constant value maintained throughout maturity. Early on, when the genetic variance is uncumulated, the rankings of individuals may be as much affected by differences in environment as by differences in genetic potential. As growing continues, the more stable genetic effects come to account for more of the individual differences in the group than do the less stable environmental effects, and rankings on the trait begin to stabilize.

During both growth and maturity, each individual's level varies up and down somewhat because of changing environmental conditions. Within the cohort as a whole, these individual shifts tend to balance one another, so in maturity the group mean and variance go unchanged. Furthermore, because individual differences are so much a product of cumulated genetic effects and because these differences still are maintained by genes in maturity, the environmental fluctuations affect the rankings of adult individuals to only a minor degree.

Nearly every feature of growth in this first application of the sequential accretion model corresponds to the development of mental ability, as defined in recent longitudinal research. The terminal drop is not accounted for, but this might be interpreted as a cessation of genetic maintenance processes in old age. (The drop anticipates death, and "natural" death is largely under genetic control; see Kallmann and Sander, 1949.)

A second case serves to illustrate that the same model is applicable when genetic determinants of a characteristic are negligible and environmental pressures cause development to occur in opposite directions, as might be the case in the development of conservative and liberal attitudes (Capel, 1967). Initiation of the process could be released at any time in life, awaiting perhaps the completion of some biological structure or the beginning of exposure to relevant environmental determinants. Assuming all members of a cohort begin development together, they start with a mean of zero and no differentiation. As development proceeds, some are drawn by environmental pressures to one side of the continuum (obtaining plus scores) and others to the other side (obtaining negative scores). Thus, if environmental pressures do not favor one pole more than the other, the mean score stays at zero throughout development and only differentiation of individuals increases. The amount of differentiation increases rapidly at first, less rapidly later on, and finally attains a constant value that is maintained thereafter. The final extent of differentiation is greater when the environmental influences impinging on different individuals are more diverse; it also is greater when environments are relatively stable rather than in constant flux. Once maturity is reached, individual rankings show moderate stability in that individual positions change but very major shifts are rare.

A third case illustrates that the sequential accretion model can be modified to provide a plausible account of social control phenomena and suppression of natural potentials; a possible instance is the suppression of aggressiveness in girls (Bayley, 1968). The model is the same as in the first case above except that each individual's environmental pressures are partially contingent on that person's attained level of development. In particular, extreme development in a particular direction releases environmental pressures for change in the opposite direction.

In this case, the mean level of a cohort tends to develop rapidly in the direction of genetic potential, and the genetic variation within the group rapidly manifests itself during early years. However, before equilibrium is reached, environmental pressures are released suppressing further development among the more extreme deviates and even causing them to pull back to earlier levels. Variation within the group suddenly declines, and the mean level swerves in the direction supported by the environment. The adjusted mean and reduced variance become the equilibrium values maintained throughout maturity, or at least as long as all the causal processes remain the same.

The characteristics of growth defined by sequential accretion models are plausible and, in fact, correspond closely to many known phenomena of development. For the present, and until research proves otherwise, the model is probably the most parsimonious way of interpreting phenomena of continuous development. Nevertheless, sequential accretion is not an adequate explanation of all changes with age, because there appear to be points when development is discontinuous.

Stage Processes

Biological Phasing

The onset of puberty disturbs the regularity of physical growth (Bloom, 1964) and leads to sudden increases in sex interests and sexual activity (Kinsey et al., 1953: chap. 13). Because of such discontinuities, a sequential accretion model does not obviously account for the onset of puberty, even though it might well describe growth processes that are initiated then. It is necessary therefore to allow for an additional mechanism in development that causes discontinuous physiological shifts.

Puberty starts when the childhood operating-genotype phases out and a new set of operative genes is released, stimulating biological maturation of sexuality. The adolescence genes seem to have their impact mainly by affecting hormone levels, which in turn nurture certain kinds of physical and psychological development (Chapter 5). Such "biological phasing" appears to be a fairly frequent phenomenon in development (Caspari, 1967). While one kind of genetic mechanism operates and effects some kind of development another genetic mechanism is suppressed. When the first mechanism ceases operation, the second is released and effects later developments, mainly by modifying the biochemical environments of existing cells.

Puberty, menopause in women, and possibly the terminal

drop (senility) are biological phases in human development with some possible relationships to psychological functioning. Both puberty and menopause involve significant hormonal changes in the body, and from these changes one could infer perhaps the kinds of personality shifts that should occur (see Chapter 5). Terminal drop is defined in terms of changes in intelligence and psychological orientation (Lieberman 1965; Riegel & Riegel, 1972), although little information is available on why these effects occur.

Critical Stage

The notion of a critical stage comes from studies of lower animals where it is found that sometimes a transitory biological condition and the environment interact dramatically to produce certain long-term psychological effects. For example, in ducks there is a short period early in life during which the infant bird is biologically ready to be imprinted with its species identification; exposed to ducks during this period, a duckling grows up attached to ducks; exposed to humans during the critical period, the duckling matures with a preference for human company (Hess, 1959). It has been suggested that a similar critical period for species identification occurs with humans early in infancy and that if unexposed to humans during this period, a child develops severe psychopathology (Moore & Shiek, 1971). Recent studies with other primates, however, suggest that the damage may not be irreversible, so the attachment process for primates, including humans, may not involve a true critical stage (Suomi & Harlow, 1972).

The imprinting notion sometimes is applied in explaining the acquisition of human gender identification since evidence does indicate that males must be exposed to elder males during a period early in life in order to develop an adequate masculine identification (Hetherington, 1966). Imprinting also has been employed to account for the development of sexual deviations and fetishes as well as normal sexual preferences (Money, 1972); the idea is that crucial exposures occurring at or around puberty determine lifelong sexual preferences, even though these attachments may be bizarre and socially undesirable.

Recent work on the psychological effects of hormones is rapidly changing ideas about the acquisition of gender identity and sexual preferences. Ultimately the imprinting principle may or may not turn out to be of value in this area, but it already is clear that critical-stage mechanisms are indeed factors in neural developments associated with sex identification and sexuality (Chapter 5).

The key difference between a biological phase and a critical stage is in the ways psychological change occurs once the phase or stage is present. Growth during a biological phase occurs as if by sequential accretion. Psychological acquisitions during a critical stage are sudden, more affected by early happenings than by later events, and differ from ordinary learning in a number of other ways (Hess, 1959).

Social Phasing

Social phasing occurs when there is a fairly sudden withdrawal of environmental support for some kinds of growth and/or the introduction of environmental pressures for other kinds of development. Such shifts can occur because an individual moves from one social status to another or because one occupies different social settings at different age levels (Barker & Wright, 1951; Barker & Barker, 1961). The transitions themselves are sociocultural phenomena defined in terms of the various "careers" that people can follow in a society (Glasser & Strauss, 1971). However, once a transition has occurred, the developmental processes probably can be described as sequential accretion processes, in which case several hypotheses follow about what should happen to a cohort after it enters a new social phase. First, the cohort should show rapid growth of differentiation in characteristics relevant to the new phase, with an eventual leveling off to a constant degree of differentiation. A possible example might be the development of achievement differences in a matched group of persons entering the occupational world at the same time. Second, traits that developed entirely as a function of environmental pressures in a previous phase should atrophy and show less differentiation once those pressures are removed. One example of this might be the reduced interest among males in cars and mechanics once they leave the supportive adolescent subcultures. Third, if a trait was a joint product of genetic and environmental factors in a previous phase, and the environmental factors are eliminated in the present phase, then a cohort should show a period of flux on the trait while individuals are shifting toward expressing their genetic potential more exactly. Increases in masculinity in middle-aged women (Chapter 9) might be an example of this.

Social phasing of a trait with significant genetic determination also could lead to the same trait being expressed in somewhat different ways at different ages. For example, it has been found that a toddler who plays autonomously, who does not seek attention or physical contact with adults, and who shows little orality tends later to be a child with high nonverbal intelligence and field independence (Wender, Pedersen, & Waldrop, 1967). Children who display social competitiveness and verbal facility grow into adults showing little dependency, little anxiety about sex, aggression, interaction, or failure, and high needs for achievement and recognition; children with loosely controlled aggressiveness who are fearless and are independent from adults grow up to have high gender identification and unconforming sexuality (Ryder, 1967). Youthful hostility and extraversion turns into later conformism for females but is continuous with impatience and aggressiveness in males (Bayley, 1968). The mechanisms involved in these kinds of shifts have not been identified with any certainty, but one plausible hypothesis is that the shifts occur as social phases interact with genetically determined dispositions.

There is little hope at this point in obtaining a definitive list of characteristics that change with age because of social phasing. However, two particularly plausible possibilities should be noted. A masculine orientation characterized by pragmatism and a preference for strong, dynamic visual forms can be enchanced by a difficult initiation or apprenticeship (Rodgers & Long, 1968). Although the trait can develop by other means as well, it is likely that many of the pre–and postadolescent differences on these characteristics are due to social phasing.

Also major ups and downs in interests over the life-span are likely to be a product of social phasing, and the development of political interests and attitudes in particular shows some correspondence to social phases: these orientations begin developing in early childhood, become fairly differentiated by early adolescence (Easton & Dennis, 1965; 1967), then show another period of development in retirement (Glenn, 1969).[2]

Hierarchical Stages

Still another form of development can be illustrated by an adult who takes up a new hobby like painting, it being understood that the person is in a stable biological phase and has a social life free from major shifts between environments or statuses. In this case there are no "outside" influences causing the person to develop modifications in personality or character, but change begins occurring nonetheless. By practicing techniques involving the use of color and brushstroke, he begins to acquire some rudimentary skills. At first, just mastering the basic techniques is the major goal; as the skills are obtained, they become reorganized and subordinated to a second set of goals, say, mastering the principles of composition. Once these additional principles are mastered they, too, are reorganized and subordinated to further goals, such as being able to express one's moods and ideals. Psychological change is occurring throughout this sequence. Yet the changes are not genetic in origin; they are not environmental in origin either, except in the sense that they grow out of the person's manipulations of the environment and inductions about how to affect the environment for specific ends. What's more, this process has a stage character (Kohlberg, 1969): the first set of learned principles is reorganized and subordinated to learn a second set, which in turn is reorganized and subordinated to the acquisition of a third goal, and so on. The stages are cumulative such that one

2 A number of authors have recorded how life-styles and orientations in old age seem to parallel adolescent modes, e.g., Lipman (1961), Barker and Barker (1961), Frenkel-Brunswik (1936).

cannot reach a higher stage without having traversed intermediate ones.

Development through hierarchical stages begins with birth, or before. Thus it inevitably occurs simultaneously with growth, with biological phasing, and with social phasing and, indeed, the initiation of a particular hierarchical stage may await developments of another kind to serve as a releaser. But the example of an adult given above at least illustrates that development through hierarchical stages is not just another way of viewing accretive growth or change through biological or social phases.

The distinction between sequential accretion and hierarchical staging perhaps is most ambiguous. Sequential accretion is concerned with the growth of a single capacity, competence, response, etc.; hierarchical staging focuses on the way these elements come to be organized—cognitively linked to one another and linked to reality so that they can be employed in planning and acting. A set of elements and its principles of organization comprise a structure, and once acquired, a person can "enter" the structure and operate within it. But a structure itself can become an element, can become linked to other structure-elements to form still a higher level structure in which a person can operate. For example, principles of visual analysis, principles of balance, and the set of principles that constitute "technique" each may be coherently organized into a structure, and together these are substructures or elements (along with others perhaps) in the larger structure of "painting." It is only theoretical conjecture at present, but probably most elemental abilities, responses, competences, etc., are acquired through processes that can be viewed in terms of sequential accretion, while the organization of these basic elements into larger wholes, allowing them to be systematically employed in interpreting and acting on the environment, is best viewed as a hierarchical stage process.

Essentially, the theory of hierarchical staging applies to the development of all kinds of "working knowledge" allowing one to think and to operate in the physical world (Ginsberg & Opper, 1969) and in the social world (Kohlberg & Kramer,

1969; Loevinger et al., 1970). As Campbell (1970) has pointed out, such practical knowledge can be acquired in the process of evolutionary adaptation and concretized in the structures of biological organisms; similarly, practical knowledge acquired in the course of cultural development can be cumulated and concretized in the structures of societies and their institutions (Carneiro, 1970). Accordingly, the theory of development through hierarchical staging is applicable at the biological and cultural levels as well as the psychological levels (Piaget, 1970).

Interrelations

The various processes described above no doubt act in concert during actual development. For example, in males the transition to a new operating genotype at puberty releases the growth of sex drive, which probably develops on a sequential accretion basis, and which possibly links to specific objects on the basis of a critical-stage mechanism. The appearance of sex drive, along with anatomical changes, may lead others to assign the new age identity of adolescent. Then, changes in psychology produced by increased sexuality and by the social changes associated with a new age identity might create existential problems that are resolved through reorganization of competencies and interests into a new hierarchical stage of ego development.

In females, transition to adulthood through becoming a mother might represent a similarly complex process. The sudden presence of the baby releases a host of environmental factors (including the baby) that begin to reinforce maternal behavior, the growth of maternalism probably proceeding as a sequential accretion process. As the woman notices the development of her feelings and patterns of action, she is stimulated to reorganize her thinking and advance to a more mature stage with regard to her concept of self. And as this change is observed by others, she tends to be awarded the age status of adult, which brings with it pressures for change in certain attitudes.

Psychological growth is a complex process indeed; and at

this time little is known in detail about how different mechanisms interact in the developments of any particular aspect of personality.

Cohort Differences

A fact complicating studies of development is that some of the psychological differences among persons of different ages are not due to processes of aging or psychological development but to historical processes that have caused cohorts to differ from one another. While the idea of generational differences is familiar, only recently has research begun to take the full measure of what is involved in "generation gaps."

Some of the earliest statements about how intelligence develops over the life-span were based on cross-sectional studies of populations (Bayley, 1970). Measurements were made of the children, adolescents, young adults, and old adults present in a population in a given year and then means were calculated for each age to chart the course of development from infancy to old age. The evidence clearly suggested that intelligence begins to decline after the early twenties. Now more recent studies, measuring the same individuals repeatedly as they age, have found no such decline as noted earlier. So it has become necessary to reconcile the two facts: in a given year, older people on the average display less mental ability than young adults; yet aging produces no significant decline in intelligence until just a few years before death. The obvious resolution of this paradox is that the mean intelligence of older generations never was as high as the average intelligence of present-day younger cohorts, and what appeared to be evidence for a decline in intelligence with advancing age is really evidence of continuous increases in mental ability among more recent generations. The details of this argument, and the methods by which it is tested, are discussed in detail in Chapter 8.

Differences in intelligence between generations are interesting in themselves, but their existence also hints that other significant psychological differences might exist between generations. Precious little rigorous research exists to support any definitive statements on this matter. Occasional evidence (e.g., Woodruff & Birren, 1972) suggests a decline in adjustment in more recent cohorts, but examination of the full range of data leaves the issue in doubt (Fried, 1964). Evidence that recent cohorts are developing more mature character also is presented occasionally (e.g., Jones, 1960). This idea is still viable and can be supported by other arguments. For example, a correlation between socioeconomic position and character development has been documented (e.g., Boehm, 1966; Kohlberg & Kramer, 1969), and a generational trend toward greater character development thus might reflect the improved position of more recent cohorts obtained through technological mobility of the entire population (Kahl, 1957).

Cohort differences are important not only because they confound our expectations about individual growth and development, as was the case for so long with intelligence, but also because they indicate in what psychological directions human populations now are moving. Although only a little is known now about such differences, research techniques have recently been developed to explore the matter, and future studies should be revealing.

References

Barker, Roger G., and Herbert F. Wright.
    1954   Midwest and Its Children. Evanston, Illinois: Row, Peterson.

Barker, Roger G., and L. S. Barker.
    1961   "The Psychological ecology of old people in Midwest, Kansas, and Yoredale Yorkshire." Journal of Gerontology 16:144–149.

Bayley, Nancy.
    1968   "Behavioral correlates of mental growth: Birth to thirty-six years." American Psychologist 23:1–17.
    1970   "Development of mental abilities." Chapter 16 in P. H. Mussen (ed.), Carmichael's Manual of Child Psychology. Volume I. New York: Wiley.

Bertalanffy, Ludwig von.
    1968   "Some aspects of system theory in biology." Chapter 7 in General System Theory. New York: George Braziller.

Bloom, Benjamin S.
    1964   Stability and Change in Human Characteristics. New York: Wiley.

Boehm, Leonore.
    1966   "Moral judgment: A cultural and subcultural comparison with some of Piaget's research conclusions." International Journal of Psychology 1:143–150.

Campbell, Donald T.
1970 "Natural selection as an epistemological model." Chapter 3 in Raoul Naroll and Ronald Cohen (eds.), A Handbook of Method in Cultural Anthropology. New York: Natural History Press.

Capel, W. C.
1967 "Continuities and discontinuities in attitudes of the same persons measured through time." Journal of Social Psychology 73:125-126.

Carneiro, Robert L.
1970 "Scale analysis, evolutionary sequences, and the rating of cultures." Chapter 41 in Raoul Naroll and Ronald Cohen (eds.), A Handbook of Method in Cultural Anthropology. New York: Natural History Press.

Caspari, Ernst.
1967 "Gene action as applied to behavior." Chapter 6 in Jerry Hirsch (ed.), Behavior-Genetic Analysis. New York: McGraw-Hill.

Easton, David, and Jack Dennis.
1965 "The child's image of government." Annals of American Academy of Political and Social Science 361:40-57.
1967 "The child's acquisition of regime norms: political efficacy." American Political Science Review 61:25-38.

Frenkel-Brunswik, Else.
1936 "Studies in biographical psychology." Character and Personality 5:1-34.

Fried, Marc.
1964 "Effects of social change on mental health." American Journal of Orthopsychiatry 34:3-28.

Ginsburg, Herbert, and Sylvia Opper.
1969 Piaget's Theory of Intellectual Development. Englewood Cliffs, New Jersey: Prentice-Hall.

Glaser, Barny G., and Anselm L. Strauss.
1971 Status Passage: A Formal Theory. Chicago: Aldine-Atherton.

Glenn, Norval D.
1969 "Aging, disengagement, and opinionation." Public Opinion Quarterly 33:17-33.

Goulet, L. R., and P. B. Baltes (eds.).
1970 Life-Span Development Psychology. New York: Academic Press.

Hess, Eckhard H.
1959 "Imprinting: An effect of early experience, imprinting determines later social behavior in animals." Science 130:133-141.

Hetherington, E. Mavis.
1966 "Effects of paternal absence on sex-typed behaviors in Negro and white pre-adolescent males." Journal of Personality and Social Psychology 4:87-91.

Jensen, A. R.
1969 "How much can we boost IQ and scholastic achievement?" Pp. 1-123 in Environment, Heredity, and Intelligence. Cambridge, Massachusetts: Harvard Educational Review Reprint Series, No. 2.

Jinks, J. L., and D. W. Fulker.
1970 "Comparison of the biometrical genetical, MAVA, and classical approaches to the analysis of human behavior." Psychological Bulletin 73:311-349.

Jones, Mary Cover.
1960   "A comparison of the attitudes and interests of ninth-grade students over two decades." Journal of Educational Psychology 51:175–186.

Kahl, Joseph A.
1957   The American Class Structure. New York: Holt, Rinehart and Winston.

Kallmann, F. J., and G. Sander.
1949   "Twin studies on senescence." American Journal of Psychiatry 106:29–36.

Kinsey, A. C.; W. B. Pomeroy; C. E. Martin; and P. H. Gebhard.
1953   Sexual Behavior in the Human Female. Philadelphia: W. B. Saunders.

Kohlberg, Lawrence.
1969   "Stage and sequence: The cognitive-developmental approach to socialization," Chapter 6 in David A. Goslin (ed.), Handbook of Socialization Theory and Research. Chicago: Rand McNally.

Kohlberg, Lawrence, and R. Kramer.
1969   "Continuities and discontinuities in childhood and adult moral development." Human Development 12:93–120.

Lieberman, Morton A.
1965   "Psychological correlates of impending death." Journal of Gerontology 20:181–190.

Linton, Ralph.
1945   The Cultural Background of Personality. New York: Appleton-Century-Crofts.

Lipman, Aaron.
1961   "Role conceptions and morale of couples in retirement." Journal of Gerontology 16:267–271.

Loevinger, Jane; Ruth Wessler; and Carolyn Redmore.
1970   Measuring Ego Development. Volume I. San Francisco: Jossey-Bass.

Money, John.
1972   "Determinants of human sexual identity and behavior." Chapter 35 in C. J. Sager and H. S. Kaplan (eds.), Progress in Group and Family Therapy. New York: Brunner/Mazel.

Moore, Dewey J., and David A. Shiek.
1971   "Toward a theory of early infantile autism." Psychological Review 78:451–456.

Owens, William A., Jr.
1953   "Age and mental abilities: A longitudinal study." Genetic Psychology Monographs 48:3–54.

Piaget, Jean.
1970   Structuralism. New York: Basic Books.

Riegel, Klaus F., and Ruth M. Riegel.
1972   "Development, drop and death." Developmental Psychology 6:306–319.

Riegel, K. F.; Ruth M. Riegel; and G. Meyer.
1967   "Socio-psychological factors of aging: A cohort-sequential analysis." Human Development 10:27–56.

Robbins, Lee N.
1966   Deviant Children Grown Up. Baltimore: Williams & Wilkins.

Roberts, R. C.
1967 "Some concepts and methods in quantitative genetics." Chapter 11 in Jerry Hirsch (ed.), Behavior-Genetic Analysis. New York: McGraw-Hill.

Rodgers, William B., and John M. Long.
1968 "Male models and sexual identification: A case from the out island Bahamas." Human Organization 27:326-331.

Ryder, Robert G.
1967 "Birth to maturity revisited: A canonical reanalysis." Journal of Personality and Social Psychology 7:168-172.

Shock, Nathan W.
1951 "Growth curves." Chapter 10 in S. S. Stevens (ed.), Handbook of Experimental Psychology. New York: Wiley.

Slater, Philip E., and Harry A. Scarr.
1964 "Personality in old age." Genetic Psychology Monographs 70:229-269.

Suomi, Stephen J., and Harry F. Harlow.
1972 "Social rehabilitation of isolate-reared monkeys." Developmental Psychology 6:487-496.

Thompson, William R.
1968 "Development and the biophysical bases of personality." Chapter 3 in E. F. Borgatta and W. W. Lambert (eds.), Handbook of Personality Theory and Research. Chicago: Rand McNally.

Wender, P. H.; F. A. Pedersen; and Mary F. Waldrop.
1967 "A longitudinal study of early social behavior and cognitive development." American Journal of Orthopsychiatry 37:691-696.

Werner, Emmy E.; Marjorie P. Honzik; and Ruth S. Smith.
1968 "Prediction of intelligence and achievement at ten years from twenty months pediatric and psychological examinations." Child Development 39:1063-1075.

Werts, Charles E., and Robert L. Linn.
1970 "A general linear model for studying growth." Psychological Bulletin 73:17-22.

Woodruff, Diana S., and James E. Birren.
1972 "Age changes and cohort differences in personality." Developmental Psychology, 6:252-259.

8

This is one of the studies that has contributed to the need for drastic rethinking about mental development in adulthood. It shows that mental abilities do not decline with age throughout most of the life-span except for those involving an element of psychomotor speed. Furthermore, the ingenious research design reveals that mental abilities have been improving on the average over the last several generations.

A Cross-Sequential Study
of Age Changes
in Cognitive Behavior
K. Warner Schaie
Charles R. Strother

One of the pervading problems troubling the developmental psychologist who is interested in studying age changes over the adult life span has been the consistent reporting of contradictory age gradients found as the result of cross-sectional and longitudinal inquiries. Many cross-sectional studies report peak performance in the early twenties or thirties with steep decrement gradients thereafter (cf. Jones & Conrad, 1933; Schaie, Rosenthal, & Perlman, 1953; Schaie, 1958; Horn & Cattell, 1966). Most longitudinal studies, on the other hand, report no decrement at all. In fact, slight gains in performance are recorded at least into the midfifties (Owens, 1953; Bayley & Oden, 1955). It has been argued that these contradictory findings can be accounted for by systematic sample attrition in the longitudinal studies, which tends to eliminate more subjects of low ability. It has been observed that none of the longitudinal studies has yet reached the sixties and seventies, the age range where the greatest decrement has been noted in the cross-

Abridged from *Psychological Bulletin*, 70, 1968, pp. 671–680, by permission of the Americal Psychological Association and the authors.

This investigation was supported by Public Health Service Research Grant HD-00367-02 from the National Institute of Child Health and Human Development. Acknowledgment is made to Betty Bostrom, Margaret Baltes, Robert F. Peterson, Judy Higgins, and Pat Sand, who assisted in the testing and data analyses.

sectional findings (Jones, 1959). The cross-sectional results also have been questioned because of the difficulties in the adequate matching of subsamples over extensive age ranges (Schaie, 1959a). All these criticisms of both the cross-sectional and the longitudinal method are well founded. They are obtuse, however, in that they overlook the methodological problem which is the crux of the difficulty.

It has been shown elsewhere that the conventional cross-sectional and longitudinal methods are simply special cases of a general developmental model (Schaie, 1965). Let us point out here that they can be expected to yield similar age gradients only under very exceptional circumstances. The basis for this statement is the fact that the cross-sectional method compares scores for samples of subjects at different ages who belong to different cohorts (generations) but are measured at the same point in time. Differences between age groups therefore could be a function of actual age differences, or they could be a function of differences between cohorts, or due to both age and cohort differences. In the longitudinal method, one compares scores for a sample of subjects, belonging to the same cohort, measured at different ages, each measure taken at a different point in time. Differences here can be a function of age changes, or of effects of the environment upon the sample over time, or due to both age changes and time differences. It follows that similar age gradients can be obtained from cross-sectional and longitudinal studies only if age differences are due to maturational phenomena alone, unrelated to any genetic or cultural variation. In most instances the cross-sectional method will confound age differences with cohort differences and the longitudinal method will confound age changes and time differences (Schaie, 1967).

It is possible to handle the above-mentioned difficulty by deriving a design which will permit the joint analysis of age, cohort, and time differences. In principle, this design would call for the longitudinal study of successive cohorts over the entire age range of interest. Such a design, of course, is not feasible due to the usual attrition problems as well as the limitations of the investigator's own life span. An efficient design, however, can be suggested which will permit a relatively short-term investigation of the problem. The proposed design will be called the cross-sequential method since it involves the sequential analysis of data from two or more cross-sectional studies. To be precise, the requisite design will involve the reexamination of a cross-sectional sample after a suitable time interval. The repeated-measurement aspect is simply a convenient rather than necessary feature of the cross-sequential method (see Schaie & Strother, 1968b).[1]

The purpose of the cross-sequential design is to obtain two or more measures from each of the cohorts included in the initial cross-sectional study so that it becomes possible to contrast the age changes occurring within generations with the age differences between generations measured at a given point in time. This can be done either by testing random splits of the original sample at successive points in time or, as was done in the present study, by obtaining repeated measures on all retrievable members of the originally measured samples.

The cross-sequential design not only permits the evaluation of cross-sectional age gradients at two or more points in time, but it also permits the construction of a composite longitudinal age gradient, each section of which will represent the age change for a given cohort over a constant time interval. Since the effect of environmental change will be constant for all age groups, it may be argued that differences in measured change ought to be due to the effect of maturational variance, and that the composite longitudinal age gradients consequently offer a more appropriate comparison with the cross-sectional findings than gradients which could be derived from a conventional longitudinal study.

Much criticism of developmental studies covering broad age ranges is based on the contention of widely differing initial characteristics of the various age groups. The population base used for the present study is thought to be one of the most representative samples of the adult population ever investigated. Nevertheless, it is obvious that successive generations must have differing characteristics in a dynamic society. The explicit purpose of the cross-sequential design strategy is to differentiate between those components of developmental change which are indeed a function of differences in initial level between generations from those which are attributable to maturational change.

Procedure

The SRA Primary Mental Abilities Test (PMA), the Test of Behavioral Rigidity (TBR), and a socioeconomic status questionnaire were administered to a stratified-random sample of 500 subjects. The popu-

1 A study with a similar design was proposed but not completed or published some years ago by John C. Flanagan (personal communication, February 29, 1968).

lation base from which subjects were sampled consisted of the approximately 18,000 members of a prepaid medical plan. The membership of this plan was fairly representative of the census figures for a large metropolitan area (although somewhat curtailed at the lower end of the socioeconomic continuum). Detailed procedures of the sampling plan have been reported elsewhere (Schaie, 1958; 1959a). Quotas of 25 men and 25 women were obtained for each 5-year age interval from 20 to 70 years. Seven years later, all subjects who could be located were contacted, and 302 subjects were retested with the same instruments. The retested subjects were distributed approximately equal by age, with a slight preponderance of female subjects. Comparison of socioeconomic data for the original and attrited sample suggested that the attrition was fairly random and not significantly biased with respect to socioeconomic factors.

The analysis of variance was used to test the significance of the age-cohort (cross-sectional) and age-time (longitudinal) differences and their interaction with sex differences. Results will be reported on the subjects tested on both occasions for variables involving intellectual ability, response tendencies, and attitudes. These include in the area of intellectual abilities the variables of Verbal Meaning, Space, Reasoning, Number, and Word Fluency.... From the TBR (Schaie, 1955; 1960), data are reported on the variables of Motor-Cognitive Rigidity, Personality-Perceptual Rigidity, Psychomotor Speed, and a scale of Social Responsibility (Gough, McCloskey, & Meehl, 1952; Schaie, 1959b). To facilitate comparisons, all scores were transformed into T scores with means (Ms) of 50 and a standard deviation (SD) of 10, using as a base the first test administration to a sample of 1,000 adult subjects (Schaie & Strother, 1968b).

Results

The results of the analysis of variance ... yielded cohort differences significant at the .001 level of confidence for all variables except for social responsibility. (Cohort differences for the latter variable, however, were significant at the .05 level of confidence.) The replicability of cross-sectional subsample differences over two administrations for measures of ability and cognitive response style was thereby demonstrated. Quite different findings occurred for the analysis of the longitudinal time differences. If the hypothesis of intellectual decrement with age is justified, then one should expect that over a 7-year interval, decrement will occur at every adult age level and for every cohort followed over such a time period. Such overall time differences, however, were found to be significant only for two variables, which are primarily measures of response speed and fluency (Verbal Meaning on the PMA and Psychomotor Speed on the TBR), and for the intellectual ability index of which the Verbal Fluency test is a component. It must be concluded, therefore, that the cross-sectional differences for all other variables represent differences between generations rather than age changes.

Matters are not quite as straightforward as they might appear at this point. An account must be rendered for the numerous significant interactions between the time and cohort levels. Such significant interactions imply that there are positive age changes for some cohorts and negative changes for others. Interactions significant at the .001 level of confidence were found for all variables except Space, Word Fluency, and Motor-Cognitive Rigidity.

Additionally, the analysis of variance revealed significant sex differences for Space and Psychomotor Speed. A significant triple interaction between time, cohort, and sex was found for Number. The latter finding suggests that the shape of the age gradient for Number will differ for men and women.

Test-retest reliability estimates also were obtained from the analyses of variance; ... [they] range from .64 for Motor-Cognitive Rigidity to .94 for the PMA estimate of intellectual ability.

Next, we must concern ourselves with the problem of constructing appropriate gradients which will permit comparisons between the cross-sectional and longitudinal findings provided by this study. The combined *Ms* for both sexes were used to construct the age gradients since none of the sex-time interactions and only one of the sex-time cohort interactions were found to be significant at or beyond the .01 level of confidence.[2] The cross-sectional estimates were obtained by averaging the two *M* scores available for each cohort. The longitudinal

2   A six-page table of mean scores separately by sex and measurement occasion as well as the estimated average cross-sectional and longitudinal means has been deposited in the American Society for Information Science. Order NAPS Document No. 00160 from ASIS National Auxiliary Publications Service, c/o CCM Information Sciences, Inc., 22 West 34th Street, New York, N.Y., 10001, remitting $1.00 for microfiche or $3.00 for photocopies.

estimates were obtained by calculating average age changes over a 5-year interval for each age interval in the range covered. To reduce sampling variability, each estimate was based on two cohorts. For example, the longitudinal age change from 25 to 30 was computed by subtracting the M scores for Cohorts 9 and 10 obtained in 1963 from the corresponding M scores in 1956, and then multiplied by 5/7 to adjust for the disparate time span. A composite longitudinal gradient can be constructed then, beginning with the known average base of the cohort. Similar predicted longitudinal gradients could also be constructed for each of the other cohorts by adding or subtracting the longitudinal age changes from their known base.

Figures 1 to 9 provide graphic representations of the various age gradients. Here we compare the age gradients obtained on the basis of the current performance of individuals at different ages who are members of different cohorts with the estimated longitudinal age gradient for a *single* cohort. If the cross-sectional age differences for a given variable are a function solely of maturational change, then one would expect the two gradients to coincide. If, on the other hand, cross-sectional differences include the effects of differential environmental opportunity and/or genetic changes in the species, then one would expect discrepancies between the two gradients. Whenever cohort differences are in the positive direction (i.e., improvement of the species with respect to a given variable) the cross-sectional gradient will have to drop below the longitudinal, since in such case the performance of an older cohort will be below that of a younger one even if there is no maturational age change whatever. Conversely, the longitudinal gradient will fall below the cross-sectional for those variables where there is decrement in ability over generations for the population samples.

In the following paragraphs we shall examine the age gradients for each of the variables included in this study and shall attempt to highlight appropriate inferences to be drawn from these findings.

Verbal Meaning (Figure 1). This is the ability to understand ideas expressed in words. It is important in any activity involving the transmission of verbal or written communication. The cross-sectional data place the peak of this ability at age 35, and suggest a decrement from peak age of as much as 1½ population SDs. The cross-sequential analysis, however, revealed that actual decrement does not occur for any cohort until age 60. The longitudinal data place the peak age for Verbal

Figure 1. Estimated age gradients for Verbal Meaning.

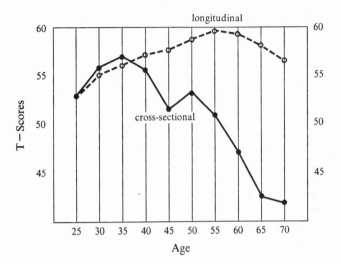

Meaning at age 55, and indicate that the decrement for the remainder of the range studied is less than half an *SD* and that the predicted *M* score at age 70 is still above the *M* score for age 25. The steep cross-sectional gradient must be attributed to increased level of verbal ability in successive cohorts, presumably due to increasingly favorable environmental experience. It will be noted that the improvement gradient is reaching an asymptote. In fact, Cohorts 8 and 9 (born in the late 1920s and early 1930s) show a more favorable position than the last cohort. Comparison of the two gradients suggests that age decrement on Verbal Meaning within generations is quite mild and probably not seriously disabling until very old age (see Strother, Schaie, & Horst, 1957).

Space (Figure 2). This is the ability to think about objects in two or three dimensions and is important in being able to see the relations of an arrangement of objects in space. Significant sex differences in favor of males occur for this ability. The age gradients, however, maintain the same shape for both sexes and joint analysis seems warranted. The peak age estimated by the cross-sectional gradient for Space is at 30 years. The decrement from the peak level to age 70 is approximately 1½ *SD*s. The cross-sequential analysis shows an ability plateau from

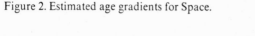

Figure 2. Estimated age gradients for Space.

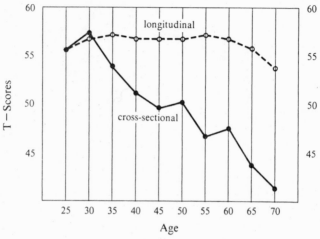

approximately 35 to 55 years. The longitudinal data place the actual peak at age 35, but also show that the age changes over the entire range studied are almost trivial and that the maximum age decrement is less than ½ *SD*. The steep cross-sectional gradient again must be attributed to increasing ability for successive cohorts on Space. Here, too, an asymptote seems to appear with the last two cohorts showing approximately comparable ability. These results may have important implications for retirement practices involving pilots, draftsmen, engineers, and other occupations which require high-level functioning on Space. Older members of such professions have in the past compared unfavorably with their younger peers, in the light of these results, not because their ability had declined, but because the younger generation had greater ability to begin with. If an asymptote has been reached, however, the apparent decrement will be lessened or will no longer appear when the present generation is compared with younger individuals.

Reasoning (Figure 3). This is the ability to solve logical problems, to foresee consequences and to make and carry out plans according to recognizable facts. The peak age for Reasoning is estimated at 25 years by the cross-sectional data and the maximum decrement exceeds 1½

Figure 3. Estimated age gradients for Reasoning.

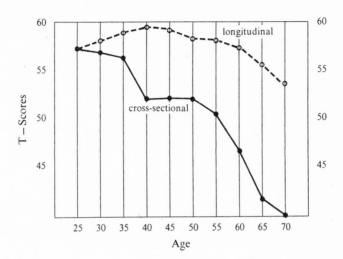

SDs. The cross-sequential data show continuing increments until age 35 and a plateau until approximately 45. The longitudinal data place the peak age for this ability at 40 years and do not show any substantial decrement until 60. There is a drop of close to ⅔ SD from peak age, a longitudinal age change which barely reaches significance at the 5 percent level of confidence. Differences among generations are again much in excess over the decrement within a given generation. The cohort gradient for Reasoning has not yet reached its asymptote, but it does show leveling off for the last three cohorts. There is some question whether the time limits imposed in this test are too stringent; it is possible that the longitudinal age gradient might flatten out further in a comparable power test.

Number (Figure 4). This is the ability to work with figures and to handle simple quantitative problems rapidly and accurately. The cross-sectional data place the peak for Number at age 50, with an approximate ½ SD gain from age 25 and an approximate decrement of 4/5 SD until age 70. Actual gain here occurs until age 65. The longitudinal gradient is considerably flatter than the cross-sectional with the 70-year-old level predicted to be above the performance of the 25-year-olds. The maximum age decrement at age 70 is less than ¼ SD

Figure 4. Estimated age gradients for Number.

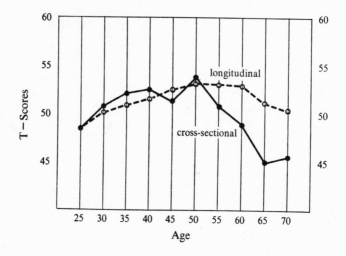

and probably of no practical consequence. The cohort gradient here is quite curvilinear and suggests that an ability peak was reached by the generation born in the early twenties with a slight but not statistically significant decline for the subsequent cohorts. There are differences in gradients for men and women, with less decrement for the female subjects.

Word Fluency (Figure 5). This is the ability to emit in writing previously learned verbal material. It is measured by asking subjects to write the largest possible number of words beginning with a given letter in a brief period of time. The cross-sectional measures for this attribute place the peak age for Word Fluency at 35 years and note a decrement of approximately 1 SD . The cross-sequential analysis, however, notes decrements for every cohort beginning at age 25, at which age the longitudinal analysis would place the peak performance. A highly significant longitudinal age difference is found here which is much in excess of differences between generations. In fact, the longitudinal estimates predict a decrement of 2½ SDs within a given cohort. The cohort gradient for this variable is negative and suggests that we are only about to reach a low asymptotic level. What is the explanation for these findings? Cattell (1963) has argued that differential gradients are to be

Figure 5. Estimated age gradients for Word Fluency.

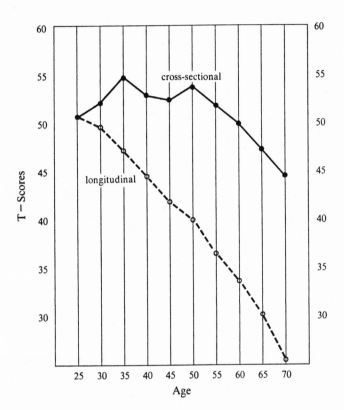

expected for fluid and crystallized forms of intelligence. Word Fluency is ambiguous in loading on both *Gc* and *Gf*, and the latter is said to be subject to decay. On the other hand, it may be suggested that Word Fluency is a highly speeded test which requires a quick response and emission of familiar material. It is well known that reaction time increases as function of age. Word Fluency perhaps may be a better measure of physiological than psychological response capacity. What about the negative cohort gradient? Just as an enriched environment leads to higher ability levels, so does it obviate the necessity for physical exertion. The present findings certainly suggest decrement in the fluency and response latency of successive generations. Similar investigations with purer measures of speed and response strength will be required, of course, to confirm this inference.

Motor-Cognitive Rigidity (Figure 6). This measure indicates the individual's ability to shift from one activity to another. It is a measure of effective adjustment to shifts in familiar patterns and continuously changing situational demands. A low score on this variable is in the rigid direction. The cross-sectional gradient for Motor-Cognitive Rigidity peaks at age 25, shows a fairly stable plateau from 30 to 50 years, and then declines steeply, with a maximum decrement of 1¼ SDs. The cross-sequential study found increments for all cohorts except the next to the oldest group. As a result, the estimated longitudinal gradient shows positive acceleration with a peak at age 60 and a virtual plateau until age 70. This variable shows a predicted longitudinal gain in excess of ½ SD. The cohort gradient is correspondingly steep and has not yet reached an asymptote. We find some difficulty in evaluating these unexpected findings. It is conceivable that as a result of a life-long practice, people do get more proficient and flexible in dealing

Figure 6. Estimated age gradients for Motor-Cognitive Rigidity.

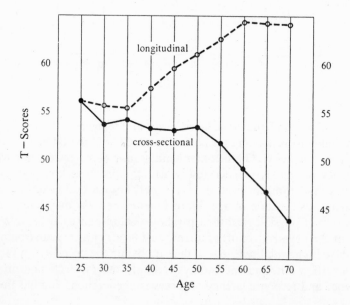

with the demands of familiar situations. We are somewhat concerned, however, that there may have been some practice effect on this measure, which involves somewhat unusual tasks which may have been remembered by the subjects. Another problem is the possibility that more careful administration and scoring might have led to some systematic increase in scores obtained for the second testing. Nevertheless, the results are such that at least it should be concluded that there is no Motor-Cognitive Rigidity increase within generations, but that there are highly significant and still ongoing positive shifts in the level of performance on this variable over successive generations.

Personality-Perceptual Rigidity (Figure 7). This measure indicates the individual's ability to adjust readily to *new* surroundings and change in cognitive and environmental patterns. It is a measure of ability to perceive and adjust to *unfamiliar* and *new* patterns and situations. The average cross-sectional peak here is placed at age 25. Personality-Perceptual Rigidity was the only variable for which the peak ages obtained in the cross-sectional gradients differed between the two testing occasions. In 1956, the peak appeared in the 31- to 35-year-old group, but the 21- to 25-year-olds obtained the highest *M* score in the retest. Maximum increment for Personality-Perceptual

Figure 7. Estimated age gradients for Personality-Perceptual Rigidity.

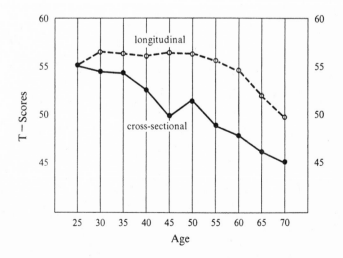

Rigidity amounts to slightly above 1 *SD*. The cross-sequential analysis shows increased rigidity beginning with age 35, but there are several reversals, with an increment appearing as late as the next to the oldest cohort. There is no distinct longitudinal peak but, instead, a peak plateau extending from 30 to 50 years. Maximum increment in rigidity is approximately ⅔ *SD*, indicating that there is some within-generation loss in flexibility in adjusting to unfamiliar patterns. This loss becomes noteworthy only in the late 60s, and even at 70 is predicted to be only approximately ½ *SD* below the status at age 25. The cohort gradient, while significant, is much less steep than for most other variables. It is positively accelerated, however, and has not yet reached its asymptote.

Psychomotor Speed (Figure 8). This measure indicates the individual's rate of emission of familiar cognitive responses. This measure is

Figure 8. Estimated age gradients for Psychomotor Speed.

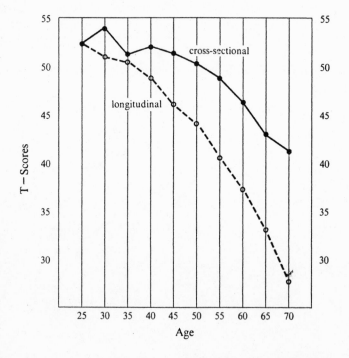

the other variable in our battery which is highly speeded, and the resulting age gradients consequently are quite similar to ones obtained for the PMA measure of Word Fluency. The cross-sectional gradient peaks at age 30 with a maximum decrement of 1.2 *SD*s. The within-generation decrement here is larger than the between-generation differences. Decrements over time were noted for every cohort studied. The longitudinal gradient peaks at age 25 and shows a predicted decrement in excess of 2 *SD*s. It appears that the cross-sectional data on Psychomotor Speed underestimate the within-generation decrement and that this is another characteristic where the level of ability for the population has declined for successive generations. The intergeneration decrement curve appears to have reached its asymptote since this ability for the last two cohorts is roughly comparable. Psychomotor Speed shows sex differences in favor of the female subjects. The age gradients, however, are similar for both sexes.

Social Responsibility (Figure 9). The final variable to be examined has slightly different characteristics from the remainder of our measures in that it is strictly an attitude scale. This is the only variable for which cohort differences failed to reach the .01 level of confidence in the variance analysis. However, cohort differences were found to be significant at the 5 percent level, and the cross-sectional gradient peaks at age 55, with an increment of ¾ *SD* from the youngest age and a decrement of ½ *SD* until age 70. Increments over time occur for Social

Figure 9. Estimated age gradients for Social Responsibility.

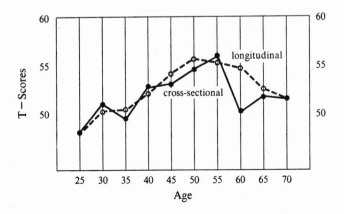

Responsibility for all cohorts until age 55. The longitudinal gradient peaks at ages 50 and 55. Increments and decrements are quite similar to the cross-sectional findings, with a somewhat smoother decrement gradient after age 55. We must conclude that the cohort differences for Social Responsibility are adequately accounted for by maturational changes in attitudes, except for the three oldest cohorts where some shift over generations in favor of more responsible attitudes seems to occur.

Conclusions

The most important conclusion to be drawn from this study is the finding that a major portion of the variance attributed to age differences in past cross-sectional studies must properly be assigned to differences in ability between successive generations. Age changes over time within the individual appear to be much smaller than differences between cohorts, and textbook age gradients may represent no more than the effects of increased environmental opportunity and/or genetic improvement in the species. The findings on longitudinal age changes suggest further that levels of functioning attained at maturity may be retained until late in life except where decrement in response strength and latency interferes.[3] The finding that many of the cohort-differences curves appear to reach asymptotic levels suggests many implications for adult education and retirement practices.

There are several serious limitations to the present study. All our estimates are based on two points in time, and it is conceivable that we have selected a particularly atypical time span for our study. The only remedy for this problem is replication over a different time span. The second problem is the possible effect of practice on test performance. A 7-year span appears long enough to resolve this problem, but it cannot be dismissed as being trivial. Moreover, it is conceivable that the subjects whom we retested do not represent a truly random sample of the original population, a problem implicit in any repeated measurement study. The latter problem is currently being dealt with by repeating the present study with an independent sampling design. A new random sample was drawn and tested in 1963, the results of

---

3   For a discussion of optimal limits of cognitive function in old age, see Schaie and Strother (1968a).

which will be compared with the entire original 1956 sample. These additional data will permit estimation of the effects of practice and contribute further information on the validity of our estimated age gradients (Schaie & Strother, 1968b).

References

Bayley, N., and M. H. Oden.
1955 "The maintenance of intellectual ability in gifted adults." Journal of Gerontology 10:91–107.

Cattell, R. B.
1963 "Theory of fluid and crystallized intelligence: An initial experiment." Journal of Educational Psychology 105:105–111.

Gough, H. G.; H. McCloskey; and P. E. Meehl.
1952 "A personality scale for social responsibility." Journal of Abnormal and Social Psychology 47:73–80.

Horn, J. L., and R. B. Cattell.
1966 "Age differences in primary mental ability factors." Journal of Gerontology 21:210–220.

Jones, H. E.
1959 "Intelligence and problem solving," in J. E. Birren (ed.), Handbook of Aging and the Individual. Chicago: University of Chicago Press.

Jones, H. E., and H. S. Conrad.
1933 "The growth and decline of intelligence: A study of a homogenous group between the ages of ten and sixty." Genetic Psychology Monographs 13:223–298.

Owens, W. A., Jr.
1953 "Age and mental abilities: A longitudinal study." Genetic Psychology Monographs 48:3–54.

Schaie, K. W.
1955 "A test of behavioral rigidity." Journal of Abnormal and Social Pscyhology 51:604–610.

1958 "Rigidity-flexibility and intelligence: A cross-sectional study of the adult life-span from 20 to 70 years." Psychological Monographs 72(9, Whole No. 462).

1959a "Cross-sectional methods in the study of psychological aspects of aging." Journal of Gerontology 14:208–215.

1959b "The effect of age on a scale of social responsibility." Journal of Social Psychology 50:221–224.

1960 Examiner Manual for the Test of Behavioral Rigidity. Palo Alto, California: Consulting Psychologists Press.

1965 "A general model for the study of developmental problems." Psychological Bulletin 64:92–107.

1967 "Age changes and age differences." The Gerontologist 7:128–132.

Schaie, K. W.; F. Rosenthal; and R. M. Perlman.
1953   "Differential deterioration of functionally 'pure' mental abilities." Journal of Gerontology 8:191-196.

Schaie, K. W., and C. R. Strother.
1968a "Cognitive and personality variables in college graduates of advanced age," in G. A. Talland (ed.), Human Behavior and Aging: Recent Advances in Research and Theory. New York: Academic Press.
1968b "The effect of time and cohort differences upon age changes in cognitive behavior." Multivariate Behavioral Research 3:259-294.

Strother, C. R.; K. W. Schaie; and P. Horst.
1957   "The relationship between advanced age and mental abilities." Journal of Abnormal and Social Psychology 55:166-170.

9

This report emphasizes a lack of dramatic personality trends
within a cohort of adults during an 18-year period of aging.
But lack of trends does not mean lack of change. In fact, over
the 18-year period a great deal of shift in specific attitudes
was found to occur; however, since one person's change
tended to be counterbalanced by another's change, the cohort
averages were mostly unaffected. Basic values and interests
were found to be considerably more stable than attitudes, but
even they could not be predicted with certainty over such a
long period. A speculative interpretation of these results is that
even where there are few general trends in personality, a great
deal happens socially to cause flux within a cohort with regard
to specific attitudes, self-conceptions, and basic values.

Consistency of the Adult Personality

E. Lowell Kelly

Within the past year I have been fortunate in obtaining a considerable amount of data concerning consistency of selected personality variables in the adult personality. This is because 21 years ago, at the youthful age of 28, I had the temerity to plan a longitudinal study. Lest I seem to take credit for a degree of foresight which I did not have at that time, let me hasten to add that the initially projected duration of this study was only seven years. For a variety of reasons, especially the disturbing effects of World War II, the definitive follow-up stage of this study had to be postponed so that it is only now being completed.

Abridged from *American Psychologist,* 10, 1955, pp. 659–681, by permission of the American Psychological Assocation and the author.

Address of the President at the Sixty-Third Annual Convention of the American Psychological Association, San Francisco, California, September 4, 1955.

In presenting this first major report growing out of this long-term project, I wish to express my appreciation to the many institutions and individuals contributing to it. Only one who has carried out an extended longitudinal study can fully appreciate the many and varied obligations incurred. To the Committee for Research in Problems of Sex of the National Research Council I am indebted for grants which made possible the initiation of the project and collection of the original data between 1934 and 1939. A grant from the Faculty Research Fund of the University of Michigan in 1952 permitted planning the follow-up which was transformed into a reality by grants during the last two years from the Foundations' Fund for Research in Psychiatry. The three universities with which I have been associated have each contributed research facilities and an atmosphere conducive to research. During the last few months the International Business Machines Corporation greatly facilitated the analysis of the data by making available one of its newer electronic computers. A score of research assistants have contributed ideas as well as helping to carry out the actual work of the investigation. Finally, I want to thank the several hundred men and women subjects whose intelligent cooperation over 20 years made this study possible.

Let me be a little more explicit. In 1934, I began a program of research designed to answer five questions:

1. How do young men and women pair off in marriage?
2. What characteristics of individuals are associated with sexual and marital compatibility?
3. What combinations of characteristics in husbands and wives are associated with sexual and marital compatibility?
4. How do individuals change during the course of marriage?
5. How are these changes related to the nature of the marriage relationship established?

During the years 1935-1938, I enlisted the co-operation of 300 engaged couples. Each of these 600 individuals was assessed with an elaborate battery of techniques including anthropometric measures, blood groupings, a battery of psychological tests, and a 36-variable personality rating scale. In addition, a personally administered questionnaire was used to obtain essential biographical data.

Each of the participating subjects agreed to advise me of the date of his marriage if the engagement eventuated in a marriage, or of the broken engagement if it did not. The original research design called for an annual follow-up questionnaire from each husband and wife for seven years, and retesting at the end of the seven-year period.

The follow-up program was initiated on the anniversary of the first marriage and followed until 1941, at which time it was interrupted by the general dislocation of all civilian activities. The subjects were advised of the writer's intention to return to these studies after the war. In spite of these good intentions I was not able to give serious attention to the project again until 1952-53. That year was spent in re-ordering all previously collected data and planning a full-scale follow-up study to be carried out in 1953-54.

Plans for this follow-up study called for recontacting as many as possible of the original 600 subjects, securing as a minimum a report on the present outcome of the marriage or of the engagement, and inviting all subjects to participate in the final follow-up phase of the study which included (a) retesting on five of the seven psychological tests used in the original battery, and (b) reporting in detail on the marriage between research partners and other intervening life experiences.

In spite of the fact that 16 to 18 years had elapsed between the time of the original testing and the initiation of this major follow-up program, we were successful in securing definitive information regarding the present outcome of all 300 engagements. Parenthetically, it may be of interest to report these outcomes: 278 of the original 300 engagements resulted in marriage of the research partners. There were 22 broken engagements; all but 5 of the 44 individuals involved later married someone else. Of the 278 marriages, 12 were terminated by death and 39 by divorce. After nearly 20 years, then, 454 of the original 600 persons are still living as husband and wife in 227 marriages.

As might be expected, the subjects, although originally contacted in the New England area, were when recontacted widely dispersed throughout the United States, and several of them live in foreign countries. It was therefore necessary to plan to collect all data in the follow-up phase of the project by mail. Because we planned to ask for approximately six hours of further participation on the part of each subject, it was decided to mail forms to the subjects in two sets. The first of these, mailed in August, 1954, included six forms: the five tests being readministered, and one new instrument, a specially prepared form of Osgood's Semantic Differential. These materials were sent to 521 subjects. The remainder of 1954 was spent in the preparation of two detailed questionnaires, one designed to permit each subject to report on the details of his own life experience during the intervening years, and the other to report the details of his marriage. The second set of forms was placed in the mail about the first of this year. Completed retest forms were returned by 446 of the 521 subjects, or 86 percent. While this return is not the 100 percent which we ideally might have hoped for, it is sufficiently large to encourage us to believe that findings based on an analysis of the data will be reasonably representative of the entire sample.

I wish that sufficient time had elapsed since the collection of these new data for me to summarize even tentatively our findings relevant to the five questions asked at the beginning of the project 20 years ago. Such, however, is not the case. In fact, all the data have not yet been coded. Fortunately, the personality retest data was obtained in time to permit a series of analyses concerning the changes in personality variables over this fairly long span of years. At this time, then, I should like to report to you the findings growing out of these analyses. Even with respect to the problem of personality consistency and change, we have not been able to complete all of the detailed analyses needed for a definitive report and interpretation.

I am sure you will want to know a little about the subjects represented in the sample studied. At the time of original testing, all were members of couples with definite anticipations of marriage. The resulting sample is obviously a select one, in that it is composed of persons who responded positively to an invitation to participate in a long-term scientific study of marriage and were willing to contribute initially six to eight hours of their time as well as enter into an agreement to report annually for seven years on the outcome of their marriage. It is not surprising, therefore, that the resulting sample turned out to be superior to the general population in education and intelligence. Only 1 percent of the men never went to high school and 75 percent had at least one year of college; nearly 20 percent had some sort of graduate or professional training. The females were somewhat less selected on the basis of education; nevertheless, approximately two-thirds of them had attended college for varying lengths of time. The I.Q. equivalent of the mean score on the Otis Self-Administering Test of Mental Ability was 115 for the males and 112 for the females at the time of the original testing. The mean age of the men at the time of the original testing was 26.7 and that of the women 24.7, with nearly 9 out of 10 of the subjects being between the ages of 21 and 30. With respect to religious affiliation, 82 percent of the males and 89 percent of the females indicated membership in some church. Approximately 11 percent of the sample indicated a preference for the Catholic and 8 percent for the Jewish faith.

We can never know in what manner and to what degree our sample is selected by virtue of its being composed of persons who volunteered to participate in a study of marriage. Admittedly, it does not include, for example, the sorts of people who marry impulsively or those who still regard marriage as a relationship inappropriate for scientific study. However, in a study such as this, one cannot hope for a sample truly representative of the general population. Our goal was that of securing a sample with sufficient variation on each of the variables studied to permit analyses of covariance. In this respect we succeeded. In spite of the operation of known selective factors, the sample studied was characterized by wide individual differences with respect to each of the roughly 200 variables on which subjects were assessed. And except for education and intelligence, the resulting distributions on the other variables were very similar to those of normative samples.

Since in any study of change it is necessary to obtain measures at two points in time, the retest data which I shall report are based on subsamples of the original samples: those subjects who accepted the invitation to participate in the retest phase of the project. These subsamples included 215 of the original 300 males and 231 of the original 300 females. Furthermore, in order to facilitate the data analyses, I have excluded all cases for whom there was missing any original or retest score on any one of the 103 scores derived from the five tests. The resulting N's are 176 males and 192 females. As might be expected, a comparison of the retested and nonretested samples revealed differences on many of the original measures. While many of these differences are statistically significant and are of interest in themselves as characterizing groups that did and did not choose to participate in the final phase of the project, they are relatively small in magnitude and do not show a systematic pattern of differences for the two sexes. It appeared defensible, therefore, to carry out our analyses of stability and change on these personality variables using the records of the 176 males and the 192 females for whom complete test-retest data were available. Admittedly, our findings will be generalizable only to a population of adults sufficiently cooperative to provide comparable data.

We should also keep in mind that whereas I shall, in most of the analyses, be treating these two samples simply as samples of men and women in general, they are further selected as being primarily the sorts of people who tend to marry. Of the 176 males, 146 were still married at the time of the retest; of the 192 women, 156 were still married at the time of the retest. And, although we shall in these analyses not be primarily concerned with the marriages of these couples, it should be pointed out that 116 of these men and an equal number of women were still married to each other at the time of the retest. To the degree that congruent assortative mating occurred, that is, to the degree that like tend to marry like, any sex differences in the original test scores will tend to be smaller than might be found for samples of men and women not married to each other. Also, since a man and woman married to each other may be assumed to have shared a large proportion of the life experiences intervening between the two testings, it is possible that sex differences in changes in test scores are smaller than would be found for samples of men and women not married to each other.

Test Battery

The original assessment battery selected in 1934 included the following standardized instruments: the Otis Self-Administering Test of Mental Ability, the Allport-Vernon Scale of Values, the Bernreuter Personality Inventory, the Bell Adjustment Inventory, Strong's Vocational Interest Inventory, and two of Remmers' Generalized Attitude Scales (Remmers et al., 1934), one designed to measure Attitude toward any Institution, the other, Attitude toward any Activity. Because it seemed likely (then as now!) that available techniques did not measure adequately all potentially important aspects of personality, we developed a 36-trait graphic personality rating scale; this was used to obtain three sets of ratings for each subject: by self, by research partner, and by five acquaintances.

While we should have liked to have obtained re-test scores on all of these measures, limitations in the total amount of time which could be requested of subjects dictated some reduction in the retest battery. The first test to be eliminated was the Otis Self-Administering Test of Mental Ability. Being a timed instrument, it was doubtful that subjects should be asked to administer it to themselves under strict time limits. Furthermore, the definitive results of the 30-year follow-up study of Army Alpha Scores by Owens in 1953 made less essential the inclusion of an intelligence test in this study. Since the original battery had included two adjustment inventories, it seemed reasonable to eliminate one of them; the Bernreuter was chosen over the Bell primarily because the items in the latter are worded primarily for high school students and approximately a quarter of the items deal with adjustment to the parental home. Finally, although we should have much liked to have obtained personality ratings by five present associates of our subjects, we decided to deny ourselves this luxury, primarily because securing such ratings proved to be one of the more difficult aspects of the original assessment program. We did, however, use the original 36-trait rating scale in the retest battery to obtain two additional sets of ratings by self and by partner.

These five instruments provided us with scores on 103 variables. Lest my audience become worried that I am about to discuss changes in each of these at length, I hasten to assure you that such is not my plan. In fact, because of probable redundancy in these variables, it was not regarded as necessary to analyze all of them in detail. Criteria for selection of variables will be mentioned as we now turn to the results, instrument by instrument. In an effort to enable you to perceive the results more rapidly, I shall present these results in the form of graphs rather than tables, even though some precision is thus lost.

Figure 1 presents the means at Time I and the mean changes after nearly 20 years in scores on the six scales of the Allport-Vernon Scale of Values. Since the Scale of Values is a relatively widely used instrument, I will remind you only that it is designed to measure the relative prominence of six basic interests or motives in personality: theoretical, economic, aesthetic, social, political, and religious. The original form of this instrument published in 1931 was used both for the original and retest.

Figure 1. Allport-Vernon Scale of Values. Means at Time I and mean changes after 20 years.

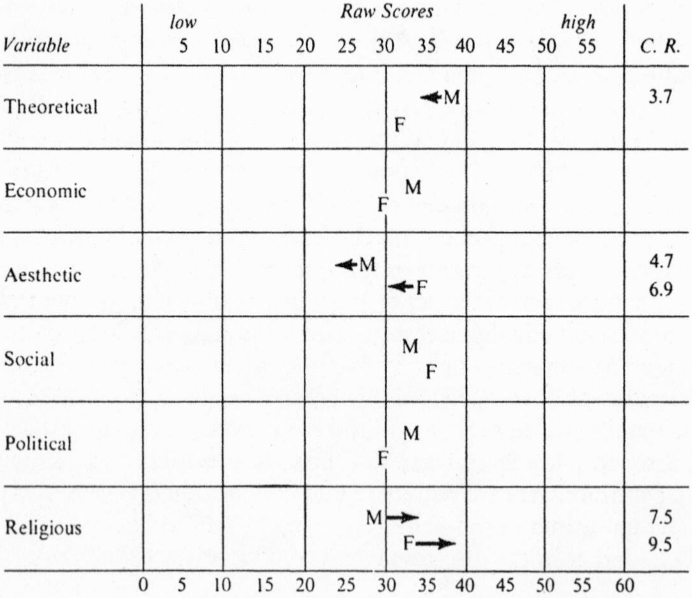

Variable	low 5	10	15	20	Raw Scores 25	30	35	40	45	high 50	55	C. R.
Theoretical						F	◄M					3.7
Economic					F	M						
Aesthetic					◄M	◄F						4.7 6.9
Social						M F						
Political					F	M						
Religious					M➤ F➤							7.5 9.5

| 0   5   10   15   20   25   30   35   40   45   50   55   60 |

Inasmuch as the same general format will be used in presenting the data for the other instruments, certain general features of the figure should be noted. The variables are indicated in the lefthand column. The scale over which scores may range is shown across the top of the figure with the high scores on the right. The letters M and F in each of the rows are placed at points corresponding to the original mean scores of the male and female samples. Mean changes in scores for each variable are indicated by arrows showing the direction and approximate magnitude of the changes. These changes have been indicated in the figure only if the difference was at least 2.5 times its standard error, in which case the critical ratio has been indicated in the column on the right-hand side of the figure.

As will be noted, only 5 of the possible 12 changes on Figure 1 are significant. By all odds the largest, and in fact the most significant, of all changes to be reported is that for Religious values. Both the men and women score about 5 points higher in their middle years than as young men and women. The change amounts to about one-half sigma of the original score distribution. Since scores derived from the Scale of Values are relative, this shift toward higher Religious values was necessarily accompanied by a downward shift on one or more of the other value scales. For the women, most of this downward shift occurred in Aesthetic values; for the men, it was about equally divided between Aesthetic and Theoretical values. Quite frankly, I do not know how to interpret this small but significant shift toward higher Religious values. Two alternate interpretations seem equally possible. The shift may merely reflect a cultural change which has taken place in the last 20 years. Perhaps people are generally more religious today than they were during the last part of the great depression. Equally possible and probably a more acceptable interpretation is that in our present-day society people tend to become more religious as they grow older. A recent personal communication from Professor Irving Bender reports a similar enhancement of religious values in a small group of Dartmouth students retested after 15 years.

One additional aspect of this figure deserves your attention, again, because it is also characteristic of those which follow. Note that while small sex differences are reflected in the original means of the men and women on certain of the scales, there is but little evidence of sex differences either in the direction or in the magnitude of the changes in scores. In fact, for the 38 variables to be discussed, the direction of the change was the same for men and women on 32 of the 38.

Figure 2 presents the story for 6 of the 8 attitudes measured. (Two of the attitude scales were omitted from the present analysis because of incomplete data on a number of the subjects.) This figure is to be read in the same way as the previous one. Note that only the upper half of the pro-con continuum is indicated and that the original scores of both the men and women were favorable toward most of these attitude objects and practices. Note, too, that the changes tended to be toward the favorable end after 20 years. The one exception is Housekeeping, shown on the fourth line of the chart. Here we find that men and women, initially mildly favorable in their attitude toward this practice, both shift toward the unfavorable end of the continuum. Whether this reflects a cultural change or the effect of 20 years of married life, we are not able to say with any certainty!

As a measure of interest, the men's form of Strong's Vocational

Figure 2. Remmers' Generalized Attitude Scales. Means at Time I and mean changes after 20 years. ($N = 176$ males, 192 females.)

Attitude toward	con			neutral			pro	C. R.
		3	6	7	8	9	10	
Marriage							M▶	3.8
							F▶	2.5
Church						M⟶		5.8
						F⟶		5.3
Rearing Children					M▶			(2.0)
					F▶			3.6
Housekeeping				◀M				2.8
					◀F			4.9
Entertaining					M			
					F			
Gardening					M▶			3.0
					F			
	2	3	6	7	8	9	10	11

Interest Blank was used for both men and women; this provided comparable measures for each pair of research partners. Both the original and retest responses to Strong's Blank were scored on 47 variables. Figure 3 presents the results for 11 of the vocational interest scores. These particular scales were selected on the basis of two criteria: first,

Figure 3. Strong V.I.B. Selected Vocational Interest Scores. Means at Time I and mean changes after 20 years.

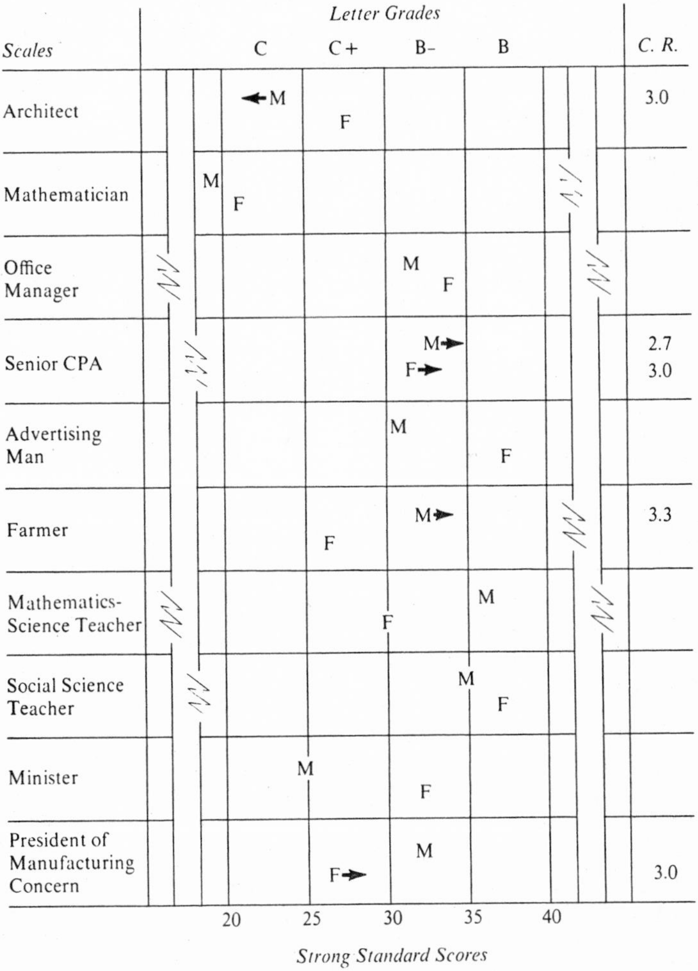

Scales	C	C+	B–	B	C. R.
Architect	◄M	F			3.0
Mathematician	M / F				
Office Manager			M / F		
Senior CPA			M► / F►		2.7 / 3.0
Advertising Man			M	F	
Farmer		F	M►		3.3
Mathematics-Science Teacher			F	M	
Social Science Teacher				M / F	
Minister		M	F		
President of Manufacturing Concern		F►	M		3.0

Letter Grades

Strong Standard Scores: 20   25   30   35   40

Strong Standard Scores

each has a relatively high plus or minus factor loading on one of the five interest factors, and second, the occupation is one which might be followed by either men or women.

While expected sex differences occur in original scores of several of the variables, it is again of interest that there are relatively few sex differences in the changes in scores. Only 5 of the 22 possible changes are statistically significant. In the case of the CPA score, both men and women score significantly higher after 20 years. The men show a small but significant shift toward a lower score on the Architect scale and the women, for reasons which I shall not attempt to explain, score significantly higher on the scale "President of a Manufacturing Concern." In general, however, note that the picture is again one of few and small score shifts for either sex.

Figure 4 presents the data for five other personality variables. The first two were derived by applying the Flanagan keys to the Bernreuter Personality Inventory, these having been used in preference to the four original keys because the two are relatively uncorrelated and account for practically all of the variance in the other four. Since there are sex differences in the raw score norms for these two scales, the means for

Figure 4. Other personality variables; means at Time I and mean changes after 20 years.

Variable	percentile score							C.R.
	20	30	40	50	60	70		
Bernreuter F1C (self-confidence)	self-confident			←—F	M	self-conscious		3.58
Bernreuter F2S (sociability)	sociable				M, F	nonsocial		
Strong MF	feminine	F→		M→		masculine		6.8 4.7
Strong IM	low			M, F		high		
Strong OL	low			M, F		high		
	10	20	30	40	50	60	70	80

the men and women have been located on a percentile scale. While there was no essential sex difference in the original score for either of these scales, the women show a small but statistically significant shift toward greater self-confidence at Time II. I shall not venture an interpretation of this change until we have had an opportunity to determine whether or not it is related to other aspects of married life.

The other three variables shown on this figure are the three non-vocational interest scales derived from Strong's Blank. The first is Masculinity-Femininity. As was to be expected, the original means for the men and women are widely separated on this scale, the letters M and F corresponding to the 30th and 3rd percentiles of the male adult norms, and to the 1st and 50th percentiles of the female norms. Not expected on the basis of the evidence reported by Strong (1943) was the small but significant shift in the masculine direction for both the men and women, especially not expected by one who had been associated with Lewis M. Terman and Catherine Cox Miles in the research reported in the volume *Sex and Personality* (1936). In fact, all the evidence reported in that volume and by Strong would have led to just the opposite prediction. The data of Terman and Miles, all based on cross-sectional comparisons of groups at different ages and with varying amounts of schooling, show that the peak of masculinity in males is reached in the high school period, and that of the females during the college period, after which time both show a trend toward more feminine scores, the trend being more pronounced for men than for women.

Again, the interpretation of this finding is hazardous. It may be that our sample studied longitudinally points to meaningful trends which were masked by cultural differences obtaining in the developmental periods of the several age groups sampled by Terman and Miles and by Strong. It may also be true that the last 20 years have been accompanied by cultural changes tending to result in more masculine scores for anyone who has lived his first 20 years of adulthood during this period. To the extent that during this period the home has become more mechanized through modern appliances, and on the assumption that women find that they like the mechanical aspects of home appliances, it is understandable that women should become somewhat more masculine in their likes and dislikes. An equally plausible explanation for the shift in masculinity scores in the men for the same period is not readily available. Perhaps our entire culture is becoming more mechanized all the time, and while both men and women react favorably to these changes, men respond a little more than women. This seemingly simple explanation may well be the correct one. As an hypothesis, it fits both our own findings and those reported by Terman and Miles, providing one is willing to assume that this mechanization of the culture is a process which has been going on gradually for several decades.

The last two scores shown on the figure are two additional personality measures derived from the Strong Blank: Interest Maturity and Occupational Level. It will be recalled that the Interest Maturity score is based on weights corresponding to the differential responses of a representative group of United States males at the ages of 15 and 25 years. At the age of 25 our subjects, both men and women scored at about the 30th percentile for 25-year-old men and no significant change occurred for either sex over the 20 years.

The Occupational Level scale is based on weights corresponding to the differential responses of representative samples of men between the ages of 18 and 60, representing what might be termed the upper and lower levels of occupations, i.e., professional men vs. unskilled men. Here again, we note practically identical scores for the men and women at the time of the original assessment with no significant shift in these scores at the time of the later test administration. This point on the continuum corresponds to a point about midway between the mean scores of foremen and office workers.

We now turn to a comparison of self ratings made by the subjects at a median age of 25 and again 20 years later. Although the rating scale used for these self ratings included 36 variables, a factor analysis of the ratings of associates showed that not more than 10 relatively independent dimensions were being tapped by the scale. We therefore selected 10 of the 36 variables, each with a relatively high loading on one of these 10 factors and each with relatively low intercorrelations with one another. The findings for these 10 variables are shown in Figure 5. Since this scale was designed for use by relatively unsophisticated raters, all of the items were originally phrased in terms of simple questions such as: "How peppy is he?" "How intelligent is he?" etc. The scale was of the graphic type with only three "landmarks": a descriptive phrase at each end of the scale with the phrase "most people" appearing at the center of the line. The high and low ends of the scales were randomly staggered in an effort to reduce halo effect.

We note first the generally comparable means for the men and women in these self ratings. While some of the sex differences in the original mean ratings are statistically significant, none of them are large. Some reason to accept the validity of these self ratings is the slight but significant difference in self ratings of intelligence by the men and women on both occasions, a difference roughly proportional to the

Figure 5. Self-ratings on personality variables: means at Time I and mean changes after 20 years.

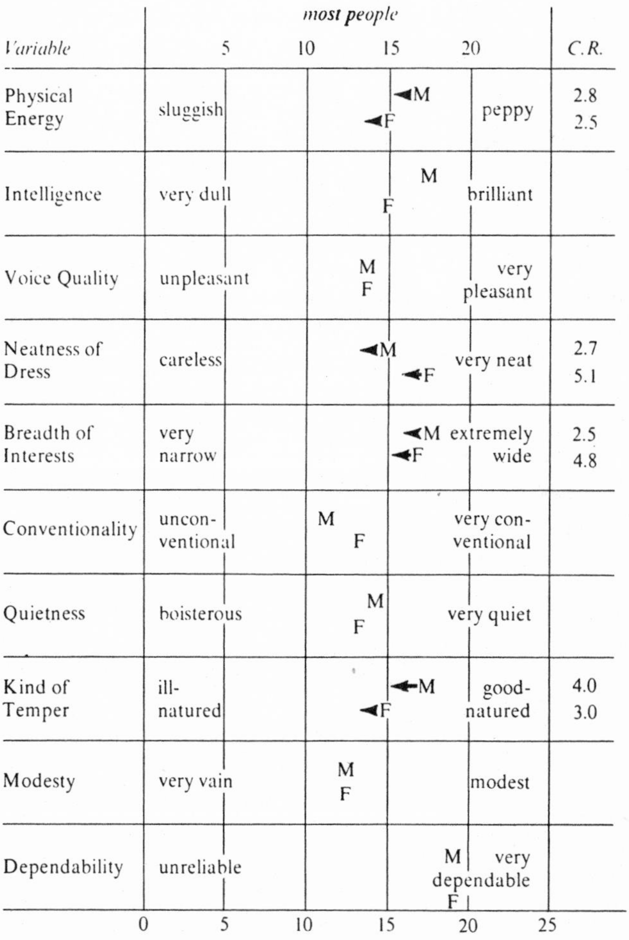

Variable	5	10	*most people* 15	20		C.R.
Physical Energy	sluggish		◄M ◄F	peppy		2.8 2.5
Intelligence	very dull		F M	brilliant		
Voice Quality	unpleasant		M F	very pleasant		
Neatness of Dress	careless		◄M ◄F	very neat		2.7 5.1
Breadth of Interests	very narrow			◄M ◄F	extremely wide	2.5 4.8
Conventionality	uncon-ventional	M F		very con-ventional		
Quietness	boisterous	M F		very quiet		
Kind of Temper	ill-natured		◄M ◄F	good-natured		4.0 3.0
Modesty	very vain	M F		modest		
Dependability	unreliable			M F	very dependable	

0   5   10   15   20   25

measured difference in intelligence of the two groups. Furthermore, self ratings on this simple continuum at Time I correlate about .45 with Otis scores.

Note that significant changes over 20 years occurred for only 8 of the 20 comparisons. Again, we find the absence of sex differences with respect to these shifts. For each variable showing a significant shift for the men there is also a significant shift for the women. Certain of these shifts, although small, are in line with general expectations. Thus, both the men and women at the age of 45 rate themselves as somewhat less peppy than 20 years earlier; they also report that they are inclined to be somewhat less neat in their dress and somewhat less broad in their interests. I am not sure what to make of the shift toward an admitted poorer temper. Perhaps by the time one gets to be 45, one is a little more objective in evaluating this aspect of one's personality!

A summary of the findings with respect to absolute changes in the mean scores of these 38 personality variables is shown in Table 1. We note that:

1. For 20 of the 38 variables, there was no significant change in mean score for either sex.
2. In the case of the 18 variables for which the mean change was statistically significant, the magnitude of the change was still relatively small.
3. These changes, though small, tend to be in the same direction for both sexes.
4. Even though small, each of the significant changes in means is of theoretical interest, but, in the absence of adequate age norms at

Table 1. Number of Personality Variables Showing Significant Changes in Means

Domain	Total	No Change	For Both Sexes	For One Sex
Allport-Vernon Values	6	3	2	1
Attitudes	6	1	4	1
Vocational interests	11	7	1	3
Other personality variables	5	3	1	1
Self ratings	10	6	4	0
Total	38	20	12	6

the two points in time, may be equally well interpreted as due to increasing age or cultural change.

Intra Individual Consistency of Personality Variables over Long Time Intervals

We now turn to an analysis of changes in scores on these same 38 personality variables for individuals. The absence of mean changes could have resulted from either of two states of affairs: for any measure, individuals could have shown little or no change, or alternately, changes in the scores of individuals could have cancelled each other.

In this analysis of change, we shall first compare the retest correlations over the 20-year time span with retest correlations on the same

Figure 6. Allport-Vernon Scale of Values.

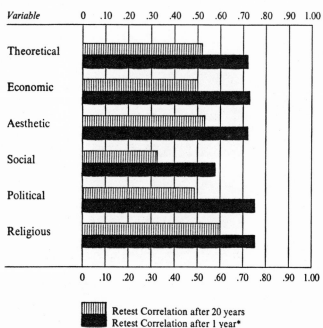

*from Whitely

measures for relatively short time intervals. Again, we shall utilize graphical presentation of the results.

Figure 6 presents the findings for the Allport-Vernon variables. For each of the variables shown on the left of the chart, the black bar indicates the retest correlation over a period of 12 months for college students tested by Whitely (1938) as juniors and again as seniors. The striped bar indicates the magnitude of the retest correlation over the approximately 20-year time span for our subjects.

In these charts we have combined the data for our men and women subjects since the values of these correlations for the men and women were generally within sampling errors of each other. In general, our data lend no confirmation to the popular belief that women are more fickle than men.

Looking again at Figure 6, it will be seen that for all of the six Allport-Vernon variables, the test-retest correlations over 20 years are considerably smaller than those for the 12-month time interval. Thus,

Figure 7. Remmers' Generalized Attitude Scales.

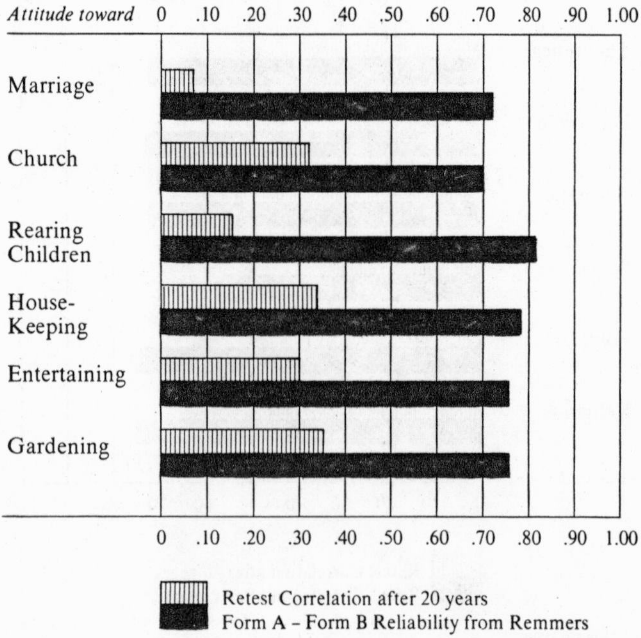

the value for the longer time interval for the Theoretical scale is .51 for our subjects as compared with .71 reported by Whitely. It is also of interest to note that the scores on Social values, which are measured less reliably than the other five values, show the lowest test-retest correlation over the 20-year period.

Figure 7 presents comparable results for the six sets of attitude

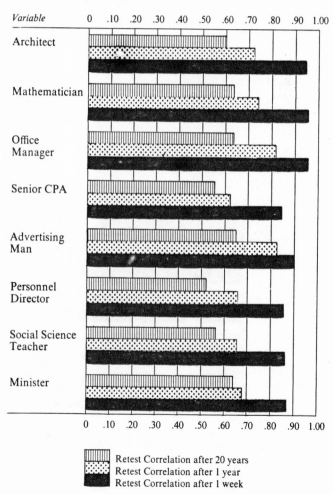

Figure 8. Strong V.I.B. Vocational Interests.

IIIIIII Retest Correlation after 20 years

░░░░░░ Retest Correlation after 1 year

██████ Retest Correlation after 1 week

scores. For these measures, we were unable to obtain any test-retest correlations over short time periods and, therefore, have plotted the black bar to correspond to the reported Form A–Form B reliability of the scales, i.e., retest correlations over a very brief time interval. It is immediately obvious that the attitude scores of our subjects were much less stable than their value scores on the Allport-Vernon. Thus we note that there is almost no relationship between scores on the attitude toward Marriage at Times I and II. The highest value shown on the figure is .33 for attitudes toward the practice of Housekeeping, as compared with a reported reliability of .79 for this particular scale.

By contrast, over this long time span, vocational interest scores for our subjects were relatively stable. Figure 8 presents the essential data for 9 of the 11 vocational interest scores used. Since for several of the scales Strong (1951:78) has provided data showing test-retest correlations for periods of one week and one year, we have incorporated both of these estimates of short-term consistency in this chart. The black bars

Figure 9. Other personality variables.

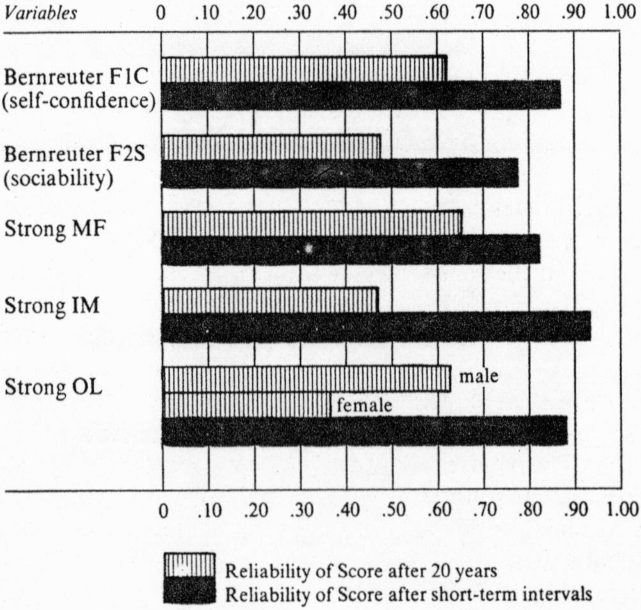

refer to retest correlations over a period of one week and the unshaded bars to correlations for a retest interval of one year.

As was anticipated on the basis of Strong's previously reported findings on the long-term stability of vocational interests, these correlations tend to be relatively high; the median is .62 for men and .57 for women. While for all scales the 20-year retest correlation is somewhat lower than the one-year correlation, the difference in the values for some occupations is rather small.

Turning now to the other personality variables (Figure 9), we find that the story is much the same. Since no retest correlations over short time intervals were available for the Bernreuter scores, the shaded bars correspond to the reported reliabilities of these scales. It is of interest to note that the retest correlations for the Masculinity-Feminity scores are of about the same magnitude as those for the vocational interest scores on the Strong Blank. By contrast, we note a much lower value (.46) for the Interest Maturity scores even though these two Strong scales have about the same reported reliabilities and show the same retest correlations over short time intervals.

The last line of this chart deserves special attention in that it shows the only significant sex difference in consistency of personality measures over this long time span: a value of .62 for our males and .37 for the females. It will be remembered that the Time I scores on this OL variable were approximately equal for the two sex samples and that neither group shifted its mean scores significantly over the 20 years. This little understood scale may measure something less relevant to women than men, it may measure an aspect of personality which stabilizes later in women than in men, or this may be just a chance difference at the .01 level of significance.

What about the consistency of the self percept as reflected in self ratings on the personality variables at two points widely separated in time? Our findings are shown in Figure 10. The black bars indicate the retest correlations between self ratings of college sophomores one week apart; the median value is .63. Again, we find our retest correlations after 20 years considerably smaller in magnitude, yet all statistically significant. The median values are .33 for men and .39 for the women.

Just as Strong found the profiles of the Vocational Interest Test scores to show considerably more long-term stability than scores on individual scales, it may be assumed that the stability of the overall self percept is considerably greater than reflected by the median values of these correlations on single dimensions. As a test of this hypothesis, we computed indices of profile congruency on these 10 self-rated dimensions at two points in time. Using a subsample of 20 cases, and Kendall's tau as an index of congruency, the median profile correlation over 20 years for these 10 traits was found to be .55. By way of comparison, the median value for the Allport-Vernon profile was found to

Figure 10. Self-ratings on personality variables.

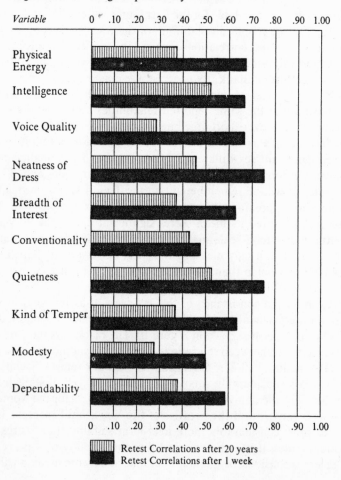

Retest Correlations after 20 years
Retest Correlations after 1 week

be .65. Strong has reported a median profile correlation of .75 for the Vocational Interest profile over 22 years.

At this point let us summarize the evidence concerning the relative consistency in adulthood of the several domains of personality variables for which data are available. In estimating the relative consistency we first corrected the median retest correlation for attenuation, thus providing an estimate of the most probable correlation between true measures at the two points in time. As an index of consistency, it seemed most appropriate to utilize the coefficient of determination, i.e., the squared values of those coefficients after correction for attenuation. The resulting values are shown in Figure 11.

It will be noted at once that the five domains of variables fall into three groups. Values and vocational interest are the most stable, each with an index of approximately .50. Self ratings and the other personality variables are also about equally consistent but with indices about .30. The lowest consistency appears for attitudes, the index being less than .10. While it is essential that any generalizations from these findings be limited to measured variables of the kind here sampled, it is my best guess that this figure fairly accurately summarizes the degree

Figure 11. Estimated long-term consistency of five domains of personality variables.

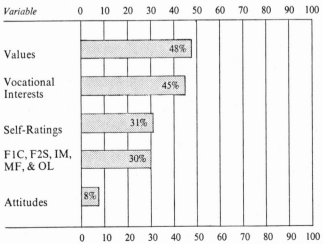

of relative consistency that characterizes the several domains of personality variables.

In view of the considerable evidence for the general constancy of I.Q., during the developmental period, and as reported by Owens (1953) and by Bayley and Oden (1955) for adult groups, it is likely that intelligence would have appeared at the top of this chart, had retest scores been available. Next in order among the personality variables we find values and vocational interests. Apparently these score: are indicative of relatively deeply ingrained motivational patterns that do not change greatly during the period of middle age. Less stable over this long period of time, but as much so as scores based on many tes items, are self ratings on specific personality variables. The relative inconstancy of attitudes during the period of adulthood came as something of a surprise. White it is possible that this relatively low index of constancy is a function of the particular and limited set of attitudes sampled or of the attitude scales utilized, I am inclined to believe that further research will indicate attitudes to be generally less stable than any other group of personality variables. The relative changeability of attitudes is probably a function of their specificity and the fact that alternative attitude objects can easily be substituted one for the other in the service of maintaining an individual's system of values. Thus a person with high social values as measured by the Allport-Vernon scale might shift his attitudes toward and even his allegiance from one to another of several alternative institutions or organizations, each dedicated to the service of humanity.

Although we have thus far been emphasizing the relative consistencies of personality variables, I would call your attention to the fact that Figure 10 has a "ground" as well as a "figure." Note the relatively wide open spaces to the right of each bar. In effect, these are the relative proportions of variance which may be expected to change during the period of life with which we are here concerned. I venture to say that the potentiality, yes, even the probability of this amount of change during adulthood is considerably greater than would be assumed from any of the current theories of personality. Similarly I suspect that these changes are larger than would be expected by most laymen.

References

Bayley, Nancy, and Melita H. Oden.
    1955   "The maintenance of intellectual ability in gifted adults." Journal of Gerontology 10:91–107.

Owens, W. A., Jr.
    1953   "Age and mental abilities: A longitudinal study." Genetic Psychology Monographs 48:3–54.

Remmers, H. H., et al.
    1934   "Studies in attitudes," in Studies in Higher Education, No. 26. Lafayette, Indiana: Purdue University.

Strong, E. K., Jr.
    1943   Vocational Interests of Men and Women. Stanford, California: Stanford University Press.
    1951   "Permanence of interest scores over 22 years." Journal of Applied Psychology 35:89–91.

Terman, L. M., and Catherine C. Miles.
    1936   Sex and Personality. New York: McGraw-Hill.

Whitely, P. L.
    1938   "The constancy of personal values." Journal of Abnormal and Social Psychology 33:405–408.

Index

Aberle, D. F., 75
Aberrant development: causes of, 32-34
Abilities: between successive generations, 192
Abnormal behavior: heritability of, 14-15
Abramson, M., 142
Achievement: heritability of, 10; Negro and white motivation for, 142; development of, 166-67
Adrenalectomy: effect of, in women, 90
Adrenalin, 89
Adrenals: and secretion of sex hormones, 89
Adrenogenital syndrome, 98-99, 100
Adult personality: research on consistency of, 196-218
Age: and psychological change, 157-72; and sequential accretion, 158-64; and stage processes, 164-68; and cohort differences, 171-72
Aggression: in Kibbutz children, 79-80; in Six Culture Socialization study, 79, 80; as related to presence of testosterone, 101-2; difficulty in defining, 103
Aggressiveness: environmental determination of, 13; in males and females, 58; and adult levels of male hormones, 87
Agricultural societies: patrilocal, 73, 74; matrilocal, 74, 75
Alexis, M., 139

Alienation: and race, 138
Alsop, S., 138
Anastasi, Anne, 123
Androstenedione (AD), 89, 96
Anomia: among whites and Negroes, 138
Antonovsky, A., 131, 142
Anxiety: in males and females, 59-60
Archetypes: Jung's concept of, 14
Armstrong, C. D., 129
Army: comparison of Negro and white personnel in, 130
Assertiveness: environmental determination of, 13
Athey, K. R., 139
Attitudes: of whites and Negroes, 136-39
Austin, L. J., 134
Ausubel, D. P., 127, 129
Authority and deference relationships, 76-79
Autocratic political states: and sexual restrictiveness, 76
Autonomic responses, 28
Avunculocal residence, 73, 75

Babchuk, N., 138
Bacon, Margaret K., 80, 81
Ball, B., 132
Ball, J. C., 131, 132
Baltes, P. B., 160
Barban, A. M., 139
Barker, L. S., 166, 168
Barker, Roger G., 166, 168
Barry, Herbert, III, 80, 81
Battle, E., 135

Index

Baughman, E. Earl, 107
Bayley, Nancy, 60, 159, 163, 167, 171, 177, 218
Bayton, J. A., 134
Beach, F. A., 76
Becker, W. C., 53
Behavioral development: biological factors in, 25–37; as related to physique, 28–31; and rate of maturing, 31–32; and physical aberrations, 32–33; and sex differences, 34–35; and effects of stigmatizing labels, 35
Behavioral genetics, 26
Bell, Richard Q., 34
Beloff, J. R., 11, 12, 13
Bender, Irving, 203
Benjamin, L., 135
Bennett, W. S., Jr., 141, 142
Berbers (North African people): authority position of women among, 77
Berdache, 82
Bernstein, Irwin, 101
Berreman, J. V., 142
Bertalanffy, Ludwig von, 161
Bezdek, William, 59
Biller, Henry B., 57, 59
Biological phasing, 164–65
Biosocial elitism, xiii–xvi
Birren, James E., 172
Bledsoe, J. C., 130
Blewett, D. B., 11, 12, 13
Blood sugar: role of hormones in maintaining, 89
Bloom, B. S., 31, 159, 164
Bodily processes: labeling of, 35
Body build: Sheldon's classification of, 28–29
Boehm, Leonore, 172
Borstelmann, Lloyd J., 57, 58
Bowerman, C. E., 140, 141
Bowlby, J., 52
Brazziel, W., 133
Bridger, W. H., 28, 44
Brink, W., 138

Brink, W., 138
Brody, E. B., 134
Broom, L., 136
Brown, J., 145
Brown, Janet L., 44
Bruch, Hilde, 35
Bullock, H. A., 139
Burke, K. R., 134
Burt, C. L., 8
Burton, R. V., 83
Butcher, J., 132
Butts, H. F., 134

Calden, G., 132
Campbell, Donald T., 170
Campbell, E. Q., 140, 141
Capel, W. C., 163
Carlsmith, Lyn, 83
Carneiro, Robert L., 170
Caspari, Ernst, 157, 164
Caste system: as means of racial accommodation, 144
Cattell, R. B., 11, 12, 13, 177
Child, I. I., 76, 79, 80, 81
Childbearing: imitation of, 82, 83
Child-rearing practices: and development of intelligence, 160
Children: ego development of, 127–29
Chinese children: and effect of ethnic and class affiliation on level of mental ability, 121–23
Christakos, A. C., 53
Christensen, Harold T., 59
Cigarette smoking: as related to maturation, 32
"Civilization": and sexual restrictiveness, 76
Clausen, J. A., 32, 145
Cognitive behavior: age changes in, 177–93
Cohort differences, 171–72
Colby, Kenneth M., 59, 84
Coleman, J. E., 139
Coles, R., 148
Color vision: genetic link to, 112

Printed in U.S.A.